Guide to
Adirondack Trails:

HIGH PEAKS
REGION

Twelfth Edition
The Forest Preserve Series (2nd ed.), Volume I

Editor, Tony Goodwin
Series Editor, Neal S. Burdick

The Adirondack Mountain Club, Inc.

1994

Copyright © 1992 by The Adirondack Mountain Club, Inc.
Design by Idee Design, Glens Falls, NY

First Edition	1934
Second Edition	1941
Third Edition	1945
Fourth Edition	1947
Fifth Edition	1988
Sixth Edition	1957
Seventh Edition	1962
Reprinted with minor revisions	1966
Reprinted with minor supplement	1968
Fourth Printing	1969
Fifth Printing	1971
Eighth Edition	1972
Reprinted with minor revisions	1973
Reprinted with minor revisions	1975
Ninth Edition	1977
Reprinted with revisons	1979
Tenth Edition	1980
Reprinted with revisions	1983
Eleventh Edition	1985
Reprinted with minor corrections	1987, 1988, 1990, 1991
Twelfth Edition	1992
Reprinted with minor revisions	1994

Library of Congress Cataloging-in-Publication Data

Guide to Adirondack Trails. High Peaks region /   editor, Tony Goodwin,
  —12th ed.
      p.   cm. — (The Forest preserve series : v. 1)
     ISBN 0-935272-62-3 : $16.95
     1. Hiking—New York (State)—Adirondack Park—Guidebooks.
2. Trails—New York (State)—Adirondack Park—Guidebooks.
3. Adirondack Park (N.Y.)—Guidebooks.   I. Goodwin, Tony, 1949–
II. Adirondack Mountain Club. III. Series : Forest preserve series.
2nd ed. : v. 1.
Gv 199.42.N652A343 1992
917.47'53—dc20   92-33420
                                                                                            CIP

ISBN 0-935272-64-X (8-Volume Set)

Printed in the
United States of America

Dedication

Orra A. Phelps

September 10, 1895–August 26, 1986

If it is possible for any one individual in her full life of achievement to personify the dual spirit and purpose of the Adirondack Mt. Club, Orra A. Phelps shines as our finest companion.

In her early seasons in the high peaks, Orra explored the mountains and the trails, then edited the first edition of this trail guide, in order to lead others to the joys and satisfaction of the wilderness experience. In subsequent years, Orra devoted her technical skills in botany and nature study to the development of our natural history program at Heart Lake, there for many years serving as Ranger-Naturalist and sharing her insights into the wondrous world around us as we climb. A whole generation of ADKers owes much of their understanding of the mountains to the educational programs presented by Orra and her associates. In the quality of her life and her service to others, Orra pioneered pathways that ever beckon others to follow, as they too explore and enjoy the many faces of the high peaks.

In that first edition, published in 1934, she proposed a series of guides to the trails throughout the Adirondacks. The eleventh edition was the first of the now-complete Forest Preserve Series and the twelfth edition is the continuation of that series. Thus, "better late than never," her dream has become an ongoing reality; and it seems only appropriate that we should rededicate this twelfth edition to our dear friend, Orra A. Phelps.

E. H. Ketchledge

High Peaks Region

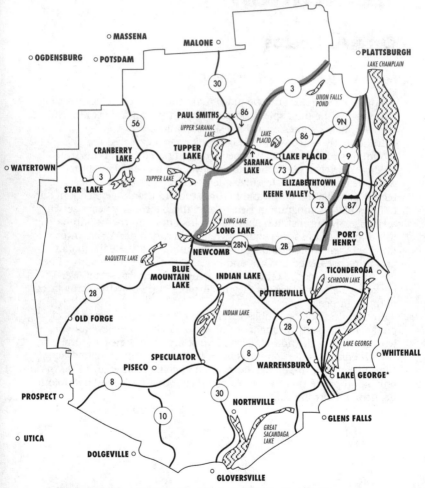

* Adirondack Mountain Club Headquarters & Information Center

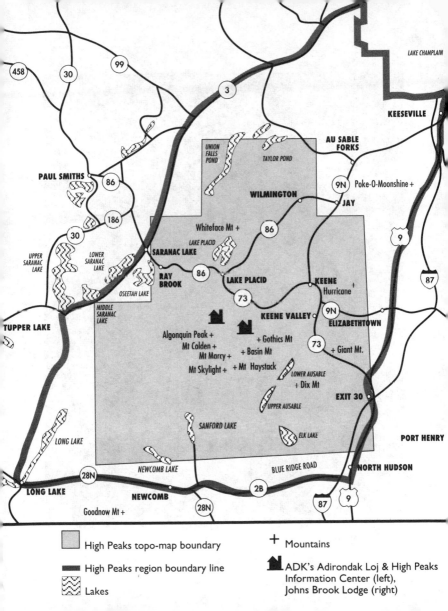

458

30

99

3

Lake Champlain

KEESEVILLE

UNION FALLS POND

TAYLOR POND

AU SABLE FORKS

PAUL SMITHS

86

WILMINGTON

9N Poke-O-Moonshine +

JAY

186

30

Whiteface Mt +

86

9

LAKE PLACID

87

UPPER SARANAC LAKE

LOWER SARANAC LAKE

SARANAC LAKE

RAY BROOK

86

Lake Placid

73

KEENE

Hurricane +

OSEETAH LAKE

MIDDLE SARANAC LAKE

KEENE VALLEY

9N

ELIZABETHTOWN

TUPPER LAKE

Algonquin Peak +

Mt Colden +

Mt Marcy +

Mt Skylight +

+ Gothics Mt

+ Basin Mt

+ Mt Haystack

73

+ Giant Mt.

LOWER AUSABLE

+ Dix Mt

UPPER AUSABLE

EXIT 30

LONG LAKE

SANFORD LAKE

ELK LAKE

PORT HENRY

NEWCOMB LAKE

BLUE RIDGE ROAD

NORTH HUDSON

28N

LONG LAKE

NEWCOMB

28N

Goodnow Mt +

2B

87

9

High Peaks topo-map boundary

High Peaks region boundary line

Lakes

+ Mountains

ADK's Adirondak Loj & High Peaks Information Center (left), Johns Brook Lodge (right)

Whiteface Mt. from Rt. 73

Preface to the Twelfth Edition

Since the publication of the 11th edition of this guide in 1985, the Adirondack Mt. Club has completed the other seven volumes in its Forest Preserve guidebook series. During this time there also have been four reprintings of the 11th edition. Each reprint incorporated all major changes, but the accumulated major changes, plus a host of minor changes, dictate that a new edition is needed. Experience has also indicated several changes in format that will make the information contained in each volume more readily accessible.

The most noticeable format change is the numbering of all trails, with the corresponding number on the map. This number is used when referring to a trail at an intersection, making it easy to find that trail's description without having to consult the index. The map now has a simple grid, and the grid coordinates of the start of each trail are included in the heading of each description. With the great increase in ski touring and other winter use, reference is also made to potential winter use of the trail. One other noticeable format change is that the descriptions for unmaintained trails and bushwhacks are now included in their respective geographical areas and not as a separate section in the guide.

Management of the High Peaks Wilderness Area has been the subject of considerable discussion during the past few years. Concerns about overuse and consequent deterioration of the resource have led to a number of suggestions regarding increased control. These possible new control measures are summarized at the end of the "Wilderness Camping" section in the Introduction.

Millions of hikers over the years, many with the help of the first 11 editions of this guide, have enjoyed the hiking in this area. Good trail work coupled with good hiker education in the past few years have meant that the trails, campsites and summits are now in generally better shape than they were 30 or even 50 years ago. I hope this momentum can be maintained so that as many people as possible can continue to enjoy this wonderful resource without undue restrictions.

Trail hardening and education can only go so far, however, and no wilderness area can infinitely absorb increased user pressure without ultimately losing its character. All hikers should thus seriously consider exploring some of the lesser-known areas. There are many lightly used trails described in this guide, and a vast majority of the trails described in the other Forest Preserve Series guides see very little use.

I hope each reader will study all the possibilities for hiking and exploring contained in this guide. Plan to do popular climbs at off-peak times and try something new on peak weekends. Such a plan hardly solves all the problems of overuse, but there is no question that a voluntary change in use patterns could go a long way toward heading off any restrictions more serious than the ones presently proposed.

TONY GOODWIN
KEENE, NEW YORK
AUGUST 1992

Attention All Hikers, Backpackers, and Canoeists!

Because trail and waterway conditions change, and new boundaries and easements are established, we revise and update our guidebooks regularly. If you have come across an error, discrepancy, or need for an update in this guidebook (be sure you are using the latest edition), we want to hear about it so a change can be made in the next edition.

Please address your comments to the publications director of the Adirondack Mountain Club, citing guidebook title, year of edition, section or trail described, page number, and date of your observation. Thanks for your help.

Note: ADK makes every effort to keep its guidebooks up to date, however, each printing can only be as current as the last press date; thus use of this information is at the sole risk of the user.

Looking SW from Hurricane

R. Meyer

x

Contents

Page Maps

Mt. Pitchoff and the Sentinels

H. D. Hammond

Introduction

The Adirondack Mountain Club Forest Preserve Series

The Forest Preserve Series of Guides to Adirondack Trails covers hiking opportunities on the more than two million acres of public Forest Preserve land in the Adirondack Park. The Adirondack Mountain Club (ADK) published the first guidebook in this series nearly sixty years ago with the idea that hiking guides would eventually cover all Forest Preserve lands; it is appropriate that the completion of this series coincides with the decade-long centennial celebration of the enactment of the Forest Preserve legislation. Each guide in this series, listed below, has been written or revised within the last few years.

Vol. I:	**Guide to Adirondack Trails: High Peaks Region**
Vol. II:	**Guide to Adirondack Trails: Northern Region**
Vol. III:	**Guide to Adirondack Trails: Central Region**
Vol. IV:	**Guide to Adirondack Trails: Northville-Placid Trail**
Vol. V:	**Guide to Adirondack Trails: West-Central Region**
Vol. VI:	**Guide to Adirondack Trails: Eastern Region**
Vol. VII:	**Guide to Adirondack Trails: Southern Region**
Vol. VIII:	**Guide to Catskill Trails**

The public lands that constitute the Adirondack Forest Preserve are unique among all other wild public lands in the United States because they enjoy constitutional protection against sale or development. The story of this unique status begins with the earliest history of the Adirondacks as recounted below, and it continues today as groups such as the Adirondack Mountain Club strive to maintain this constitutional safeguard. The protection of many of the scenic and aesthetic resources of the Forest Preserve also rests with the individual hiker who has the responsibility not to degrade these resources in any way while enjoying their wonders. The Forest Preserve Series of trail guides seeks not only to show hikers where to hike, but also to interpret the area's natural and social history and offer guidelines whereby users can minimize their impact on the land.

The Adirondacks

The Adirondack region of northern New York is unique in many ways. It contains the only mountains in the eastern U.S. that are not geologically Appalachian. In the late 1800s it was the first forested area in the nation to benefit from enlightened conservation measures. At roughly the same time, it was also the most prestigious resort area in the country. In the 20th century, the Adirondacks became the only place in the Western Hemisphere to host two Winter Olympiads. In the 1970s the region was the first of significant size in the nation to experience comprehensive land use controls. The Adirondack Forest Preserve (see below) is part of the only wild lands preserve in the nation whose fate lies in the hands of the voters of the entire state in which it is located.

Geologically, the Adirondacks are part of the Canadian Shield, a vast terrain of ancient Precambrian igneous and metamorphic rock that underlies about half of Canada and constitutes the nucleus of the North American continent. In the U.S., the Shield bedrock mostly lies concealed under younger Paleozoic sedimentary rock strata, but it is well exposed in a few regions, among them the Adirondacks. The Adirondacks are visibly connected across the Thousand Islands to the Grenville Province of the eastern side of the Shield, which is around one billion years old. Upward doming of the Adirondack mass in the past few million years—a process that is still going on—is responsible for the erosional stripping of the younger rock cover and exposure of the ancient bedrock. The rocks here are mainly gneisses of a wide range of composition. One of the more interesting and geologically puzzling rocks is the enormous anorthosite mass that makes up nearly all of the High Peaks region. A nearly monomineralic rock composed of plagioclase feldspar, this peculiar rock was apparently formed at depths as great as fifteen miles below the surface. It is nearly identical to some of the rocks brought back from the moon.

The present Adirondack landscape is geologically young, a product of erosion initiated by the ongoing doming. The stream-carved topography has been extensively modified by the sculpturing of glaciers which, on at least four widely separated occasions during the Ice Age, completely covered the mountains.

Ecologically, the Adirondacks are part of a vegetation transition zone, with the northern, largely coniferous boreal forest (from the Greek god Boreas, owner of the north wind, whose name can be found on a mountain peak and series of ponds in the High Peaks region) and the southern deciduous forest, exemplified by beech/maple stands, intermingling to present a pleasing array of forest tree species. Different vegetation zones are also encountered as one ascends the higher mountains in the Adirondacks; the tops of the highest peaks are truly arctic, with mosses and lichens that are common hundreds of miles to the north.

A rugged and heavily forested region, the Adirondacks were generally not hospitable to native Americans, who used the region principally for hunting and occasionally for fighting. Remnants of ancient campgrounds have been found in some locations. The native legacy survives principally in such place names as Indian Carry, on the Raquette River-Saranac Lake canoe route, and the Oswegatchie River in the northwest Adirondacks.

The first white man to see the Adirondacks was likely the French explorer Jacques Cartier, who on his first trip up the St. Lawrence River in 1535 stood on top of Mont Royal (now within the city of Montreal) and discerned high ground to the south. Closer looks were had by Samuel de Champlain and Henry Hudson, who came from the north and south, respectively, by coincidence within a few weeks of each other in 1609.

For the next two centuries the Champlain Valley to the east of the Adirondacks was a battleground. Iroquois, Algonquin, French, British and eventually American fighters struggled for control over the valley and with it supremacy over the continent. Settlers slowly filled the St. Lawrence Valley to the north, the Mohawk Valley to the south, and somewhat later the Black River Valley to the west. Meanwhile the vast, rolling forests of the interior slumbered in virtual anonymity, disturbed only by an occasional hunter, timber cruiser or wanderer.

With the coming of the 19th century, people discovered the Adirondacks. Virtually unknown as late as the 1830s (the source of the Nile River was located before the source of the Hudson), the Adirondacks by 1850 made New York the leading timber-producing state in the nation. This distinction did not last for long, though, as the supply of timber was quickly brought close to extinction. Meanwhile, mineral resources, particularly iron, were being exploited.

After the Civil War, people began to look toward the Adirondacks for recreation as well as for financial gain. An economic boom, increasing acceptability of leisure time, and the publication of a single book, *Adventures in the Wilderness* by Rev. William H. H. Murray in 1869, combined to create a veritable flood of vacationers descending upon the Adirondacks. To serve them, a new industry, characterized by grand hotels and rustic guides, sprang up. Simultaneously, thanks to the pioneering work of Dr. Edward Livingston Trudeau, the Adirondacks, particularly the Saranac Lake area, became known far and wide as a mecca for tubercular patients.

In the decades following the Civil War the idea of conservation began to take on some legitimacy, thanks in large part to the book *Man and Nature* written by George Perkins Marsh in 1864. In this remarkably influential book, which noted historian Lewis Mumford once called "the fountainhead of the American conservation movement," Marsh called for the implementation of such practices as reforestation and watershed protection, and suggested that the Adirondacks were a good laboratory for testing these ideas.

Another trend in the middle decades of the 19th century was an increasing acceptance of wilderness. This was brought about partly through the work of poets such as William Cullen Bryant, writers such as Henry David Thoreau, and artists such as Frederick Church. Also contributing to this trend was the fact that, as the frontier moved steadily westward, the wilderness was no longer seen as a physical threat, at least not in the more populous, affluent East.

Vacationers, tubercular patients, conservationists, wilderness devotees—all of these people wanted to see the resources of the Adirondacks preserved. This was partially achieved in 1885, when, after much political wrangling, the New York State legislature created the Adirondack Forest Preserve and directed that "the lands now or hereafter constituting the Forest Preserve shall be forever kept as wild forest lands." This action marked the first time a state government had set aside a significant piece of wilderness for reasons other than its scenic uniqueness.

In 1892, the legislature created the Adirondack State Park, consisting of Adirondack Forest Preserve land plus all privately owned land within a somewhat arbitrary boundary surrounding the the Adirondacks, known as the "blue line" because it was drawn in blue on a large state map when it was first established. In 1894, in response to continuing abuses of the Forest Preserve Law, the state's voters approved the inclusion of the "forever wild" portion of that law in the constitution of New York State, thus creating the only wild land preserve in the nation that has constitutional protection. Today the Forest Preserve consists of 2.5 million acres, being those lands owned by the people of the State of New York that are within the 6-million-acre Adirondack State Park, which is the largest park in the nation outside of Alaska.

In the first decade of the 20th century, raging fires consumed hundreds of thousands of acres of prime Adirondack forest lands; the scars from these fires can still be seen in many locations, both in exposed rock and in vegetation patterns. After World War I, tourism gradually took over as the primary industry in the Adirondacks. The arrival of the automobile, the invention of theme parks (some of the very first of which were in the Adirondacks), the development of winter sports facilities (with Lake Placid hosting the Winter Olympics in 1932), the increasing popularity of camping and hiking, and the growth of the second-home industry all brought such pressures to bear on the region that in 1968 Governor Nelson Rockefeller created a Temporary Study Commission on the Future of the Adirondacks. This commission made 181 recommendations, chief among them that a comprehensive land use plan, covering both public and private lands, be put in place and administered. This was accomplished by 1973, with the creation of the land use plans and the Adirondack Park Agency to manage them. Although the plans and the Agency have remained controversial, they are indicative of the need to address the issues facing the Adirondacks boldly and innovatively.

In 1990 there were 130,000 permanent residents and nearly 100,000 seasonal residents in the 9,375-square-mile Adirondack Park, which is roughly the size of Vermont. Recreation, forestry, mining and agriculture are the principal industries in the Park.

The High Peaks Region

Using This Guidebook

The trails described in this book are all in the High Peaks region of the Adirondacks, which derives its name from the fact that it contains all of the Adirondack peaks with elevations over 4000 feet, as well as numerous other mountains under 4000 feet. The region is located in the interior of the northeastern quadrant of the Adirondack State Park (see accompanying map) and includes the villages of Lake Placid, Saranac Lake, Keene, Keene Valley and Newcomb. The principal highways in the region are NY 73 in the north and northeast, and NY 28N and Essex County Road 2B in the south; US 9 and Interstate 87, "The Adirondack Northway," establish the region's eastern boundary for the most part.

Like all the books in the Adirondack Mountain Club Forest Preserve Series of guides to Adirondack trails, this book is intended to be both a reference tool for planning trips and a field guide to carry on the trail. All introductory material should be read carefully, for it contains important information regarding the use of this book, as well as numerous suggestions for safe and proper travel by foot in the Adirondacks. For campers, there is an important section on the relevant rules and regulations for camping in the Adirondacks.

The introduction to each of the sections in this book gives hikers an idea of the varied opportunities available in the High Peaks region. There are many beautiful and seldom-visited places aside from the most popular hiking, climbing and camping areas; this guide will enable you to find and explore these remote spots.

Mount Marcy

Mt. Marcy, the highest peak in the Adirondacks, rises 5344 ft. above sea level. It was named in 1837 in honor of Governor William Learned Marcy by Ebenezer Emmons, Professor of Chemistry at Williams College and Geologist-in-Chief of the second District of the Geological Survey of New York. Emmons was the leader of the party that made the first recorded ascent on August 5, 1837. An Indian name, "Tahawus," has also been applied to this peak; but in reality this name was not used by local Indians and was first used by a writer of that era in referring to the recently climbed peak. Pronounced "Ta-HA-wus," the name means "cloud-splitter."

The first trail up Marcy was cut by "Old Mountain" Phelps and other guides about 1861 from Upper Ausable Lake. This trail roughly followed the current trail from the Warden's Camp to the top of Bartlett Ridge, from which it slabbed the side of Haystack and dropped down to cross Panther Gorge NE of the present Panther Gorge Lean-to. From the bottom of Panther Gorge, the trail ascended Marcy via some slides on the SE slopes to timberline. This trail was abandoned after 1873 when men working on Verplanck Colvin's Adirondack Survey cut a trail up the valley of Marcy Brook and up to Four Corners, similar to the route of the present Elk Lake-Marcy Trail.

The last 800 ft. of its crest rises above timberline—an irregular rocky dome with alpine growing in the crevices and depressions where soil has accumulated. A copper bolt was set into the actual summit at the time of the Colvin Survey in 1875, but it has since been removed and only the drill hole now remains. A brass disk set in place in the 1940s has also regrettably been removed by souvenir hunters. On a vertical rock wall just below the summit is a bronze plaque (see below) commemorating the first recorded ascent of this "High Peak of Essex."

1837—MARCY—1937
Also Known by the Indian Name
TAHAWUS
Meaning "Cloud Splitter"

ON AUGUST 5, 1837 THE FIRST RECORDED
ASCENT OF THIS MOUNTAIN WAS MADE AND ITS
HEIGHT MEASURED. IT WAS NAMED MT. MARCY IN
HONOR OF GOVERNOR WILLIAM LEARNED MARCY,
WHO HAD APPOINTED A COMMISSION TO MAKE
THE FIRST GEOLOGICAL SURVEY OF THE
NORTHEASTERN DISTRICT.

The following made the ascent:
    Prof. Ebenezer Emmons of Williams, and
    James Hall, state geologist;
    Prof. John Torrey, botanist;
    Professors Strong and Miller, geologists;
    William C. Redfield, engineer and meteorologist;
    C.C. Ingham, artist and Ebenezer Emmons, Jr.;
    Archibald McIntyre and David Henderson,
    original explorers and early owners of this region;
    Harvey Holt and John Cheney, guides;
    and three unknown woodsmen.

Erected by the Adirondack Mountain Club in conjunction
with the Conservation Department of New York State.

Editors's note: The Conservation Department mentioned above is
presently the Department of Environmental Conservation of New
York State. Also, more recent research indicates that three of the
individuals named on the plaque—Strong, Miller and McIntyre—did
not actually make the ascent.

The view from Marcy on a clear day is of an endless wilderness of irregular mountaintops and miles of unbroken forest. Only to the N and far E are farmlands and villages visible. To the ESE near at hand is Haystack, the third highest Adirondack summit, with its long rocky crestline. Between Marcy and Haystack is the precipitous Panther Gorge. From Haystack, the Great Range runs NE toward Keene Valley. Prominent in this range, ENE from Marcy, is Gothics with its bare rock slides. Directly over Gothics is the col between Giant on the L and Rocky Peak Ridge on the R. Through this col on a clear day may be seen Camel's Hump in the Green Mountains of Vermont, about 54 mi. away. Directly to the R of Gothics is its third summit, Pyramid, beyond which a long, low col leads to Sawteeth. On spectacularly clear winter days, the White Mountains of New Hampshire can be seen beyond.

To the NNE, across the Johns Brook Valley from the Great Range, the rock face of Big Slide stands out against a background of Porter and Cascade to the L. In the distance to the N the waters of Lake Placid shine below the regular cone of Whiteface, with the village of Lake Placid just to the L of Lake Placid. The large white structure in the village is the Olympic Center field house with the ski jump complex visible closer at hand and practically in line with the field house. Nearer and NNW lies little Heart Lake at the foot of Mt. Jo. Slightly W of NW, Colden, with its rock slides, stands out against the broad side of the MacIntyre Range, with Boundary Peak directly above Colden, Iroquois to the L, and Algonquin, the second highest Adirondack summit, to the R. To the R of Algonquin is Wright Peak with a prominent slide; through the col between these two peaks may be seen Street.

Due W, about 0.8 mi. away, is Gray Peak, seventh highest peak and the highest trailless summit. By walking to the SW of the summit, about 200 feet one can see little Lake Tear of the Clouds, the highest pond source of the Hudson River, directly below Marcy to the SW. In line with Lake Tear stands Redfield, while near at hand, SSW, is Skylight, the fourth in order of height. Between Redfield and Skylight, and about 38 mi. away, may be seen Snowy Mt., the highest peak in the southern Adirondacks, elevation 3899 ft.

Slightly to the L and behind Skylight is Allen with its two summits, while almost due S the Boreas Ponds gleam in a forest setting. Boreas Mt. may be seen to the E of the ponds, and the long, low, tree-covered ridge with many bumps SE from Marcy is the Colvin-Pinnacle Ridge. In all, the summits of 43 of the other 45 major peaks can be seen; only little Couchsachraga, hidden behind Panther Mt., is totally invisible. The highest point seen on East Dix appears to be the summit, but is actually a point 200 yds. NE of the true summit.

There are four main approaches to Marcy. These start from Keene Valley, Heart Lake, Upper Works near Tahawus, and Elk Lake. As the following summary shows, the shortest approach is from Heart Lake. The most difficult is from Elk Lake, due to the rough nature of the trail and to the extra vertical ascent caused by the presence of the Colvin Range before the start up Marcy. There are almost unlimited possibilities for backpackers to approach Marcy, including a very rugged traverse of the Great Range on the way to the summit, or a long, relatively flat approach from the W from Long Lake or Coreys.

Summary of Principal Trails to Marcy	Miles
Keene Valley:	
Phelps Trail via Slant Rock from Garden	9.1
Phelps Trail via Hopkins Tail from Garden	9.1
Great Range via Rooster Comb from Keene Valley	13.5
Heart Lake:	
Via Va Hoevenberg Trail	7.4
Via Avalanche Pass and Lake Colden	10.7
Via Lake Arnold	8.8

Summary of Principal Trails to Marcy	Miles
Elk Lake:	
Elk Lake-Marcy Trail	11.0
Upper Works:	
Via Calamity Brook Trail	10.3
Via Hanging Spear Falls and Flowed Lands	14.2
Western Approaches:	
From Coreys via Duck Hole and Henderson Lake	26.8
From Long Lake via Shattuck Clearing, Duck Hole and Henderson Lake	40.2

Mt. Marcy from Keene Valley via the Complete Great Range:

This is an extremely rugged trip with very rough trail for most of the distance. For more information, see Mt. Marcy section of Introduction.

The following table of information is included for those who wish to traverse the entire Great Range from Keene Valley to Mt. Marcy. As the distance and vertical ascent figures indicate, this is an extremely rugged trip with very rough trail for most of the distance. Allow several days with backpacks, and be aware that there are no longer any lean-tos along this route and that there is only one designated camping area. Unless camping at this one designated campsite (at the site of the former Sno-Bird Lean-to), one must camp at least 150 ft. away from any trail or water supply. Camping is further prohibited anywhere above 4000 ft. in elevation.

The following are the applicable trail descriptions in the Keene Valley Section: Rooster Comb, Hedgehog, and Lower Wolf Jaw from Keene Valley (trail 18); Lower Wolf Jaw (trail 5); ADK Range Trail to Upper Wolf Jaw, Armstrong and Gothics (trail 4); State Range Trail to Saddleback, Basin, Haystack and Marcy (trail 9). One can return by either the Phelps or Hopkins Trail.

Summary of Distances from bridge 0.6 mi. W of Keene Valley to:

Point	Distance Miles	(Kms)	Approx. Feet	Total Ascent (Meters)
Rooster Comb	1.8	(2.8)	1640	(500)
Hedgehog	3.1	(5.0)	2530	(700)
W.A. White Trail	3.5	(5.6)		
Lower Wolf Jaw	5.0	(8.0)	3670	(1120)
Wolf Jaws Notch	5.4	(8.8)		
Upper Wolf Jaw	6.4	(10.4)	4510	(1375)
Armstrong	7.2	(11.7)	5030	(1530)
ATIS Trail to St. Huberts	7.7	(12.3)		
Gothics	8.1	(13.1)	5530	(1685)
Gothics Col	8.8	(14.1)		
Saddleback	9.4	(15.0)	6130	(1870)
Basin	10.3	(16.5)	6800	(2070)
Shorey Short Cut	11.1	(17.8)		
Site of former Sno-Bird Lean-to	11.2	(18.0)		
Haystack Trail	11.7	(18.8)	7630	(2235)
Phelps Trail	12.2	(19.6)		
Van Hoevenberg Trail	12.7	(20.7)	8440	(2570)
Marcy	13.5	(21.7)	9000	(2740)

Maps

The map enclosed in the back of this book is a composite of U.S. Geological Survey quadrangles with updated overlays of trails, shelters and private land lines. The maps in this guide and in the companion guides are especially valuable because of their combination of contour lines from the original base maps and recent trail information, updated with each printing of the guides. The High Peaks map covers most of the terrain described in this guidebook, but a few isolated trails not conveniently shown on it are shown on individual page maps within the text. Extra copies of the two-sided High Peaks map are available from many retailers or directly from the Adirondack Mountain Club, RR 3, Box 3055, Lake George, NY 12845.

There are now two series of USGS maps covering this area. The first is the familiar 15-minute series produced in the mid-1950s; the newer series are 7.5 by 15-minute sheets with metric elevations and contours. The USGS produced this second series in the late 1970s in anticipation of the 1980 Winter Olympics, and the metric units reflect the international nature of that event. The map enclosed with this guidebook uses both of these series of base maps. The "High Peaks" map (on one side), which has been a part of this guide for years, continues to be based on the older 15-minute series maps, while the new "High Peaks—North" map (opposite side) is based on the newer metric maps.

For the "High Peaks" map the actual quadrangles used are the Santanoni, Mt. Marcy, and Elizabethtown (eastern half). (The corresponding metric series sheets are the Ampersand Lake, Santanoni Peak, Keene Valley, Mt. Marcy, Elizabethtown and Witherbee sheets.) The "High Peaks—North" map is based on the Saranac Lake, Wilmington, Lake Placid and Lewis 7.5' by 15' metric sheets. (The corresponding 15-minute series quadrangles are Lake Placid, SE corner of Saranac Lake, and SW corner of Ausable Forks).

Trail Signs and Markers

With normal alertness to one's surroundings, trails in the Adirondacks are easy to follow. In most cases, where trails leave a highway or come to a junction there will be a sign to direct the hiker. As much as possible, descriptions in this guidebook are detailed enough so that a hiker can find the correct route even in the rare case when signs are temporarily down.

In addition to a map, all hikers should carry a compass and know at least the basics of its use. In some descriptions, this guide uses compass bearings to differentiate the trail at a junction or to indicate the direction of travel above timberline. More importantly, a compass can be an indispensable aid in the unlikely event that you lose your way.

The trails themselves are usually marked with metal or plastic disks bearing the insignia of the organization responsible for them. Trails maintained by the DEC are marked with blue, yellow or red disks; the particular color for each trail is indicated on the signs and in the guidebook description. Trails maintained by ADK are marked with red and white or orange and black disks. Trails maintained by ATIS are marked with their markers, now mostly orange and black, although some older blue or white markers remain.

Hikers must be aware that some trails are easier to follow than others due to the level of use. While one could practically "sleepwalk" from Adirondak Loj to Marcy Dam, for instance, considerable care is needed to follow other trails though the pattern of marking is similar. Although this guidebook does mention particularly tricky turns in the trail descriptions, each hiker must remain alert at all times for changes of direction and group leaders have a particular responsibility not to let inexperienced members of the party travel by themselves. A trail that seems obvious to a more experienced person may not be that way at all to an inexperienced member of the group.

Finally, it should go without saying that one should never remove any sign or marker. Hikers noticing damaged or missing signs should report this fact to the appropriate group: Adirondack Mt. Club, RR 3, Box 3055, Lake George, NY 12845, for ADK trails; Department of

Environmental Conservation, Ray Brook, NY 12977, for DEC trails; and the Adirondack Trail Improvement Society, P.O. Box 565, Keene Valley, NY 12943, for ATIS trails.

All trails described in this guide are on public land or along public rights of way, but there may be "posted" signs at some points. These are usually there to remind hikers that they are on private land over which the owner has kindly granted permission for hikers to pass. In most cases, leaving the trail, camping, fishing and hunting are not permitted on these lands, and hiker should respect the owner's wishes.

Distance and Time

Except where noted, all trails in this guidebook have been measured with a professional surveyor's wheel. While this instrument is accurate to a hundredth of a mile, distances are expressed to the nearest tenth since that is as close as most hikers can estimate in the field. Shorter distances are expressed as yards although the number of yards has usually been derived from a wheel measurement in the field.

At the start of each section of this guide there is a list of trails in the region, the mileage unique to the trail, and the number of the page on which the trail description is located. All mileage distances given in the trail description are cumulative, the beginning of the trail being the 0 mi. point. A distance summary is given at the end of each description, with a total distance expressed in kilometers as well as in miles. If a trail has climbed significantly over its course, its total ascent in both feet and meters is provided. To the inexperienced hiker, these distances will seem longer on the trail, but he or she will quickly learn that there is a great difference between "sidewalk" miles and "trail" miles.

The distances given in this guide are often at odds with the distances given on the DEC trail signs. The DEC has used a variety of measuring methods over the years and has not always updated every sign after every change of distance caused by rerouting, etc. In all cases where there is a disagreement, the guidebook distance can be assumed to be correct; the DEC is currently in the process of revising all of its sign distances based on the wheel measurements found in this guide.

No attempt has been made to estimate times for these trails. A conservative rule to follow in estimating time is to allow an hour for every 1.5 mi., plus 1/2 hour for each 1000 ft. ascended, with experience soon indicating how close each hiker is to his standard. Most day hikers will probably hike faster than this, but backpackers will probably find they go more slowly. Some time will usually be saved on the descent, but on a rough trail the descent may take nearly as long as the ascent, especially with heavy packs.

Abbreviations and Conventions

In each of the books in the Forest Preserve Series, R and L, with periods omitted, are used for right and left. The R and L banks of a stream are determined by looking downstream. N, S, E, and W, again without periods, are used for north, south, east, and west. Some compass directions are given in degrees, figuring from true N, with E as 90 degrees, etc.

The following abbreviations are used in the text and on the maps:

ADK	Adirondack Mt. Club
AMR	Adirondack Mountain Reserve
ATIS	Adirondack Trail Improvement Society
DEC	New York State Department of Environmental Conservation
JBL	Johns Brook Lodge

N-P	Northville-Placid (Trail)
PBM	Permanent Bench Mark
USGS	United States Geological Survey
ft.	Feet
mi.	Mile
yds	Yards

Hiking with Children

Most hikers with children want to start them hiking as early as possible, but one needs to be aware that children can have very different perceptions of what it means to go on a hike. Given the range of physical abilities and mental outlooks, there is no one "right" way to introduce a child to the concept of struggling up a steep hill only to turn around and return to the starting point. The guidelines below may help avoid a few of the common pitfalls. Also, see Appendix III for a table of short hikes in the region.

Attitude:

Having a positive experience is more important than reaching one's destination. At least at first, children are not goal-oriented, so that the promise of reaching the view at the top does not have the same motivation factor it has for adults. Be prepared to stop short of the original goal; as one experienced father put it, "You are where you are." Make an adventure out of the tough spots ("we're almost to the 'mountain goat pitch'") and a game out of boring spots ("how many trail markers can you see?"). Be prepared to stop and look at anything of interest, whether it is you or the child who notices the plant, frog, moss, stick, leaf or whatever. A lady slipper along the trail may be an adult's greatest treat, but a child will take even greater pleasure in finding a stick that looks vaguely like a dinosaur.

Make sure to reward the child for completing a hike. Make it a special occasion, perhaps a reason for a call to the grandparents or a favorite dessert with dinner. You may want to keep a chart or map of hikes done to show progress. Show the child the day's trip on a map, and get it out again to plan the next one. Over time, most children will come to appreciate the satisfaction of a fun hike, and will want to do more.

Distance and Destination:

Three-year-olds (and even strong two-year-olds) can hike as much as a mile, and a mile will get you to the top of some small mountains. Walking uphill can be a problem, however, and many children are just as excited to hike a flat route to a stream where they can throw rocks and sticks. Four-to six-year-olds are more likely to be able to focus on making an ascent of over a mile to a summit—but again, too much steep going can prove discouraging.

Time:

At least double your own time for a particular hike. Children not only walk more slowly but also want to take frequent breaks. Have an open-ended time schedule so that you don't become impatient with slower-than-expected progress. Adult hikers know that a steady pace with fewer stops is usually the most efficient, but children need to take "mental" breaks as well as physical rests. While actually hiking, however, encourage steady progress as opposed to the "20 running steps followed by a complete stop" type of pace that many children will try at first.

Equipment and Supplies:

Even small children should be encouraged to carry at least some of their own gear, but be prepared to take it if the pack seems to be the only thing causing an unpleasant time. Bring plenty of water and food and don't feel that your goal is to instill toughness by forcing the march to the summit before the first sip of water can be had. On a hot day, freeze a few plastic water bottles beforehand. Not only will you have cool water, but watching the ice melt and telling others about a "special hiking trick" will add to the hike in ways an adult could never understand. Likewise, avoid using food (i.e. candy) as a bribe too often, but I doubt if there are many parents who can claim never to have promised a treat for just a little more effort. Bring insect repellent; a cap can be very helpful in keeping the bugs off the back of the head.

Hiking boots are the preferred footwear, but running shoes are fine as long as they are sturdy enough to offer protection from sharp rocks underneath and sticks above. Make sure the child wears socks and has a sweater and raincoat at all times. Add a wool hat and mittens if it is at all cold because a summit can be much colder. Long pants offer protection from twigs and brambles as well as reducing the exposed skin area for insect bites, but don't push it if the child prefers shorts.

Most importantly, double-check that every needed item is indeed packed. One forgotten cookie can ruin the whole trip.

Safety:

Children have very little judgment and, at first, virtually no ability to stay on even an "obvious" trail. Let them lead but keep them in sight, and be ready to take the lead near any cliffs, bridges or other dangerous areas. Be especially careful on top of ledges, and keep them from throwing anything over the edge of a cliff. Not only is it very easy for a child to throw himself off as well, but there may be others below. Children love to hike with the family dog, but large, rambunctious dogs pose the danger of knocking a child down or even off the trail as they race back and forth checking on everyone or chasing sticks.

Above all, keep the group together and never solve the problem of a reluctant hiker by sending him back down the trail alone. The above list of safety concerns is hardly complete, but it may alert parents to a few of the potential problems unique to hiking.

Wilderness Camping

It is not the purpose of this series to teach one how to camp in the woods. There are many good books available on that subject that are more comprehensive and useful than any explanation that could be given in the space available here. The information below should, however, serve to make hikers aware of the differences and peculiarities of the Adirondacks while giving strong emphasis to currently recommended procedures to reduce environmental damage—particularly in heavily used areas.

Except for Johns Brook Lodge, 3.5 mi. up the Marcy Trail from Keene Valley, there are no huts in the Adirondacks. There are, however, lean-tos at many convenient locations along the trails, and there are also many possibilities for tenting along the way. The regulations regarding tenting and the use of these shelters are simple and unrestrictive when compared to those of other popular backpacking areas in the country; but it is important that every backpacker know and obey the restrictions that do exist, because they are designed to promote the long-term enjoyment of the greatest number of people.

General Camping Guidelines:

Except for groups of ten or more (see below), no camping or fire permits are required in the Adirondacks, but campers must obey all DEC regulations regarding camping. Listed below are some of the most important regulations. Complete regulations are available from the DEC and are posted at most access points.

1) No camping within 150 ft. of a stream, other water source, or trail, except at a designated campsite. Most areas near an existing lean-to are considered designated campsites; other areas are designated with the following symbol:

New York State Dept. Environmental Conservation

" CAMP HERE "

2) Except in an emergency, no camping is permitted above 4000 ft. in elevation. (This rule does not apply from December 1 to April 30.)

3) All washing of dishes must be done at least 150 ft. from any stream, pond, or other water source. **No soap,** even so-called "biodegradeable" soap, should ever get into the water, so use a pot to carry water at least 150 ft. away from your source and wash items and dispose of water there. One can also take a surprisingly effective bath by taking a quick dip and then using a pot for soaping and rinsing away from the stream or pond.

4) All human excrement must be buried under at least four inches of soil at a spot at least 150 ft. away from any water source, and all toilet paper likewise buried or burned. Use established privies or latrines when available.

5) No wood except for **dead** and **down** timber may be used for fire building. Good wood is often scarce at popular campsites, so a stove is highly recommended.

6) No fire should be built near or on any flammable material. Much of the forest cover in the Adirondacks is composed of recently rotted twigs, leaves, or needles and is **highly flammable.** Build a fire at an established fireplace or on rocks or sand. Before leaving destroy all traces of any new fireplace created.

7) All refuse must be completely burned or carried out of the woods. **Do not bury** any refuse and be sure that no packaging to be

burned is an air pollutant or contains metal foil—it will not burn no matter how hot the fire. Plastic packaging is also best carried out. When burned it can pollute the air and often does not burn completely.Remember—if you carried it in, you can carry it out.

8) In general, leave no trace of your presence when leaving a campsite, and help by carrying out *more* than you carried in.

Lean-tos:

Lean-tos are available on a first-come, first-served basis up to the capacity of the shelter—usually about seven persons. A small party cannot therefore claim exclusive use of a shelter and must allow late arrivals equal use. Most lean-tos have a fireplace in front (sometimes with a primitive grill) and sanitary facilities. Most are located near some source of water, but each camper must use his own judgment as to whether or not the water supply needs purification before drinking.

It is in very poor taste to carve or write one's initials in a shelter. Please try to keep these rustic shelters in good condition and appearance.

Because reservations cannot be made for any of these shelters, it is best to carry a tent or other alternate shelter. Many shelters away from the standard routes, however, are rarely used, and a small party can often find a shelter open in the more remote areas.

The following regulations apply specifically to lean-tos, in addition to the general camping regulations listed above:

1) No plastic may be used to close off the front of a shelter.

2) No nails or other permanent fastener may be used to affix a tarp in a lean-to, but it is permissible to use rope to tie canvas or nylon tarps across the front.

3) No tent may be pitched inside a lean-to.

Groups:

Any group of ten or more persons must obtain a permit *before* camping on state land. This system is designed to prevent overuse of certain critical sites and also to encourage groups to split into smaller parties more in keeping with the natural environment. Permits can be obtained from the DEC forest ranger closest to the actual starting point of one's proposed trip. The local forest ranger can be contacted by writing to him directly; if in doubt about whom to write, send the letter to the Department of Environmental Conservation, Ray Brook, NY 12977. They will forward the letter, but you should allow at least two weeks for the letter to reach the appropriate forest ranger.

One can also make the initial contact with the forest ranger by telephone, but keep in mind that rangers' schedules during the busy summer season are often unpredictable. Forest rangers are listed in the white pages of local phone books under "New York, State of; Environmental Conservation, Department of; Forest Ranger." Bear in mind when calling that most rangers operate out of their own homes, and observe the normal courtesy used when calling any private residence. Contact by letter is much preferred, and, as one can see, camping with a large group requires careful planning several weeks before the trip.

The camping regulations as described here are those in effect as of the date of publication. However, the DEC is in the process of preparing a unit management plan for the High Peaks Wilderness Area; and there *may* be some significant changes in these regulations in the near future in order to better protect this popular area from potential further damage. These regulations may or may not be extended to the Dix, Giant, Sentinel and McKenzie Mountain Wilderness Areas at the same time they are implemented for the High Peaks. On the adjacent "wild forest" and "primitive" areas, however, the regulations will not likely change. The highlights of the possible new regulations include:

1) Camping groups of ten will be allowed without a permit, but *no permits* will be written for groups larger than that.

2) No fires will be permitted at Marcy Dam, Lake Colden, or in the Johns Brook Valley. Stoves will therefore by required.

3) No winter camping will be permitted above 4000 feet. (The summer prohibition will continue.)

4) A limit (probably of less than 20, and possibly as low as 10) will be placed on day hiking groups. These groups must either start at different trailheads or split to different destinations. Groups cannot simply separate themselves on the same trail. There also may be a limit on the total number (probably 50) of members of the same "affinity" group permitted in the High Peaks at any one time.

5) No glass containers will be permitted.

6) Registration will be mandatory, and all camping parties may be required to carry a camping "trip ticket."

The unit management plan and its proposed new restrictions must still pass through several stages of public review and comment before it is enacted. If, however, any of the above changes might affect one's planned trip in any of the wilderness areas in this guide, check with either the DEC or ADK to ascertain the current regulations.

Drinking Water

For many years, hikers could trust practically any water source in the Adirondacks to be pure and safe to drink. Unfortunately, as in many other mountain areas, some Adirondack water sources have become contaminated with a parasite known as *Giardia lamblia*. This intestinal parasite causes a disease known as Giardiasis—often called "Beaver Fever." It can be spread by any warm-blooded mammal when infected feces wash into the water; beavers are prime agents in transferring this parasite because they spend so much of their time near water. Hikers themselves have also become primary agents in spreading this disease because some individuals appear to be unaffected carriers of the disease, and other recently infected individuals may inadvertently spread the parasite before their symptoms become apparent.

Prevention: Follow the guidelines for the disposal of human excrement as stated in the "Wilderness Camping" section (above). Equally important, make sure that every member of your group is aware of the problem and follows the guidelines as well. The health of a fellow hiker may depend on your consideration.

Choosing a Water Source: While no water source can be guaranteed to be safe, smaller streams high in the mountains which have no possibility of a beaver dam or temporary human presence upstream may be safe to drink. If, however, there is any doubt, treat the water before drinking.

Treatment: Boil all water for 2-3 minutes (rolling boil), administer an iodine-based chemical purifer (available at camping supply stores and some drug and department stores), or use a commercial filter designed specifically for Giardiasis prevention. If after returning from a trip you experience recurrent intestinal problems, consult your physician and explain your potential problem.

Safety in the High Peaks

Unlike other regions of the Adirondacks, the High Peaks region presents an abundance of extremely steep terrain as well as exposed alpine environments with the potential for arctic weather conditions. On these exposed summits, one must be prepared for either a sudden loss of visibility, a rapid drop in temperature, or both, even in the summer. Hikers should therefore always carry extra clothing when traveling above timberline and also should pay close attention to their location in the event that visibility is suddenly reduced.

Summer temperatures in the High Peaks can drop below freezing at night, particularly in late August, and snow or ice, though rare, is not unknown on the summits in any month of the year. From early September through the end of May, hikers should always consider the possibility of considerable snow or freezing temperatures on the summits. True winter conditions can commence in early November and last until May. During the winter, weather conditions in the lowlands can be relatively benign while at higher elevations, and especially above timberline, conditions may be so severe that a single miscue or a momentary lapse of concentration could prove fatal. It is imperative that persons travel in groups of not less than four and be outfitted properly when winter conditons prevail. Be advised that the DEC requires High Peaks users to have snowhoes or skis in "snow season." For more information on winter travel, see the Adirondack Mountain Club publication *Winterwise* by John Dunn.

Hunting Seasons

Hikers should be aware that, unlike the national park system, sport hunting is permitted on all public lands within the Adirondack and Catskill state parks. There are separate rules and seasons for each type of hunting (small game, waterfowl, and big game); but it is the big game season, i.e. deer and bear, that is most likely to cause concern for hikers.

For those hikers who might be concerned, the following is a list of all big game hunting seasons—running from approximately mid-September through early December.

Early Bear Season: Begins the first Saturday after the second Monday in September and continues for four weeks.

Archery Season (deer and bear): September 27 to opening of the regular season.

Muzzleloading Season (deer and bear): The seven days prior to the opening of regular season.

Regular Season: Next to last Saturday in October through the first Sunday in December.

During any of these open seasons, prudence dictates the wearing of at least one piece of brightly colored clothing, although the chance of actually encountering hunters on mountain trails is relatively small given that the game being pursued, and consequently the hunters themselves, do not favor the steeper mountain slopes. Although hunters might use portions of marked hiking trails as access, they recognize that hiker traffic along the marked trail frightens game animals so that their best chance of success is far from those areas frequented by hikers.

The Adirondack Mt. Club does not promote hunting as one of its organized activities;, but it does recognize that sport hunting, when carried out in compliance with the game laws administered by the Dept. of Environmental Conservation, is a legitimate and necessary method of managing game populations. The harrassment of hunters engaged in the legitimate pursuit of their sport is not appropriate. Suspected violations of the game laws should be reported to the nearest DEC Forest Ranger or Conservation Officer.

Emergency Procedures

An ounce of prevention is always worth a pound of cure, but if one is in need of emergency assistance, the DEC forest rangers are the first people to contact for help. The names and phone numbers of the local rangers are often posted inside each trail register. Forest rangers are listed in the white pages of the local phone book under "New York, State of; Environmental Conservation, Department of; Forest Ranger." If this fails, one should try (during business hours) DEC headquarters in Ray Brook, NY: (518) 891-1370, or (after business hours) the DEC Ranger Dispatch: (518) 891-0235. The third place to call would be the New York State Police (518-897-2000) in Ray Brook. They will use whatever means needed to contact persons able to help. Make sure that the person going for help has the above information plus a complete *written* description of the type and exact location of the accident.

Peaks Without Maintained Trails

Of the 46 peaks in the Adirondacks determined to be 4000 feet or more above sea level by the United States Geological Survey at the turn of this century, 20 lack trails. Though all of them now possess rough paths beaten out by many climbers, these so-called "herd paths" are not marked. Any of these trails can become blocked by blowdown at some key point, causing the formation of false herd paths. In some places there are veritable mazes of herd paths with not all leading to one's destination. (There are several instances, for example, of hikers inadvertently ascending Street or Tabletop a second time the same day—all the while thinking they were headed somewhere else). Thus, ascents of these peaks still call for considerable route-finding and tracking skills and are not for the inexperienced.

The current interest in trailless climbing dates back to Robert and George Marshall, who in 1924, with their friend and guide Herbert Clark, completed climbing the 46 peaks indicated as over 4000 feet on USGS maps available at that time. Since then, following completed ascents of the same mountains nine years later by Fay Loope, thousands of recreationists have sought out this special outdoor activity. These mountaineers have organized a unique climbing society known as the Adirondack Forty-Sixers. They have their own articles of organization, by-laws, and a distinctive shoulder patch. The Forty-Sixers meet twice a year near the High Peaks and publish a newsletter known as *Adirondack Peeks*.

In deciding what constituted an individual peak, the Marshalls set an arbitrary rule that it should rise 300 ft. on all sides or be at the end of a ridge at least three-quarters of a mile from the nearest peak. Since then, more recent surveys using better equipment and aerial photography have indicated that four of the peaks—Blake, Cliff, Nye and Couchsachraga—are under 4000 ft. and that some peaks fail to qualify if the above rule on separate peaks is strictly applied to the new survey data. The 1953 survey raised MacNaughton Mt., originally indicated as being 3976 ft., to the 4000 foot peerage only to have the most recent survey in 1979, which produced the 1:25,000 scale 7.5 by 15 minute metric scale maps, lower the mountain once again below the 4000 ft. line.

Because the Adirondack Forty-Sixers was founded to bring together those who had climbed the same 46 peaks climbed by the Marshalls and Herb Clark, it has been resolved that the climbing of these same 46 peaks, regardless of their corrected elevations, still shall be considered a prerequisite for membership in that organization. Technically, however, climbers of the 108 4000-footers in the northeastern United States are correct in recognizing only 42 peaks in the Adirondacks over 4000 ft.

If you seriously intend to become a Forty-Sixer, write to The Adirondack Forty-Sixers, Adirondack, NY 12808. It is not necessary to belong to the Adirondack Mountain Club (and in fact the Forty-Sixers and ADK are completely separate organizations), but many Forty-Sixers are also members of ADK.

Climbing the peaks without maintained trails calls for leadership by people experienced in map reading and use of the compass along with possessing a feeling for route-finding in forested mountain terrain. Fog and rain can complicate staying on course, and dealing with injuries and illness is obviously more difficult away from formal trails. Know the location of all trails in the vicinity of a climb. Know your mountain peaks and be able to recognize them from any viewpoint. Before you make your trip, learn to read a topographic map and to use a compass. Carry with you a guidebook, USGS topographic map, compass, flashlight with extra batteries and bulb, first-aid kit, insect repellent, matches, extra food and clothing (not 100% cotton) and raingear designed to keep you as dry and warm as possible in case bad weather sets in and you are forced to spend the night out.

Climbers of these peaks without maintained trails have a special obligation not to climb alone, to sign in as well as out at all DEC registers on approach trails, and to let other responsible people know of planned climbing routes. Such consideration is due the people who possibly might have to participate in a rescue party.

It has been Adirondack Mountain Club policy and more recently DEC policy to favor keeping a considerable number of Adirondack peaks free of formal trails so that those desiring it may enjoy the adventure of route-finding on their own in less frequented areas. Climbers of these peaks have taken pains to leave the routes, bivouac areas and summits as free as possible of human presence. This includes refraining from placing any markings such as blazes or surveyor's flagging along the route since climbers are expected to be able to find their own route back to civilization.

In the near future there may be a shift in the above policy, as the experience of the past few years has shown that earlier efforts to control erosion on these peaks have not been as successful as hoped. Also, on several peaks the number of "herd paths" has continued to multiply. To try and solve these problems there may in the future be some official marking of the desired route so as to keep hikers on the route where the least damage will occur. Where possible, this marking will be totally natural, such as placing brush strategically to block off a less desirable route or the limbing of a down tree to encourage hikers to continue to use the established route. This possible policy change in no way sanctions the marking of existing routes, and it may be several years before the policy is implemented and even more before there is much noticeable change.

The descriptions of routes on the peaks without trails are included with the descriptions of neighboring trails and not in a separate section. The descriptions are general, both to encourage individual route-finding and in recognition that blowdowns, beaver dams and many other natural changes can likewise change the exact route of the herd paths over time. Even if these routes become more fixed, the descriptions will likely remain general to help continue the sense of adventure one should feel when venturing off the marked trails. Each peak description includes a brief discussion of other possible approaches to the peak.

Finally, for those who desire even greater challenge than afforded by the trailless 4000 footers, there are an almost infinite number of other trailless peaks in the Adirondacks without so much as a hint of a herd path. Where appropriate, mention of these trailless peaks is made in this guide; but by consulting the maps much like the Marshalls did 70 years ago one will realize that the possibilities are still practically limitless for true exploration in the Adirondacks.

Alpine Zones

The actual land area that is above timberline in the Adirondacks is a very small part of the Forest Preserve, but it is one of the most unique and precious natural resources in the state. The alpine vegetation of moss, grasses, lichen, and rare flowers is very sensitive to human interference, and any damage done is extremely slow to heal. Hikers are therefore urged to stay on the designated trails and in all cases to walk only on the solid rock. Even exposed dirt and gravel must be avoided because these areas may grow back again if left undisturbed. Because of the precious and irreplaceable nature of these alpine areas, ADK and the Nature Conservancy have funded, in cooperation with the DEC, a Summit Steward program to put naturalists on Marcy, Algonquin, and occasionally other summits for the purpose of educating the hiking public about the importance of protecting this fragile resource. For this plus safety reasons, camping above 4000 feet elevation is forbidden; and hikers camping in open areas between 3000 and 4000 feet are urged to camp only at established sites or on rock or gravel, which cannot be destroyed by wear.

The Adirondack Mountain Club

The Adirondack Mountain Club (or ADK, the initials AMC having been claimed by the previously formed Appalachian Mountain Club) was organized in 1922 for the purpose of bringing together in a working unit a large number of people interested in the mountains, trails, camping, and forest conservation. A permanent club headquarters was established, and with an increasing membership, club chapters were organized. The chapters are as follows: Adirondak Loj (North Elba), Albany, Algonquin (Plattsburgh), Black River (Watertown), Cold River (Long Lake), Ct. Valley (Hartford), Finger Lakes (Ithaca-Elmira), Genesee Valley (Rochester), Glens Falls, Hurricane Mt. (Keene), Iroquois (Utica), Keene Valley, Knickerbocker (New York City and vicinity), Lake Placid, Laurentian (Canton-Potsdam), Long Island, Mid-Hudson (Poughkeepsie), Mohican (Westchester and Putnam counties, NY and Fairfield county, Ct), New York metropolitan area), Niagara Frontier (Buffalo), New Jersey, North Woods (Saranac Lake-Tupper Lake), Onondaga (Syracuse), Penn's Woods (Harrisburg, PA), Ramapo (Rockland and Orange counties), Schenectady, Shatagee Woods (Malone), and Susquehanna (Oneonta). In addition, there is an extensive membership-at-large.

Most chapters do not have qualifying requirements; a note to the Membership Director, Adirondack Mountain Club, RR 3, Box 3055, Lake George, NY 12845, will bring you information on membership in a local chapter (e.g., names and addresses of persons to be contacted) or details on membership-at-large. Persons joining a chapter, upon payment of their chapter dues, *ipso facto* become members of the club. Membership dues include a subscription to *Adirondac*, a bimonthly magazine; ADK's quarterly newsletter; and discounts on ADK books and at ADK lodges. An application for membership is in the back of this book.

Members of the Adirondack Mountain Club have formulated the following creed, which reflects the theme of the club and its membership:

I support the Club's work to insure that the lands of the State constituting the Forest Preserve shall be forever kept as wild forest lands in accordance with Article XIV, Section 1, of the New York State Constitution. I wish to be a part of the Club's volunteer-based conservation, education, and recreation activities aimed at protecting the Forest Preserve and encouraging outdoor recreation consistent with its wild forest character.

In the 1990s, approx. 19,000 "ADKers" enjoy the full spectrum of outdoor activities, including hiking, backpacking, canoeing (from floating on a pond to whitewater racing), rock climbing, cross-country skiing and snowshoeing. Most chapters have an active year-round outings schedule as well as regular meetings, sometimes including a meal, and programs featuring individuals ranging from chapter members to local and state officials. Many ADKers are also active in service work ranging from participation in search-and-rescue organizations to involvement in the ongoing debate over the best use of our natural resources and forest or wilderness lands, not only in the Adirondacks but also in their immediate localities.

ADK Facilities

ADK Information Center and Headquarters:

At the southernmost corner of the Park is the long log cabin that serves as ADK's Adirondack Park Information Center and Headquarters. The building, located just off exit 21 of I-87 ("the Northway") about 0.2 mi. S on Route 9N, is open year-round. Hours: June 15 to Columbus Day, Monday–Saturday, 8:30 a.m.–5 p.m.; Tuesday after Columbus Day–June 14, Monday–Friday, 8:30 a.m.–4:30 p.m.

ADK staff at this facility provide information about hiking, canoeing, cross-country skiing, climbing and camping in the Adirondack Park. In addition, they host lectures, workshops, and exhibits; sell publications and ADK logo items; and provide membership information. For further information, call or write ADK, RR 3, Box 3055, Lake George, NY 12845-9522 (telephone: 518-668-4447). For information about ADK accommodations, see below.

High Peaks Information Center:

Located on the Heart Lake property near the trailheads for many of the region's highest peaks, the High Peaks Information Center (HPIC) offers backcountry and general Adirondack information, educational displays, publications, some outdoor equipment, and trail snacks.

Adirondack Mountain Club Lodges:

The Adirondack Mountain Club, Inc. owns and operates two lodges for overnight guests in the High Peaks region. Johns Brook Lodge (Keene Valley Section) is accessible only by foot, whereas Adirondak Loj (Heart Lake Section) can be reached by car.

Johns Brook Lodge: Johns Brook Lodge (JBL) is on the trail to Mt. Marcy 5.1 mi. from Keene Valley and 3.5 mi. from the trailhead at the Garden. The lodge is open to all comers for meals and lodging daily from mid-June until Labor Day, during which it has a resident staff, and weekends from Memorial Day weekend until late June and the weekend after Labor Day until Columbus Day on a caretaker basis. During the summer season, the hutmaster in charge will make every effort to accommodate transients, but only reservations in advance will guarantee space in one of the two bunkrooms. Available all year long in the immediate vicinity of JBL are other accommodations owned by the Adirondack Mountain Club, Inc.: three lean-tos, and two cabins with cooking facilities—Camp Peggy O'Brien, housing 12, and Grace Camp, housing six. For further details and reservation information, contact Johns Brook Lodge, c/o Adirondak Loj, P.O. Box 867, Lake Placid, NY 12946.

Adirondak Loj: This facility, whose unusual spelling is explained in the Heart Lake Section of this guidebook, is 9 mi. by car from the village of Lake Placid. In addition to the Loj, the Adirondack Mountain Club owns the square mile of surrounding property, including all of Heart Lake and most of Mt. Jo. The Loj offers accommodations to all comers by the day or week, all year long, either in private bedrooms or in bunkrooms. Other accommodations include cabins, lean-tos with fireplaces, and numerous tent sites, for which nominal charges are made. Basic camping supplies may be purchased at the High Peaks Information Center located at the entrance to the parking lot at the Loj. A nominal parking charge is made for nonmembers not registered at the Loj or using the lean-tos and tent sites.

Several cross-country ski trails are located on the property and on nearby Forest Preserve land. This extensive network is a center of much wintertime activity. Snowshoers find much territory in which to enjoy their particular sport.

Of special interest at Adirondak Loj is a Nature Museum where one may find specimens of mosses, lichens, birds' nests, rocks and other Adirondack features. A modest library is available to help those who wish to identify their own samples.

A ranger-naturalist program is offered during the summer months. The leader conducts walks along a special nature trail and furnishes talks and slide shows on conservation and natural history topics. The latter are generally conducted in a scenic outdoor amphitheatre especially constructed for this purpose.

For full information about reservations, rates, or activities, address the Manager at Adirondak Loj, P.O. Box 867, Lake Placid, NY 12946 (telephone: 518-523-3441).

> Neal S. Burdick, Forest Preserve Series Editor
> Tony Goodwin, Editor, *Guide to Adirondack Trails:
> High Peaks Region*

Keene Valley Section

The village of Keene Valley has for many years been a favorite resort for those who love the mountains. From a multitude of trailheads, all within a few miles of each other, there is a tremendous variety of hikes available, ranging from short afternoon jaunts to rugged multiday backpacking trips. The most popular destinations are Mt. Marcy and other peaks of the Great Range, but there are also many shorter hikes whose views are dominated by Marcy at the head of the Johns Brook Valley.

Keene Valley is located on Rt. 73, 12 mi. N of Exit 30 on the Adirondack Northway or approx. 28 mi. S of Exit 34 via Rt. 9N and 73. There is daily bus service through Keene Valley on Adirondack Trailways, starting from Albany to the S or from Massena and Ottawa to the N. In the village are a grocery store, mountaineering store, diner, and bar/restaurant. Overnight accommodations are available at several local inns.

Johns Brook Lodge, 3.5 mi. up from Phelps Trail to Marcy, offers overnight accommodations from mid-June through Labor Day and is open on a caretaker basis Memorial Day Weekend until late June and the weekend after Labor Day until Columbus Day. (See section on Adirondack Mountain Club Lodges in Introduction for more information.) Staying at Johns Brook Lodge before climbing Marcy is perhaps the easiest way to ascend this peak since it is only 5.5 mi. from JBL to the summit, compared with over 7 mi. or more from any trailhead. The trails in this area are maintained by the DEC, the Trails Committee of ADK, or various chapters of ADK.

Trails in winter: Unless otherwise noted, trails in this section are not suitable for skiing. Winter ascents of the higher peaks usually require crampons, perhaps the use of an ice axe, and possibly a rope in addition, of course, to snowshoes.

The following are some suggested hikes among the many excellent possibilities:

Short Hikes:

Baxter from Rt. 9 N on Spruce Hill—2.2-mi. round trip. Mostly easy to moderate grades lead to a series of blueberry-covered ledges with nice views of Keene Valley, the Great Range, and Marcy.

First Brother—3.0-mi. round trip. This trail, though steep in spots, ascends via a beautiful series of ledges to a summit with good views of Keene Valley, Giant, the Great Range, and Marcy. See description for Big Slide via Brothers from Garden.

See also—Table of Short Hikes in Appendix III.

Moderate Hikes:

Porter Mt. from Garden with return via Ridge Trail to Airport—8.4 mi. point to point. An ascent with relatively easy grades and a nice view from Little Porter, with a return via the Ridge Trail and its many views including the ledges on aptly named Blueberry Mt. See description for Porter from Johns Brook Rd. near Garden and Porter from Keene Valley Airport via Ridge Trail.

Big Slide via Brothers with return via Slide Mt. Brook Trail and Southside Trail—9.5 mi. round trip. An ascent over three summits with good views, culminating in the spectacular view from Big Slide. Return down pretty Slide Mt. Brook and the Southside Trail with a swim at Tenderfoot Pool. See description for Big Slide via Brothers, Big Slide via Slide Mt. Brook Trail, and Southside Trail.

Harder Hikes:

Gothics via ADK Range Trail—14.7-mi. round trip. A rugged loop including two peaks before Gothics' spectacular summit, followed by an even more spectacular descent of the W face. See descriptions for Johns Brook Lodge and Mt. Marcy via Phelps Trail; ADK Range Trail to Upper Wolf Jaw, Armstrong and Gothics, and Gothics via Orebed Brook Trail.

Haystack Mt.—17.7-mi. round trip. Too many hikers come to the Adirondacks to climb Mt. Marcy and don't realize that it is far better to sit in relative solitude on the finest summit in all of the Adirondacks and gaze at Marcy. See descriptions for Johns Brook Lodge and Mt. Marcy via Phelps Trail and Haystack from Range Trail.

(1) Johns Brook Lodge and Mt. Marcy via Phelps Trail   Map: F-8

This route to Marcy was established by Ed Phelps, son of the famous Keene Valley guide Old Mountain Phelps. This trail is also called the Johns Brook Trail, Northside Trail or, in its upper sections, Slant Rock Trail. This approach to Marcy leads up the Johns Brook Valley past Johns Brook Lodge, which offers the closest overnight accommodations to the summit of Marcy. This approach to Marcy is the best to use if you are traveling by public transportation, because the bus route through Keene Valley is only 1.6 mi. from the trailhead, as compared to 5 mi. or more from all other Marcy trailheads.

Trailhead: The trail starts at the Garden parking lot W of Keene Valley.

From the center of Keene Valley at the DEC sign, "Trail to the High Peaks," follow yellow markers along a paved road, going straight at

0.3 mi. onto Interbrook Rd. At 0.6 mi. the road turns sharp R across a bridge over Johns Brook. (Private road straight ahead is the start for Rooster Comb and an approach to the complete Range Trail.) The road now begins a steady climb, bearing L at the two junctions with other paved roads. At 1.3 mi. the road surface becomes gravel, and the Garden is reached at 1.6 mi., where there is parking for about 60 cars. On many busy weekends this parking lot can be full, and hikers should be aware that parking is not permitted on the private land next to the road. Once the capacity of the lot has been reached, hikers must park in Keene Valley and walk the 1.6 mi. up to the trailhead. In winter, the road may be plowed only as far as the end of the pavement at 1.3 mi. As in the summer, parking is not permitted along the road; if one cannot make it to the Garden, one must park in Keene Valley, because even one car parked in the wrong place will prevent the large snowplows from turning around. In this instance, the threat to tow cars away is not an idle one.

Leaving the register at the far end of the Garden (0 mi.), the trail with yellow DEC disks crosses a small stream and begins a moderate climb for a few hundred yds. Easing off, it dips to cross a small stream and then continues mostly on the level to a junction at 0.5 mi. with the Southside Trail (trail 3), an alternate route to Johns Brook Lodge. Bearing R, the Phelps Trail continues mostly on the level, crossing one brook and then crossing Bear Brook just before reaching Bear Brook Lean-to on the L at 0.9 mi. Still mostly on the level, the trail continues to Deer Brook Lean-to on the R at 1.3 mi. Just beyond, the trail dips down, crosses Deer Brook on two bridges, and climbs steeply up the far bank. Again mostly on the level, the trail passes three large boulders on the R and comes to a small stream at 1.5 mi.

The trail now begins a steady, moderate climb which eases at 2.0 mi. Proceeding mostly on the flat and crossing several small brooks, the trail turns R at 2.9 mi. Here a newer section follows near the edge of a bank for 200 yds. until a more recent (1991) relocation takes it R and up to a designated campsite at 3.0 mi. before dropping down to a junction just above the DEC Interior Outpost at 3.1 mi. (Trail L leads 50 yds. to the Interior Outpost and 200 yds. to a suspension bridge over Johns Brook, connecting at the far side with the Southside Trail (trail 3), ADK Range Trail (trail 4), and the Orebed Brook Trail (trail 8)).

Bearing R, the trail passes several good campsites and the Howard Memorial Lean-to on the L before crossing Slide Mt. Brook with a junction just beyond at 3.2 mi. Trail R with ADK markers leads 2.4 mi. to Big Slide Mt. (trail 13). There are also some good campsites just up this trail on the R bank of Slide Mt. Brook. Continuing on the flat, the trail soon passes a private bridge leading L across Johns Brook to ADK's Camp Peggy O'Brien (formerly Winter Camp) and Grace Camp—both camps part of Johns Brook Lodge. Continuing past this bridge, the trail crosses a bridge over Black Brook at 3.4 mi. and reaches Johns Brook Lodge at 3.5 mi. Johns Brook Lodge is owned and operated by the Adirondack Mt. Club and offers overnight accommodations, meals, candy and drinks, and information to hikers. For further information, see section on Overnight Accommodations.

Just past JBL is a junction at a signpost. Trail L is the State Range Trail (trail 9) with blue DEC markers leading to Gothics and the Upper Great Range as well as the Woodsfall Trail (trail 6) which connects with the ADK Range Trail (trail 4). Trail R is the Klondike Trail (trail 12) leading to South Meadows near Lake Placid and also connecting with the trail to Big Slide via Yard (trail 14).

Going straight at the signpost, the Phelps Trail to Marcy proceeds on the level, coming to the former site of Johns Brook Lean-to on the L at 3.6 mi. [Camping is now permitted only on the R (N) side of the trail.] Past this point the trail continues at an easy grade near the L bank of Johns Brook to the former site of Hogback Lean-to at 4.5 mi.

Crossing Hogback Brook just beyond, the trail climbs a steep ridge known as a hogback, the remnant of a lateral moraine of a valley glacier that came down the Johns Brook Valley for a short time after the last ice age. The steep climbing eases at 4.6 mi. and the trail continues at easier grades to a junction at 5.0 mi., just before reaching the first Bushnell Falls Lean-to. A vague spur trail L leads 250 yds. very steeply down to the base of the falls, a favorite spot of Rev. Horace Bushnell, and named in his honor by the Keene Valley guides as he was a very well-liked summer resident of the valley.

At the lean-to, just past the junction with the spur trail to the falls, is another junction. The yellow markers continue to the R on the Hopkins Trail (trail 2). Turning L and now with red DEC markers, the Phelps Trail descends at a moderate grade to Johns Brook at 5.2 mi. The trail crosses on the rocks to the R bank just above the confluence of Chicken Coop Brook with another lean-to located just beyond. There is also a high-water bridge located 125 yds. upstream of the regular crossing.

From the upper Bushnell Falls Lean-to, the trail swings away from Johns Brook at a moderate grade near the L bank of Chicken Coop Brook. Swinging R and away from Chicken Coop Brook, the grade moderates at 5.8 mi. and the trail crosses a large brook at 6.4 mi. Now mostly on the level, the trail comes to Johns Brook again with Slant Rock just beyond at 6.8 mi. This large rock which forms a natural shelter was a famous early camping spot. A lean-to now faces the natural shelter. Other camping in this area is generally limited to sites on the side of the trail away from the brook.

Swinging L just past Slant Rock, the trail follows close to the L bank of Johns Brook to a junction at 6.9 mi. Trail L with yellow markers is the Shorey Short Cut (trail 11) leading 1.1 mi. to the Range Trail between Basin and Haystack; see below. Past this junction, the climbing becomes steep in spots, with a last crossing of Johns Brook at 7.4 mi. From here, the trail is quite wet and rough as it climbs at a moderate grade with some steep pitches to a junction with the State Range Trail (trail 9) at the top of the pass between Marcy and Haystack at the head of Panther Gorge at 7.8 mi. The Phelps Trail bears R and continues to climb steeply to a junction at 8.5 mi. with the Van Hoevenberg Trail from Heart Lake (Trail 61.)

Bearing L with blue markers, the trail climbs a few yards to some bare rocks with a view of the summit and then dips down and crosses a wet area before climbing onto another rocky shoulder at 8.7 mi. From this point the trail is level for a short stretch before beginning the final climb over open rocks. The trail is marked with cairns and yellow paint blazes and care is needed to follow it in fog or rain. The trail passes over a slightly lower eastern summit and then on the flat to the base of the summit rock with a plaque commemorating the first ascent of the peak. The actual summit is reached at 9.1 mi. (For a description of the view and history of the mountain see section on Marcy in the Introduction.) The artic-alpine vegetation on the summit is fragile. For more information on how to protect it, see Introduction. The trail continues over the summit and down the SW side toward Lake Tear and connects with the Elk Lake-Marcy Trail and the trail to Lake Colden and Upper Works near Tahawus. (See Southern Section.)

Trail in winter: Suitable for skiing as far as JBL with a foot of snowcover, although the bridges are narrow and a few brook crossings may require removing one's skis.

Distances: Garden parking lot to DEC Interior Outpost, 3.1 mi.; to Johns Brook Lodge, 3.5 mi.; to Bushnell Falls Lean-to and junction with Hopkins Trail, 5.1 mi.; to Slant Rock, 6.8 mi.; to junction with State Range Trail, 7.8 mi.; to junction with Van Hoevenberg Trail, 8.5 mi.; to summit of Marcy, 9.1 mi. (14.6 km). Ascent from Garden, 3821 ft. (1165 m). Elevation, 5344 ft. (1629 m). Order of height, 1.

(2) Marcy via Hopkins Trail   Map: E-9

This trail was laid out by Arthur S. Hopkins, former director of Lands and Forest for the Conservation Department, as a short cut for his survey crews during some major land acquisitions in 1920. It leads from the Phelps Trail at Bushnell Falls to the Van Hoevenberg Trail and offers an alternate route for those heading between the Johns Brook valley and Heart Lake. The trail is, however, much rougher than the Phelps Trail as it has not received the same degree of maintenance in recent years. The upper end is generally very wet.

Leaving the Phelps Trail at Bushnell Falls (0 mi.), the Hopkins Trail, with yellow markers, climbs at an easy grade to a descent across a small ravine at 0.4 mi. After a short, steep climb up the far bank, the trail levels out until it dips to cross another brook at 0.9 mi. After another steep climb, the grades are easy to moderate until the trail comes to the L bank of the L fork of Johns Brook at 1.5 mi. Now the climbing increases as the trail remains near the L bank of the brook before finally crossing it at 2.1 mi. Shortly after this crossing, the grade moderates and then levels out through some swampy terrain at 2.8 mi. After a few more short climbs and some more wet areas, the trail joins the Van Hoevenberg Trail (trail 61) with blue markers at 2.8 mi.

Distances: Bushnell Falls to Van Hoevenberg Trail, 2.8 mi.; to summit of Marcy, 4.0 mi. (6.4 km). (From JBL, 5.5 mi. [8.9 km]. From Garden parking lot, 9.1 mi. [14.6 km]. Ascents are the same as for the Phelps Trail.)

(3) Southside Trail to Johns Brook Lodge   Map: F-8

This trail offers an alternate route to Johns Brook Lodge and the Range trails. It follows an old tote road along the R bank of Johns

Brook, offering many views of this characteristic mountain stream. The grades are easy throughout and some consider this a less difficult approach to Johns Brook Lodge than the Phelps or Northside-Trail, but it can be very wet in spots and there is a stretch of rock-hopping next to the brook. The crossing of Johns Brook near the Garden can also be quite difficult in times of high water.

From the Garden (0 mi.), follow the Phelps Trail (Trail 1) 0.5 mi. to the junction with the Southside Trail. Turning L with ADK markers, the trail descends a steep hogback at first and then turns sharp R and down off the hogback at the second flat area. From the bottom of the hogback, the trail is level to Johns Brook at 0.7 mi., which is crossed on stones. Some care is needed to find the trail on the far side. Climbing the bank, the trail comes to the old tote road at 0.8 mi., now a bulldozed tractor road. (Note: this turn is easy to miss coming down the trail; watch for it shortly after crossing a large tributary and climbing a short, steep grade.)

Turning R, the trail follows the bulldozed road, drops down across a large tributary, and turns L at the far side. Now at an easy grade, the trail follows the road until 1.6 mi., where the road goes up and L. Continuing straight ahead on the level, the trail descends slightly into the brook bed at 1.9 mi. and proceeds on the rocks for 175 yds. Leaving the brook bed, the trail climbs above a small flume known as the Rock Cut, swings L, and then drops down over some ledges to cross a tributary at 2.0 mi. Again mostly on the level, it rejoins the bulldozed road from the L at 2.1 mi.; 100 yds. later a side trail leads R and down to some beautiful flat rocks with good swimming holes called Tenderfoot Pools.

Continuing at easy grades and swinging away from the brook, the trail crosses several brooks and comes to a junction at 2.9 mi. with the ADK Range Trail (trail 4) leading to Wolf Jaws Lean-to and the Great Range. Beyond this junction, the bulldozed road branches L shortly before the trail comes to the suspension bridge and a junction at 3.0 mi. Trail L with blue markers is the Orebed Brook Trail to

Gothic (trail 8). Turning R and crossing the bridge, the trail reaches the DEC Interior Outpost at 3.1 mi. Just beyond, it rejoins the Phelps Trail from the Garden. Continuing straight ahead, Johns Brook Lodge is reached at 3.5 mi.

Trail in winter: The descent to and crossing of Johns Brook may be difficult, but the old tote road is much better for skiing than Phelps Trail provided there is a foot or more of snowcover. For skiing, stay on the bulldozed road around the washout even though it involves a little extra climbing.

Distances: Garden to junction with Southside Trail, 0.5 mi.; to ADK Range Trail, 2.9 mi.; to DEC Interior Outpost, 3.1 mi.; to JBL, 3.5 mi. (5.7 km).

(4) ADK Range Trail to Upper Wolf Jaw, Armstrong and Gothics   Map: E-9

The ADK-maintained Range Trail leads from Johns Brook over Upper Wolf Jaw, Armstrong and Gothics with a side trail leading to Lower Wolf-Jaw. See Gothics via Orebed Brook Trail (trail 8) for information on the naming of this peak. Information on the naming of Wolf Jaws is found with the Wedge Brook Trail (trail 33) description. Armstrong was named for Thomas Armstrong, a prominent lumberman in Plattsburgh, who with his partner Almon Thomas in 1866 acquired title to Township 48, Totten and Crossfield Purchase, a parcel that included much of the Great Range and Marcy. In 1887 they sold it to the Adirondack Mountain Reserve, which still owns the part near the Ausable lakes.

Previous editions of this guidebook have described this trail as starting from Johns Brook Lodge via the Woodsfall Trail; but when approaching these peaks from the Garden, the shortest route to Upper and Lower Wolf Jaw is from the DEC Interior Outpost via this route—formerly described as the High Water Route. Those hikers starting from Johns Brook Lodge should follow the Woodsfall Trail to the ADK Range Trail at the Wolf Jaws Lean-to. Total distances and ascents for those starting at JBL are the same as described below.

From the DEC Interior Outpost (0 mi.), head E and down a slight grade through the open field to the suspension bridge across Johns Brook. At the far side of the bridge, turn L and follow ADK markers down the Southside Trail to a junction at 0.2 mi. Southside Trail (trail 3) leads straight ahead 2.9 mi. to the Garden. Turning R, the Range Trail climbs at a moderate grade and comes out on the L bank of Wolf Jaws Brook at 0.4 mi. after which the grade eases. The trail swings back away from the brook, and then climbs steadily to a junction at 1.1 mi. with the Woodsfall Trail (trail 6). Wolf Jaws Lean-to is about 50 yds. past this junction on the L.

From this junction, the trail continues at a steady, moderate climb generally along the L bank of Wolf Jaws Brook. After the second of two small tributaries at 1.7 mi., the grade steepens until the junction at the top of the pass is reached at 2.0 mi. ADK trail L leads to Lower Wolf Jaw (trail 5). Turning R, the trail begins a steep to very steep climb, switchbacking up through the many ledges on the steep slope. At 2.3 mi. there is a good view of Big Slide and Whiteface with the trail reaching the lesser summit of Upper Wolf Jaw at 2.5 mi. From here, the trail descends easily to a col and then ascends to a junction at 2.9 mi. with a spur trail R leading 20 yds. to the summit lookout.

From the summit there are good views to the S and E. A vague trail leads NW from the summit a few yards to another ledge with good views of the Johns Brook Valley. Upper Wolf Jaw ascent from DEC Interior Outpost, 2000 ft. (610 m). Elevation, 4185 ft. (1276 m). Order of height, 29.

The ADK Range Trail continues straight ahead from the junction with the spur trail and drops to a col at 3.1 mi., after which it climbs over an intermediate bump before descending to the base of Armstrong at 3.4 mi. A long ladder and a hanging cable takes the trail up over some steep ledges after which the climbing remains steep nearly to the summit at 3.9 mi. (6.2 km). A large ledge on the R offers views of the Johns Brook Valley and the upper Great Range. Armstrong total ascent from DEC Interior Outpost, 2500 ft. (760 m). Elevation, 4400 ft. (1341 m). Order of height, 22.

Continuing on, the trail descends over a few steep ledges to a col and then climbs to the S peak of Armstrong at 4.2 mi. where the trail swings R and descends to a junction at 4.3 mi. with ATIS-marked trail to Lake Road and St. Huberts (trail 34). Continuing with ADK markers, the trail is level for a few yards before it climbs steeply to the summit of Gothics at 4.8 mi. (7.7 km). The view is unobstructed with about 30 major peaks discernible. The boathouse at the Lower Ausable Lake can be seen, but to see any of the Upper Lake one must proceed past the summit 0.1 mi. to the ATIS trail over Pyramid and go L on this trail a few yards to a wide ledge with views to the S and W. Gothics total ascent from DEC Interior Outpost, 3000 ft. (914 m). Elevation, 4736 ft. (1444 m). Order of height, 10.

The trail continues over the summit and along the ridge to the W peak of Gothics and then down the very steep and open W face with two cables in place to aid passage. At the bottom of this face, the trail joins the Orebed Brook Trail at 5.4 mi. (trail 8).

Distances: DEC Interior Outpost to junction with Woodsfall Trail, 1.1 mi.; to junction with trail to Lower Wolf Jaw, 2.0 mi.; to summit of Upper Wolf Jaw, 2.9 mi.; to summit of Armstrong, 3.9 mi.; to summit of Gothics, 4.8 mi.; to Orebed Brook Trail junction, 5.4 mi. (8.7 km).

(5) Lower Wolf Jaw   Map: F-9

From Wolf Jaws Notch, a branch of the ADK Range Trail leads to the summit of Lower Wolf Jaw and connects with the W.A. White Trail to St. Huberts or Keene Valley.

From the notch (0 mi.), the trail heads E on the flat for 50 yards to a junction with the cut-off to the Wedge Brook Trail (trail 33), which goes R. Turning L, the trail begins to climb steeply to a junction at 0.2 mi. where the main Wedge Brook Trail comes in from the R. From this junction, the trail continues to climb to the summit at 0.5 mi., where there are good views from the lookout on the L. Trail straight ahead is the W.A. White Trail (trail 32) to St. Huberts with connections to Keene Valley via Hedgehog and Rooster Comb.

Distances: DEC Interior Outpost to Wolf Jaws Notch, 2.0 mi.; to summit of Lower Wolf Jaw, 2.5 mi. (4.0 km). Ascent, 2000 ft. (610 m). Elevation, 4175 ft. (1273 m). Order of height, 30.

(6) Woodsfall Trail   Map: E-9

This ADK-maintained trail offers the most direct approach from Johns Brook Lodge to the Wolf Jaws and the ADK Range Trail. For the first 0.3 mi. this route coincides with the blue-marked State Range Trail. From the signpost at JBL (0 mi.), the trail descends and crosses Johns Brook on stones. (High-water route via DEC Interior Outpost.) Turning R and then immediately L on the far bank, the trail leads up over two small ridges to Orebed Brook at 0.2 mi. Climbing the far bank in two steep pitches with some wooden steps, the trail reaches a five-way junction at 0.3 mi. Trail sharp R and sharp L is the blue-marked Orebed Brook Trail (trail 8) leading from the DEC Interior Outpost to Gothics and the upper Great Range. Trail nearly straight ahead at 110 degrees is the ADK trail to Short Job (trail 7).

The Woodsfall Trail bears slightly R, heading away from this junction at 170 degrees on an easy to moderate grade. Crossing several small brooks, it reaches a height of land at 0.9 mi. and descends gradually, crossing two brooks before joining the ADK Range Trail (trail 4) near Wolf Jaws Lean-to at 1.1 mi.

Distances: JBL to junction with Orebed Brook Trail, 0.3 mi.; to junction with ADK Range Trail, 1.1 mi. (1.8 km).

(7) Short Job   Map: E-9

This small knoll across the valley from JBL offers some interesting views for a short hike. From JBL (0 mi.), follow the Woodsfall Trail description (trail 6) to the five-way junction at 0.3 mi. From here, take the trail heading at 110 degrees, which climbs gradually at first but then up more steeply to the first lookout toward the Range at 0.7 mi. The trail continues with a slight descent to a lookout over the Johns Brook Valley at 0.7 mi.

Distances: JBL to Orebed Brook Trail at five-way junction, 0.3 mi.; to end of trail at second lookout, 0.7 mi. (1.2 km).

(8) Gothics via
Orebed Brook Trail   Map: E-9

According to legend, the arched peaks of this triple-crested mountain, with their great slides and bare rock, suggested Gothic architecture to Frederick Perkins and Old Mountain Phelps one day in 1857 when they sat on the top of Marcy and christened Skylight, Basin, Saddleback and Gothics with characteristic names. More recent evidence, however, has surfaced to indicate that Gothics had been named as early as 1850 in a poem written by a minister from North Elba (Lake Placid).

The Orebed Brook Trail is the most direct route to Gothics from the Johns Brook Valley. It connects at Gothics Col with the State Range Trail to Saddleback, Basin and Haystack (trail 9). Like the

ADK Range Trail, the shortest approach to this trail from the Phelps Trail is from the DEC Interior Outpost, but one can also approach from Johns Brook Lodge via the Woodsfall Trail.

From the DEC Interior Outpost (0 mi.), the trail goes E and down gradually through an open field a few yards to a suspension bridge over Johns Brook. On the far side of the brook at 0.1 mi. there is a junction with the Southside Trail (trail 3). Orebed Brook Trail with blue markers leads R and up steeply and joins a bulldozed road which is followed to the R on an easy grade about 100 yards from the bridge. The Orebed Brook Trail swings L away from the road (be alert as this turn is not well marked) and continues to climb on an older tote road to a five-way junction at 0.6 mi. Woodsfall Trail (trail 6) goes R to JBL and L to Wolf Jaws while Short Job Trail (trail 7) goes sharp L.

Continuing straight ahead on the old tote road at an easy grade, the Orebed Brook Trail crosses a large brook at 1.2 mi., with Orebed Lean-to just beyond to the L of the trail. There are some designated campsites down and to the R at this point as well. Continuing at an easy grade, the trail passes a huge boulder on the R at 1.5 mi. and continues on past two small brooks before descending to cross a larger brook at 1.8 mi. The trail climbs a steep bank on the far side and then continues at moderate grades along the R bank of the main branch of Orebed Brook. At 2.3 mi. the trail comes to a large new slide coming down off the small peak to the L. There is a view of Saddleback from this slide, which the trail crosses by turning L for a few yds. and then R across the slide to join the original trail at the far side.

The trail is now close to the R bank of Orebed Brook with several attractive mossy falls visible. The trail crosses the brook at 2.6 mi. and continues up the L bank around several large boulders. Some care is needed to follow the trail in this section, both going up and coming down, as the trail and brook often look remarkably alike.

The climbing soon becomes much steeper with a very steep pitch commencing at 2.7 mi. The trail climbs on bare rock for much of the time, with a steep open slide just to the R which offers some views back to the Johns Brook Valley. The grade eases slightly as the trail veers L and traverses across the side hill. The grade finally eases back to moderate at 3.0 mi. at the base of a small slide with a view of the W peak of Gothics and the summit beyond. The junction at Gothics Col is reached at 3.1 mi. Trail R is the State Range Trail (trail 9).

Turning L and now with ADK markers, the trail climbs quite steeply up the mostly bare W ridge of Gothics. The first of two cables fastened to the rocks is reached at 3.2 mi., and above the second cable the trail continues to climb steeply around to the L of a final steep step to gain the W summit at 3.4 mi., where there are good views. Crossing over this summit , the trail descends slightly and then climbs to a junction at 3.6 mi. with ATIS Trail to the Lower Ausable Lake via Pyramid (trail 35). From here, the trail continues mostly on the flat to the summit of Gothics at 3.7 mi. See ADK Range Trail for notes on views.

Distances: DEC Interior Outpost to five-way junction, 0.6 mi.; to Orebed Lean-to, 1.3 mi.; to Gothics Col and Range Trail, 3.1 mi.; to summit of Gothics, 3.7 mi. (6.0 km). Ascent from Johns Brook, 2360 ft. (719 m). Elevation, 4736 ft. (1444 m). Order of height, 10.

(9) State Range Trail to Saddleback, Basin, Haystack and Marcy
Map: E-10

This section of trail is perhaps the most spectacular of any in the Adirondacks as it goes over the bare summits of Saddleback and Basin and connects to the spur trail to Haystack. It is also a very rugged trail and is a serious undertaking, especially with backpacks. There are many sections of steep rock, particularly on the W sides of

Basin and Saddleback, which can be very uncomfortable to negotiate with a heavy pack. Day trips are suggested for those wishing to climb these peaks, and backpackers may want to consider hiking this trail in reverse direction so as to ascend the most precipitous and dangerous sections.

As described here the trail starts at Gothics Col (0 mi.) at a junction with the Orebed Brook Trail (trail 8). It climbs steeply up the E side of Saddleback with many good views back at the spectacular slides on Gothics. At 0.3 mi. the grade eases on the E peak of Saddleback, after which the trail dips to the "saddle" at 0.4 mi. with a side trail L to a good view just beyond. The trail then climbs two rock steps to the summit at 0.5 mi. (0.9 km) where a broad ledge offers good views. Saddleback ascent from Johns Brook, 2200 ft. (670 m). Elevation, 4515 ft. (1376 m). Order of height, 17.

The trail turns sharp R at the summit and follows along a ledge marked with yellow paint blazes. Turning L at the end of the ledge, the trail descends precipitously over ledges where extreme caution is needed. The trail reaches the bottom of the col at 0.8 mi., after which it begins a moderate ascent through open firs with views back at Saddleback. The grade becomes progressively steeper and remains steep until it eases on a shoulder of Basin at 1.1 mi. The trail descends gradually to a col and then begins steep climbing again at 1.3 mi. At 1.4 mi., the trail crosses a spectacular narrow ledge and then turns L and up to the summit of Basin at 1.5 mi. Here in the rock is embedded the bolt placed by Verplanck Colvin during the Adirondack Survey in 1876. The view is unobstructed in all directions except to the S, but with a little walking around one can see this view as well. Gothics to the E, Marcy to the W, and Haystack to the SW are the most prominent peaks visible, with Upper Ausable Lake to the S and the valley to the SE forming an almost perfect basin from which the peak got its name. Basin total ascent from Johns Brook, 2870 ft. (875 m). Elevation, 4827 ft. (1471 m). Order of height, 9.

The trail goes straight over the summit, turns L at the base of the summit rocks and then descends generally easy to moderate grades along a SW shoulder to the top of a ledge at 1.9 mi. There used to be a ladder leading down this face, but now the trail detours R to get around the ledge, arriving at the bottom at 1.9 mi. The trail now descends very steeply for 75 yds. to a second ledge which still does have a hidden ladder, but after descending this pitch the trail levels out for a few hundred yards before descending steeply to a junction at 2.3 mi. with the Shorey Short Cut to the Phelps Trail (trail 11).

The Range Trail continues its steep descent for another 100 yds. to the headwaters of Haystack Brook and then begins climbing steeply to the former site of Sno-Bird Lean-to at 2.4 mi., now a designated campsite. Just past the former lean-to site, the trail crosses a small stream to a junction with the ATIS Haystack Brook Trail (trail 59) to Upper Ausable Lake . The Range Trail now begins a very rough and eroded climb to a trail junction at 2.9 mi. (trail L with yellow markers, trail 10, leads 0.6 mi. to the summit of Haystack.) Turning R, the Range Trail climbs steeply to the top of a ridge at 3.0 mi., with a bare spot offering views just beyond on the R. Now the trail starts down at a moderate grade, getting progressively steeper until at 3.3 mi. it descends a near-vertical pitch to the pass at the head of Panther Gorge where the Phelps Trail (trail 1) comes in from the R at 3.4 mi. Turning L with red markers, the route from here to the summit of Marcy is the same as the Phelps Trail.

Distances: DEC Interior Outpost at Johns Brook to Gothics Col, 3.1 mi.; to summit of Saddleback, 3.6 mi.; to summit of Basin, 4.5 mi.; to junction with Shorey Short Cut, 5.2 mi.; to former site of Sno-Bird Lean-to, 5.3 mi.; to junction with trail to Haystack, 5.8 mi.; to Phelps Trail 6.3 mi.; to Van Hoevenberg Trail, 7.0 mi.; to summit of Marcy, 7.6 mi. (12.2 km). Total ascent from Johns Brook via Range Trail, about 4890 ft. (1490 m).

(10) Mt. Haystack from the Range Trail
Map: E-10

This third highest peak in the Adirondacks was named by Old Mountain Phelps in August 1849 when he made the first recorded ascent with Almeron Oliver and George Estey. Phelps remarked to his companions that the mountain was a great stack of rock but that he would call it Haystack; and Haystack it has been ever since.

Haystack is approached from the Range Trail either over Saddleback and Basin or more directly via the Phelps Trail to the head of Panther Gorge. The distance to the junction with the Haystack Trail is 5.8 mi. from the DEC Interior Outpost via Saddleback and Basin, or 5.2 mi. (and a lot less climbing) via the Phelps Trail and Slant Rock. This trail is not as well marked as some others above timberline, and care is needed to follow it in fog or rain. Hikers should be careful to stay on the trail to avoid trampling the fragile alpine vegetation.

From the junction with the Range Trail (trail 9) (0 mi.) , the trail follows yellow markers to the first ledge, after which it is marked by cairns. After a few sharp zig-zags through the ledges, the trail reaches the summit of Little Haystack (actually just W of the summit) at 0.2 mi. Then bearing slightly L, the trail descends a diagonal ledge for 150 yds. before turning sharp R and down to the few trees in the col at 0.3 mi. Ascending at an easier grade from the col, the trail sticks fairly close to the crest of the ridge, bears slightly R as it approaches the summit to avoid the sharpest part of the ridge, and reaches the totally bald summit at 0.6 mi. The view from the summit is considered one of the finest in the mountains, with the yawning abyss of Panther Gorge and the steep cliffs on Marcy dominating the view. The trail from the S is the Bartlett Ridge Trail (trail 57), giving access to the Upper Lake and Panther Gorge.

Distances: Range Trail to summit of Haystack, 0.6 mi. (0.9 km). From Johns Brook Interior Outpost via Saddleback and Basin, 6.3 mi. (10.1 km); total ascent, 4170 ft. (966 m). From Johns Brook Interior Outpost via Phelps Trail and Slant Rock, 5.8 mi. (9.3 km); total ascent, 2790 ft. (850 m). Elevation, 4960 ft. (1512 m). Order of height, 3.

(11) Shorey Short Cut from Range Trail to Phelps Trail   Map: E-10

This trail was cut by A. T. Shorey, former chair of the ADK Guidebook Committee, when he was with the Conservation Department. It connects the Range Trail (trail 9) at the base of Basin with the Phelps Trail (trail 1) near Slant Rock and offers a shorter return from the Range Trail to the Johns Brook Valley. This trail has been much maligned by hikers over the years because it climbs well above the height of land needed to gain access to the Johns Brook Valley and it is rough going throughout. It does, however, lead past a viewpoint that is a perfectly framed "portrait" of Haystack and Little Haystack.

Leaving the Range Trail (0 mi.), the trail with yellow DEC disks climbs a moderate to steep grade to a lookout on the L at 0.2 mi., after which the grade eases a bit up past a large boulder, and finally to a height of land on the shoulder of Haystack at 0.3 mi. Now descending steep to moderate grades, the trail passes several other glimpses of the Johns Brook Valley through the trees. The descent continues to the old Slant Rock Lean-to site on the R bank of Johns Brook with the junction with the Phelps Trail on the other side of the brook at 1.1 mi. This point is 0.1 mi. above Slant Rock.

Distance: Range Trail to Phelps Trail, 1.1 mi. (1.79 km).

Mt. Marcy from Keene Valley via the Complete Great Range

This is an extremely rugged trip with very rough trail for most of the distance. For more information, see Mt. Marcy section of Introduction.

(12) Klondike Notch Trail to South Meadow   Map: E-9

This route leads from Johns Brook Lodge through Klondike Notch to South Meadow, where it meets a road coming in from the Heart Lake Road providing access to Adirondak Loj. (See Heart Lake Section.) Klondike Notch between Howard and Yard mts. has also been called Railroad Notch at times, but this name rightfully belongs to the lower notch between Porter and Big Slide which once was actually surveyed for a railroad. Contrary to legends that have even been printed in various Adirondack histories, this route was not part of the Underground Railroad for escaped slaves to reach John Brown's Farm. His farm was for freed slaves and Canada was the only safe haven for an escaped slave.

Leaving the JBL signpost (0 mi.), the trail with red DEC disks heads across the back yard of JBL, crosses Black Brook, and climbs along the L bank of the brook at a moderate grade with occasional steep pitches to a junction at 1.3 mi. with ADK trail to Big Slide via Yard (trail 14). Continuing at a moderate grade, the trail soon descends slightly to cross a swampy area and then resumes the climb to the height of land at Klondike Notch at 1.7 mi., having gained 866 ft. (264 m) in elevation from JBL.

Descending now at easy to moderate grades, the trail crosses Klondike Brook at 2.7 mi. The new (1990) Klondike Lean-to is just beyond and up to the L. The trail swings R, follows a tote road up a short climb, and then continues mostly on the level to 3.7 mi. where it starts down a moderate grade. Occasionally swinging away from the tote road to avoid eroded sections, the trail reaches the level shortly before a junction with the Mr. Van Ski Trail (trail 80) goes R at 4.6 mi.

At 4.8 mi. the Mr. Van Trail diverges to the L (distance to Adirondak Loj, 1.9 mi., but sections of this portion of the trail can be very wet and practically impassable). Continuing on, the Klondike

Trail reaches South Meadow at 5.1 mi., turns upstream to a good bridge, and reaches the end of the South Meadow Road at 5.3 mi. Continuing W on this road, it is slightly over a mile to the Heart Lake Road, and another mile to Adirondak Loj.

Trail in winter: Although steep in spots, the Klondike Trail and the Phelps Trail make a good 10-mi. traverse. The JBL side of the pass has the most difficult pieces of trail to ski, so many skiers choose to ascend this side and enjoy the easier hike down the N side, even though the reverse direction produces a net loss of altitude.

Distances: JBL to ADK Big Slide Trail, 1.3 mi.; to Klondike Lean-to, 2.7 mi.; to South Meadow Rd., 5.3 mi. (8.5 km); to Adirondak Loj, 7.3 mi. (11.8).

(13) Big Slide Mt. via Slide Mt. Brook Trail   Map: E-9

This trail starts from the Phelps Trail (trail 1), 0.1 mi. above the DEC Interior Outpost and 0.3 mi. below JBL. Leaving the Phelps Trail (0 mi.) and marked with ADK markers, the trail starts at an easy grade and crosses Slide Mt. Brook at 0.2 mi., and then twice more before it comes to the base of an old slide. The trail climbs away from the brook on this slide, at the top of which, at 0.5 mi., is a good view of Gothics and some of the rest of the Great Range. Now the trail returns to the brook and follows close to it with several more crossings, finally ending up on the R bank and leaving the brook at 1.0 mi.

The climbing is now moderate through open hardwoods with some glimpses of the Range back through the trees. Gradually becoming steeper, at 1.8 mi. the trail comes to a good view of the bare rock slide which occurred in 1830 and from which the mountain takes its name. The climbing is now quite steep to a junction at 2.1 mi. (Trail R with ADK markers leads over the Brothers to the Garden in 3.6 mi.; see below.) The climbing becomes very steep with a side trail L to a view of the slide at 2.2 mi. Swinging sharp R just above this side trail, the grade eases a bit as the trail works onto the N side of the peak, swings L and climbs on past another view on the L to the summit at 2.4 mi. There are magnificent views of the Great Range, Giant and Algonquin, with only the view to the N blocked by trees. The trail with ADK markers continues over the summit and down over Yard Mt. to JBL in another 4.0 mi. (trail 14).

Distances: Phelps Trail to trail over Brothers, 2.1 mi.; to summit of Big Slide, 2.4 mi. (3.8 km). Ascent from Phelps Trail, 2000 ft. (610 m). Elevation, 4240 ft. (1292 m). Order of height, 27.

(14) Big Slide via Yard Mt.   Map: E-8

This trail starts from the Klondike Notch Trail (trail 12), 1.3 mi. from JBL or 0.4 mi. below the height of land coming from South Meadow. Combined with the Slide Mt. Brook Trail, it makes an interesting loop of 6.3 mi. from JBL.

Leaving the Klondike Notch Trail (0 mi.) with ADK markers, the trail climbs moderately and then more steeply until at about 0.5 mi. it swings L on a long traverse heading NW. After this traverse, the trail again climbs steeply onto the W ridge of Yard Mt. with a view of Marcy at 0.9 mi. and reaches the summit of Yard Mt. at 1.3 mi. Yard's elevation is 4018 ft., but it is not one of the 46 peaks as it is too close to Big Slide.

From the summit of Yard, the trail drops slightly and then begins a generally easy climb along the ridge with a profile view of Big Slide at 1.4 mi. Continuing the easy climb, the trail reaches the summit of Big Slide at 2.7 mi. (See above for description of the view.)

Distances: JBL to junction with Big Slide Trail, 1.3 mi.; to summit of Yard Mt., 2.5 mi.; to summit of Big Slide, 4.0 mi. (6.4 km). Ascent from JBL, 1924 ft. (586 m). Elevation, 4240 ft. (1292 m). Order of height, 27.

(15) Big Slide via The Brothers

Map: F-8

This trail offers a spectacular approach to Big Slide Mt. from the Garden parking lot over the three Brothers, all of which offer excellent views. Combined with the Slide Mt. Brook Trail and the Phelps Trail, an interesting loop of 9.5 mi. from the Garden is possible. The First and Second Brother at 1.5 mi. and 1.8 mi. are good objectives for shorter hikes. This trail is currently maintained by the Long Island Chapter of ADK.

Trailhead: See Phelps Trail (trail 1) for trailhead description.

From the trail register at the end of the Garden (0 mi.), the Big Slide trail with ADK markers goes sharp R and up along the edge of the parking lot and then climbs moderately for a few hundred yards before easing off. At 0.4 mi. the trail swings L and drops down to cross Juliet Brook before beginning a steady, moderate climb to the base of a steeper pitch at 0.7 mi. Here the trail traverses to the R to avoid the steepest climbing and then switchbacks L and up to the first ledge at 0.8 mi., where there are good views of Keene Valley and the Great Range. The climbing is easier for a while over some more ledges, but it soon begins to increase as the trail goes up a series of open ledges until it moderates on a large, flat ledge at 1.2 mi. Turning R at the end of this ledge, the trail enters the woods and climbs a few steep, rocky pitches to a summit which the trail skirts on the L (W) side. Turning R just past this first summit, the trail passes a natural rock shelter and soon climbs to the bare summit of the First Brother at 1.5 mi. (2.4 km). Elevation, 2940 ft. (896 m). Ascent from Garden, 1437 ft. (438 m).

Dipping slightly, the trail soon climbs steeply up open rocks to the apparent summit of Second Brother at 1.7 mi., where there are good views to the E, S, and W. Turning L, the trail is mostly level to a junction at 1.8 mi. (2.8 km). Here a side trail R leads 20 yds. to the true summit of the Second Brother, where a rock offers views to the N. Elevation, 3120 ft. (950 m). Ascent from Garden, 1600 ft. (488 m).

Swinging L, the trail descends an easy grade over more open ledges with a few short rises until finally dipping down to the col between the Second and Third Brother at 2.0 mi. The trail now climbs moderately with a few short dips to the summit of the Third Brother at 2.6 mi. (4.2 km), where there is a spectacular view of Big Slide. Elevation, 3681 ft. (1122 m). Ascent from Garden, 2160 ft. (658 m).

From the summit of the Third Brother, the trail descends gradually, passes a rock shelter on the L at 2.7 mi. and soon flattens out in a mature spruce forest. The trail continues flat or gently down to a small stream where it swings L and up gradually and soon comes to a larger stream at 3.2 mi. Crossing the stream, the trail is wet for a few yards, and then climbs moderately to steeply to a junction at 3.7 mi. with the Slide Mt. Brook Trail (trail 13).

Turning R, the trail now becomes very steep with a side trail L to a view of the slide at 3.8 mi. The trail swings sharp R just above this side trail, and the grade soon eases a bit as the trail works onto the N side of the peak, swings L, and climbs on past another view on the L to the summit at 3.9 mi. There are magnificent views of the Great Range, Giant, and Algonquin with only the view to the N blocked by trees. The trail, with ADK markers, continues over the summit and down over Yard Mt. to JBL in another 4.0 mi. (trail 14).

Distances: Garden to First Brother, 1.5 mi.; to Second Brother, 1.8 mi.; to Third Brother, 2.6 mi.; to junction with Slide Mt. Brook Trail, 3.7 mi.; to summit of Big Slide, 3.9 mi. (6.3 km). Total ascent from Garden, 2800 ft. (853 m). Elevation, 4240 ft. (1292 m). Order of height, 27.

(16) Porter Mt. from Johns Brook Road near Garden   Map: F-8

Once called West Mt., Porter is named for Dr. Noah Porter, President of Yale University from 1871 to 1886, who was a summer resident of Keene Valley and who made the first recorded ascent of the peak in 1875 with guide Ed Phelps. Although Porter does not have a bald summit, it offers 360-degree views. (This trail is currently maintained by the Schenectady Chapter of ADK and is marked with ADK markers.)

Trailhead: On Interbrook Rd. (also known as Johns Brook Rd.) 0.3 mi. below the Garden. Because parking is not permitted on this part of the road, hikers must park at the Garden and walk back down. See Phelps Trail (trail 1) for directions to reach the Garden.

Leaving Interbrook Rd. (0 mi.), the trail follows the dirt road, bearing R at a private driveway at 0.2 mi. and then turning sharp R and crossing Slide Brook on a bridge. The trail now climbs along an old road at easy to moderate grades to the site of an old sugar camp at 0.9 mi., where it intersects a private jeep road. Turning L, the trail crosses the jeep road and climbs moderately to steeply to a level section near a private camp at 1.3 mi. The trail soon climbs again, gains the top of a ridge and comes to the end of another private jeep road coming in from the R at 1.5 mi. (In descending this section, care is needed to stay on the marked trail and not end up on the jeep road.) Continuing on past the jeep road, the trail passes another private camp on the L and soon enters state land. Now going up and down on a generally open ridge, the trail reaches the summit of Little Porter at 1.8 mi., where there are excellent views.

After a short descent, the trail is level through open woods to a stream crossing at 2.1 mi. Following up the L bank, the trail begins climbing again at a moderate grade, crossing a small brook at 2.3 mi. A slight dip is followed by more climbing through an open, grassy glade until the trail enters thicker woods just before dipping to cross another larger brook at 2.9 mi. The trail now begins to slab across the side of Porter with moderate grades alternating with short descents and several small brook crossings. Much of this section of trail is through grassy glades, a legacy of the 1903 fire. The trail finally climbs to a junction with the Ridge Trail from the Keene Valley Airport (trail 17) at 3.4 mi. Turning L, the trail continues at easy to moderate grades to the E summit, after which it is mostly flat to the summit of Porter at 3.8 mi. A trail marked with red DEC disks continues over the summit and on to Cascade and Rt. 73 in Cascade Pass (trail 90).

Distances: Interbrook Rd. to Little Porter, 1.8 mi.; to junction with Ridge Trail, 3.4 mi.; to summit of Porter, 3.8 mi. (6.2 km). Ascent from road, 2700 ft. (825 m). Elevation, 4059 ft. (1237 m). Order of height, 38.

(17) Porter Mt. from Keene Valley Airport via Ridge Trail   Map: F-7

This trail is the longest route to Porter and there is some steep climbing in its lower sections, but the variety of views makes it a worthwhile route. The first mile of the trail passes through some recent lumbering, but the route is now cleared and marked through this area. This trail is currently maintained by the Schenectady Chapter of the ADK and is marked with ADK markers.

Trailhead: From the High Peaks sign in the center of Keene Valley, proceed N on Rt. 73 for 2.0 mi. to a side road opposite the Town of Keene highway *garage, marked with a small sign for Porter. Turn down this road for 150 yds., turn R and park at the entrance to a dirt road.*

Leaving the paved road (0 mi.), the trail follows the road across the open field and then up until the trail turns sharp L off the road at 0.2 mi. and climbs across a side hill to the lower edge of the lumbered area at 0.3 mi. Soon after entering the lumbered area, the trail crosses a small height of land, descends slightly, and proceeds on the flat to a brook crossing at 0.6 mi. The trail now follows an eroded logging road up the R bank of the brook, bearing L at 0.7 mi. and then almost immediately turning R off the road and heading for some standing timber. Now on the edge of a bank above the brook, the trail reaches state land and the end of the lumbering at 1.1 mi. (Care is needed to follow this trail on the descent, but there are enough markers if one is careful to look for them.)

Above the lumbered area, the trail follows an old tote road until it turns sharp R and crosses the brook at 1.2 mi. The trail traverses to the R on a moderate grade but after crossing a brook bed at 1.3 mi. begins a steep climb. Reaching a view of Hurricane at 1.5 mi., the trail continues to a better view at a ledge at 1.7 mi. Now marked with both trail markers and red paint blazes, the trail climbs steeply to very steeply to a lookout at the E end of a ridge at 1.8 mi., where there are good views of Keene Valley. Now mostly on the flat, the trail comes to an open ledge on the S side of the ridge at 1.9 mi. and then drops slightly to a sag before climbing easily to the summit of Blueberry Mt. at 2.4 mi.

After descending to a col at 2.6 mi., the trail winds through a spruce forest and then climbs steeply up a ravine to a grassy summit at 3.1 mi. Now it continues along a beautiful ridge at easy grades, passing over two fine lookouts before joining the trail from Johns Brook Rd (trail 16) at 4.1 mi. Continuing straight ahead along the ridge, the trail climbs at easy to moderate grades to the E summit and then is mostly flat to the summit of Porter at 4.5 mi. A trail with red DEC disks continues over the summit and on to Cascade and Rt. 73 in Cascade Pass (trail 90).

Distances: Keene Valley Airport to Blueberry Mt., 2.4 mi.; to ADK trail from Interbrook Rd., 4.1 mi.; to summit of Porter, 4.5 mi. (7.3 km). Ascent from Airport, 3275 ft. (998 m), Elevation, 4059 ft. (1237 m). Order of height, 38.

(18) Rooster Comb, Hedgehog and Lower Wolf Jaw from Keene Valley   Map: F-8

This trail leads first to the rocky summit of Rooster Comb, a popular short hike, and then on over Hedgehog via a trail cut in 1953 to join the W. A. White Trail to Lower Wolf Jaw. This is the first portion of a traverse of the entire Great Range. (See "Mt. Marcy from Keene Valley via the Complete Great Range" under Mt. Marcy subhead in Introduction.) This trail is currently maintained by the Glens Falls Chapter of ADK and is marked with ADK markers.

Trailhead: On Interbrook Rd. (also known as Johns Brook Rd.), 0.6 mi. W of the High Peaks sign in the center of Keene Valley on the approach to the Phelps Trail and the Garden (trail 1). Just before the bridge over Johns Brook, a narrow driveway goes straight ahead. No parking is permitted anywhere on the private driveway beyond the stone gates, so cars must be parked on the road near the bridge.

From the stone gates (0 mi.) proceed up the driveway past one house on the R and bear L at the driveway to a second house. At 0.1 mi. bear L on a recent (1991) reroute and follow the road past a summer cottage and up a gradual grade to a sign at 0.5 mi. where the route turns L to rejoin the original route just before a bridge over a small stream. The trail now begins to ascend an eroded lumber road. The grade becomes steeper at 0.5 mi. on a very eroded section, but soon eases. At 0.8 mi. the trail turns sharp R off the lumber road and crosses a small brook. Now the trail begins to climb easily, but soon ascends at a steady, steep grade until there is a short breather at a small height of land at 1.5 mi. Turning L here, the trail resumes its steep climb to a ledge at 1.7 mi., where there are views of Porter and the Johns Brook Valley. Easier climbing leads to the summit of Rooster Comb at 1.8 mi. (2.8 km). A side trail leads R for 75 yds. to a broad open ledge with excellent views of Marcy, the Johns Brook Valley and Chapel Pond Pass. Ascent from road, 1640 ft. (500 m). Elevation, 2762 ft. (842 m).

Swinging sharp L at the summit, the trail descends steeply over ledges and then down very steeply through a gully for 50 yds. to the foot of the cliff and a junction near some large boulders at 2.0 mi. Trail straight ahead with ADK markers is the Sachs Trail (trail 19). Turning R at this junction, the Hedgehog Trail climbs at moderate to steep grades with occasional glimpses out through the trees of the cliffs on Rooster Comb. The trail dips slightly at 2.4 mi., but soon resumes the climb to the summit of North Hedgehog at 2.7 mi. Both this and the main summit of Hedgehog are wooded, offering no views. The trail now descends, crosses a brook at 3.0 mi., and then climbs to the summit of Hedgehog at 3.1 mi. (5.0 km). Total ascent from road, 2530 ft. (771 m). Elevation, 3369 ft. (1027 m).

From Hedgehog, the trail descends toward the W and SW to a brook with a junction just beyond at 3.5 mi. Trail coming in from the L with ATIS markers is the W.A. White Trail (trail 32). Turning R and now following ATIS markers, the trail continues to the crest of a ridge and climbs at moderate to easy grades to a slight sag, after which the climbing increases to the top of the Wolf's "chin" at 4.5 mi. The trail then descends steeply to a col and soon begins an exceedingly steep climb to the summit of Lower Wolf Jaw at 5.0 mi. There are good views from the summit lookout to the N and W. The trail continues over the summit and on to connect with the ADK Range Trail in Wolf Jaws Notch (trail 4).

Distances: Interbrook Rd. at Johns Brook bridge to Rooster Comb, 1.8 mi.; to junction with Sachs Trail to Rt. 73, 2.0 mi.; to summit of Hedgehog, 3.1 mi.; to junction with W.A. White Trail, 3.5 mi.; to summit of Lower Wolf Jaw, 5.0 mi. (8.0 km). Total ascent from road, 3670 ft. (1119 m). Elevation, 4175 ft. (1273 m). Order of height, 30.

(19) Rooster Comb
from Rt. 73
Map: F-8

Known as the Sachs Trail, this trail to Rooster Comb is slightly longer than the trail from Keene Valley but has roughly equivalent grades. This trail also gives access to Snow Mt.

Trailhead: The start is rather difficult to find because the landowner has requested that no signs be placed on the highway. The trail starts on Rt. 73, 0.8 mi. S of the High Peaks sign in the center of Keene Valley. There is a small red fire hydrant just S of a private driveway with two old stone gate posts nearly hidden in thick bushes. Park on the highway.

From the highway (0 mi.) proceed 0.1 mi. up the driveway to a junction with a sign pointing R for Rooster Comb. The trail follows this road at easy grades past another house on the R to a sharp L turn off the road at 0.3 mi. at a point where the road swings R. The trail now climbs moderately through open hemlocks to the L bank of Rushing Brook above a small flume, and then swings R and continues the climb to a short flat area at 0.5 mi. Crossing a small stream, the trail swings R and up to a junction at 1.2 mi. with ATIS trail L to Snow Mt. (trail 53).

Continuing past this junction, the grade moderates at 1.4 mi. and continues mostly easy to a junction at 1.7 mi. with trail L to Hedgehog and Lower Wolf Jaw (trail 18). Continuing straight ahead, the trail passes several large boulders and begins a very steep climb up a gully for 50 yds., after which the grade eases a bit as the trail switchbacks up through small ledges to the summit at 1.9 mi. A side trail L from the junction at the summit leads 75 yds. to the broad summit ledge, where there are excellent views of Marcy, the Johns Brook Valley and Chapel Pond Pass. Trail with ADK markers continues over the summit and on down to Interbrook Rd. just W of Keene Valley (trail 18).

Distances: Rt. 73 to junction with ATIS trail, 1.2 mi.; to junction with Hedgehog Trail, 1.7 mi.; to summit of Rooster Comb, 1.9 mi. (3.1 km). Ascent from Rt. 73, 1720 ft. (524 m). Elevation 2762 ft. (842 m).

(20) Baxter Mt. from Rt. 9N on Spruce Hill   Map: G-7

There are three trails to this popular summit, of which this approach is the easiest. The many ledges on Baxter offer both good blueberrying and outstanding views of Keene Valley, the Great Range and Marcy at the head of the Johns Brook Valley. This trail is currently maintained by the Algonquin Chapter of ADK and is marked with ADK markers.

Trailhead: Start on Rt. 9N, 2.0 mi. from the intersection of Rts. 9N and 73 between Keene and Keene Valley, at the top of a long climb. The trail begins 20 yds. to the E of the junction of Hurricane Rd. and Rt. 9N.

From the road (0 mi.), the trail heads SW through some pines, crosses under a power line, and begins an easy to moderate climb to a height of land at 0.7 mi., after which it is level to a junction 40 yds. later with trail from Beede Farm (trail 21). Turning R, the trail starts a steep climb which moderates at 0.8 mi., after which there are many side trails leading L to numerous views and blueberry patches. The trail continues with alternating steep pitches and flat areas to the SE summit of 0.9 mi. The trail now descends into a col and climbs to the NW summit at 1.1 mi., where there are more views. The trail continues over this summit and down to the Upham Road near Keene Valley (trail 21).

Distances: Rt. 9N to junction with Beede Farm Trail, 0.7 mi.; to NW summit, 1.1 mi. (1.8 km). Ascent from Rt. 9N, 770 ft. (235 m). Elevation, 2440 ft. (744 m).

(21) Baxter Mt. from Beede Farm   Map: F-8

This slightly longer approach to Baxter can be combined with a descent via the Upham Trail to make a nice loop. Since most hikers making this circuit do so in this direction, the Upham Trail is described going down. The Upham Trail is not well-used, however, and it requires considerable care to follow.

Trailhead: From the High Peaks sign in the center of Keene Valley go N 0.6 mi. and turn E on Beede Rd. After crossing the Ausable Rive, bear L across a small bridge, then bear L again at the junction with Phelps Brook Rd., 0.4 mi. from Rt. 73. The third driveway on the L from Phelps Brook Rd. is the approach for the Upham Trail, but no cars may be driven up this driveway. Beyond this driveway, Beede Rd. turns to gravel to a junction at 0.9 mi. from Rt. 73, just below Beede Farm. Cars should be parked here and not at the farm as in the past.

From the junction (0 mi.), the trail goes L up the driveway past the Beede Farm and continues up across an old pasture. There are few markers on this section, but in general the trail takes every L after the top of the pasture. At the top of the old pasture, the trail follows a grassy road and bears L at 0.3 mi. continuing to bear L onto an older road, the trail becomes a footpath and is maked with occasional yellow paint blazes along with a few trail markers. At 1.1 mi. the trail comes to a junction with a trail from Rt. 9N (trail 20). Turning L, the trail starts a steep climb which moderates at 1.2 mi., after which there are many side trails leading L to numerous views and blueberry patches. The trail continues with alternating steep pitches and flat areas to the SE summit at 1.4 mi. It now descends into a col and climbs to the NW summit at 1.5 mi. (2.5 km) where there are more views. Ascent from Beede Farm, 1150 ft. (350 m). Elevation, 2440 ft. (744 m).

The Upham Trail continues over the summit and descends to the W shoulder where there are good views to the W. Descending steeply off this shoulder, it flattens out at 1.8 mi. and comes to some more views at 2.0 mi. Swinging L off the end of the ridge, the trail descends steeply through an open forest of red pines and then into thicker trees and down to a small book at 2.3 mi. After climbing over a small hogback on the far side of the brook, the trail swings R on an old tote road and descends gradually along a shelf above the brook valley. Bearing L where another old road diverges R, the tail takes a sharp L off the tote road at 3.0 mi. and goes over a low ridge and down to the Upham driveway at 3.1 mi., just below the house. (Hikers ascending via this route should watch for this sharp R just before the house at the end of a switchback on the driveway.) The trail now descends the driveway to Beede Rd. at 3.3 mi.

Distances: Beede Farm to junction with trail from Rt. 9N, 1.1 mi.; to summit of Baxter, 1.6 mi.; to Beede Rd. via Upham Trail, 3.3 mi. (5.2 km).

(22) Spread Eagle and
Hopkins   Map: F-8

The parking area and fist 0.6 mi. of trail as described in previous editions have been closed at the request of a private landowner. To date (August 1992) the Keene Valley Chapter of ADK has been unable to reach an agreement with an adjoining developer regarding either hiker parking or marking of a new route through the road system of the real estate development. Foot travel is, however, still permitted on the roads leading from the end of Beede Rd. (see trail 21), but no formal marking exists to guide hikers through the road system. From the upper end of the road system, both the Direct Trail to Hopkins and the trail over Spread Eagle are intact and marked. Thus, hikers confident of their ability to navigate through this road system may continue to climb and descend these peaks via this route. The only changes are that the old start is closed altogether and that public vehicular traffic is not permitted beyond Beede Rd., making the distance to Hopkins and Spread Eagle 0.5 mi. longer than the old route—2.9 mi. for Spread Eagle and Hopkins and 2.7 mi. for Hopkins via Direct Trail.

(23) Hopkins via
Direct Trail   Map: F-8

See above.

(24) Hopkins via
Ranney Trail   Map: F-8

This trail to Hopkins is rarely used, but it has moderate grades throughout and generally good footing. The trail joins the Mossy Cascade Trail to Hopkins 0.9 mi. below the summit of Hopkins.

Trailhead: *Start at an iron bridge over the Ausable River, 0.5 mi. S of the High Peaks sign in the center of Keene Valley on Rt. 73. Because this is a prive drive, cars should be parked on Rt. 73.*

From the highway (0 mi.), follow the driveway on the flat to the far end of the clearing at 0.3 mi., where a sign pointing R marks the start of the trail. The trail enters the woods on a lumber road following along the R bank of a stream on easy to moderate grades. Crossing the brook at 0.7 mi., it climbs steeply along an old lumber road and then turns sharp L at 0.9 mi., now climbing moderately along the L bank of the brook. The trail crosses a yellow-blazed property line at 1.0 mi. and continues at a moderate grade with a few steeper pitches to the junction with Mossy Cascade Trail (trail 51) coming in from the R at 1.8 mi.

Distances: *Rt. 73 to Mossy Cascade Trail, 1.8 mi.; to summit of Hopkins, 2.7 mi. (4.3 km). Ascent from Rt. 73, 2140 ft. (652 m). Elevation, 3183ft. (970 m).*

H. Hammond

Mt. Haystack from Mt. Marcy

St. Huberts Section

St. Huberts is located on Rt. 73, 2.5 mi. S of Keene Valley. There are over 90 mi. of trails in this area, offering a wide variety of hikes, from woodland walks along beautiful streams to ascents of Giant, Gothics and other peaks. One must be aware, however, that many of the hikes in this section are on the land of the Adirondack Mountain Reserve (AMR)/Ausable Club, a private preserve stretching over 10 mi. to the SW and incorporating both the Upper and Lower Ausable lakes. Hikers should consult the map accompanying this guide for the exact boundaries of the AMR and should follow carefully all special regulations regarding parking and use of AMR land.

As part of the sale of higher land by the AMR to the State of New York in 1978, the state acquired permanent public easements for foot travel over all of the hiking trails on AMR land with the exception of certain trails near the shores of the Upper Ausable Lake. (See Upper Ausable Lake Area, below.) These easements guarantee public access to the summits of Colvin, Blake, Dial, Nippletop, Sawteeth and the Great Range, but while still on AMR land, hikers must obey the following rules:

1) No camping, fishing or hunting.
2) No off-trail travel including rock climbing or bushwhacking along the shores of the Lower Ausable Lake.
3) No boating or swimming, including portable boats brought by the public; there are no boats for rent by the public.
4) NO DOGS or other pets are permitted in this game preserve.

These restrictions do not apply to approaches to Snow, Hopkins, Giant, Round, Noonmark, Dix or Lower Wolf Jaw (if approached via Deer Brook); and once past the private boundaries one may camp and fish. Hikers starting backpacking trips from St. Huberts must therefore plan an early enough start so that they can reach state land in time to set up camp. The warden of the AMR may turn backpackers away if they clearly cannot reach a legal campsite by nightfall.

The approaches to trails 26–42 are from the Lake Road (trail 25). Read this description carefully and be aware that since drop-offs and pick-ups are not permitted along the road in front of the clubhouse, all hikers must start and finish at the designated parking area. Also, as of 1995, the summer bus service will no longer be available to the public.

Except for the Dix Trail from Rt. 73, all trails described in this section are maintained by the Adirondack Trail Improvement Society and marked with ATIS markers—mostly orange but with a few old blue or white disks still evident.

Trailheads: Hikers approaching Round, Noonmark, or any of the climbs off the Lake Road, are required to park their car at the designated hikers' parking lot just off Rt. 73 opposite the parking lot for the Roaring Brook Trail. This spot is 3.0 mi. S of the High Peaks sign in Keene Valley (0.5 mi. S of the main access road to the Ausable Club) or 5.9 mi. N of the junction of Rts. 9 and 73 in Underwood. From this parking lot, it is 0.5 mi. W along the gravel road and past the golf course to the start of the Lake Road (see below). The designated parking accommodates 35–40 cars, but on busy weekends this parking lot may be full. Because parking is not permitted along the gravel road leading up to the golf course and clubhouse, hikers must find parking across Rt. 73 or at other designated parking areas.

Trails in winter: With the exception of the Lake Road, none of the trails in this section are suitable for skiing. In addition to snowshoes, crampons may be required to ascend any of the peaks, with an ice axe possibly required.

The Lake Road is a classic ski tour and is often skiable early in the season. Skiers must be aware, however, that this is a private road and is used to haul supplies to the Upper Lake when the lake ice makes this possible. Vehicles of all types may be encountered, even on weekends, and the snow surface may be less than ideal for skiing as a result. In spite of these potential problems, the skiing is often fine and the destination makes it a worthwhile ski even if conditions underfoot aren't perfect.

Below are listed a few suggested hikes to help first-time visitors to the area choose among the many possibilities.

Short Hikes:

Snow Mt.—3.4-mi. round trip. An easy trail along a pretty brook with a waterfall leads to an open summit with good views and plenty of blueberries. See description for Snow Mt. via Deer Brook Trail.

Giant's Nubble via the Washbowl —3.0-mi. round trip. This rocky summit offers a spectacular view of the slides on Giant and of Chapel Pond Pass with a unique mountainside pond on the way. See descriptions for Giant via Ridge Trail and Giant's Nubble.

See also—Table of Short Hikes in Appendix III.

Moderate Hikes:

Hopkins via Mossy Cascade—6.3-mi. round trip. A seldom-used approach to a popular rocky summit, passing by a beautiful 50-ft.-high waterfall and several interesting lookouts.

East and West River Trails— 7.4 mi. round trip. A relatively flat walk through some beautiful forests along the banks of the Ausable River, making a loop trip to the Lower Ausable Lake and back. See descriptions for lake Road, East River Trail and West River Trail.

Harder Hikes:

Giant via Ridge Trail with return over Green and Hopkins—9.4-mi. point to point. An ascent of Giant along the open rocks of the ridge trail with a descent through some lovely virgin forests and a variety of additional views enroute. See descriptions for Giant via Ridge Trail, Giant from Hopkins via Green, and Hopkins via Mossy Cascade.

Gothics with return via Sawteeth "Scenic Trail"—13.5-mi. round trip. A rugged loop but one offering unforgettable views from the summits of Gothics, Pyramid, and Sawteeth, plus five more lookouts on the way down Sawteeth. See descriptions for Gothics from Lake Road, Gothics from Lower Ausable Lake via Pyramid, and Sawteeth from lower Ausable Lake via Scenic Trail.

Trail Described	Total Miles	Pages
Road to Lower Ausable Lake	3.3	79
East River Trail	3.3	81
Ladies Mile	0.9	82
West River Trail	3.8	82
Cathedral Rocks and Bear Run	1.9	84
Lost Lookout	1.5	85
Rainbow Falls	0.2	85
W. A. White Trail to Lower Wolf Jaw	4.5	86
Wedge Brook Trail to Lower Wolf Jaw	2.1	87
Gothics from the Lake Road	3.4	88
Gothics from the Lower Lake via Pyramid	2.7	90
Sawteeth from Lower Lake via Scenic Trail	3.0	91
Sawteeth via Pyramid-Gothics Trail	0.5	92
Indian Head	0.8	93
Fish Hawks Cliffs	0.6	94
Colvin from Lake Road and Gill Brook	2.9	95
Nipple Top via Elk Pass from Lake Road	3.5	96
Dial and Nipple Top via Bear Den from Lake Road	5.9	97
Noonmark via Stimson Trail from Ausable Club	2.1	99
Noonmark from SE via Felix Adler Trail	2.7	100
Round Mt.	3.0	101

(25) Road to Lower Ausable Lake   Map: F-9

This private road, known as the Lake Road, runs SW from the main club building to the boathouse at the foot of Lower Ausable Lake, gaining about 700 vertical ft. in 3.5 mi. A quarter mile from the club is a locked gate, beyond which private vehicles (except those of members in the off-season) are not permitted. Bicycles are also prohibited, but foot traffic is permitted.

For many years the AMR allowed the hiking public to use the summer bus service on this road on a space-available basis. However, recent increases in use of the bus, by both AMR members and hikers, has caused the AMR to decide reluctantly that, as of the summer of 1995, public use of the bus service will end. Hikers also are reminded that both the main clubhouse and the boathouse area at the Lower Lake end of the road are off limits to public hikers. As in the past, all hikers must sign in and sign out at the trail register located at the watchman's hut at start of the Lake Road (see below).

From the clubhouse, the road drops down between two tennis courts then past the golf house and some private cottages. Three hundred yds. beyond the clubhouse the W.A. White Trail to Lower Wolf Jaw (trail 32) and the West River Trail (trail 28) diverge R at a small watchman's hut. Continuing straight ahead, the trail reaches the gate in another 90 yds. Constructed as part of the AMR's centennial observances in 1986, the present gate is a replica of the original gate on the Lake Road.

From the gate (0 mi.), the Ladies Mile (trail 27) branches R at both 45 yds. and 0.3 mi. Just beyond this second junction the East River Trail (trail 26) also branches R. At 0.7 mi. the Henry Goddard Leach Trail to Dial and Nipple Top (trail 42) branches L, and at 0.9 mi. a bridge leads across Gill Brook to connect with the East and West River Trails. Continuing on, the road crosses Gill Brook at 1.1 mi. with a side trail L leading past a small flume on Gill Brook. At 1.8 mi. a trail leads R to Beaver Meadow Falls and Gothics (trail 34) with the Gill Brook Trail to Colvin and Nipple Top (trail 40) diverging L a few yards beyond. The shorter trail to Colvin and Nipple Top diverges L at 2.5 mi., and at 3.1 mi. the road reaches a height of land where the Indian Head trail (trail 38) diverges L. Just beyond the Indian Head trail, the trails to Rainbow Falls, Gothics, and Sawteeth (trails 31, 35, and 36) diverge R down a side road, past some sheds, and down to the Lower Lake dam. (The Lake Road continues to the lake, but public hikers are not permitted beyond this point.)

Distances: Gate to Lower Ausable Lake, 3.3 mi. (5.2 km). Ascent, 700 ft. (213 m).

(26) East River Trail   Map: F-9

This trail follows the R bank of the Ausable River to the dam at Lower Ausable Lake. It offers some very pleasant walking and some lovely views of various falls and pools in the river as well as a few of the surrounding peaks. The trail diverges R from the Lake Road 0.3 mi. from the gate (see above). From the road (0 mi.) the trail veers away from the road and reaches the Ausable River at a bridge at 0.2 mi. Bearing L, it follows along the river bank, climbs the bank of the river, and quickly descends to cross Gill Brook on a bridge at 0.5 mi.;and then follows up Gill Brook's L bank for a few yards before bearing R and reaching a gravel road at 0.7 mi. (Road R leads to Canyon ford across the Ausable River and connection to West River Trail (trail 28) in 0.3 mi. Road L leads 0.1 mi. to Lake Road).

Crossing the gravel road, the East River trail climbs to the top of a bank high above the river and levels out at 0.9 mi. After some other lesser climbs, the trail heads R and down across a steep side hill at 1.6 mi. and soon comes to a lookout over the gorge at 1.7 mi. The trail now draws slowly closer to the river, passing some other views of falls before coming to a crossing of a large plastic water line which transfers water from the Ausable to Gill Brook to supplement the Ausable Club's water supply. At 2.2 mi. the trail reaches a junction with the Beaver Meadow Falls Trail to Gothics (trail 34). The two trails are together until 2.3 mi., where the Gothics Trail goes sharp R and down to a bridge. Continuing straight ahead, there is a view of Sawteeth across Beaver Meadow at 2.4 mi., and the trail continues mostly on the flat to the bridge below the dam at 3.3 mi.

Distances: Lake Road to Beaver Meadow Falls Trail to Gothics, 2.2 mi.; to bridge and dam at Lower Ausable Lake, 3.3 mi. (5.3 km); to Lower Lake Boathouse, 3.5 mi. (3.8 mi. from the gate).

(27) Ladies Mile   Map: F-9

This is a short jaunt through the woods to the bank of the Ausable River and back, making about a mile round trip from the clubhouse. There are many possible variations using the East or West River Trail to return.

Leaving the road (0 mi.) 45 yds. past the gate, the trail descends a short flight of steps, crosses a bridge over the usually dry bed of Leach Brook, and turns L past a large woodshed at 0.1 mi. Here the Ladies Mile forks with the L branch following the L bank of Leach Brook for 200 yds. to the upper bridge leading back to the Lake Road. The R branch crosses a small brook, reaches the bank of the Ausable and follows this up to a junction at 0.4 mi. The trail straight ahead connects with the East River Trail while the trail L returns to the Lake Road at 0.6 mi.

(28) West River Trail   Map: F-9

This trail follows the L bank of the Ausable River to the dam at Lower Ausable Lake. It offers pleasant walking through some virgin stands of timber, as well as some views of the pools and falls in the river and some of the surrounding peaks. Combined with either the East River Trail or the Lake Road, this provides a lovely woodland walk of about 7 mi. with relatively little climbing.

The start is on the Lake Road 300 yds. past the clubhouse at the small green watchman's hut. Leaving the road (0 mi.), the trail starts on a private driveway and descends slightly to the river, which is crossed on a bridge to a junction at 1.2 mi. with the W.A. White Trail (trail 32).

Turning L, the trail proceeds along the river to another junction at a bridge at 0.6 mi. with Cathedral Rocks and Bear Run (trail 29). (Bridge L leads to East River Trail and Ladies Mile; see above.)

Continuing straight, the West River Trail crosses Pyramid Brook at 1.1 mi. with the upper end of the Cathedral Rocks Trail joining the trail 25 yds. farther on. Soon climbing above the river, the trail comes to a junction with the "direct" trail to Pyramid Brook (trail 29) coming in from the R and another junction 60 yds. beyond at 1.3 mi. (Trail L descends steeply and crosses the river at a ford to connect with East River Trail and Lake Road; see above.)

Continuing straight ahead, the grade becomes easy at 1.4 mi., where there is a lookout into the gorge below. The grade soon steepens again, and there is another lookout at 1.7 mi. with views of Colvin, Nipple Top, and the river; with a third lookout of Giant at 1.9 mi. Now swinging away from the river, the trail crosses Wedge Brook at 2.0 mi. and reaches a junction with the Wedge Brook Trail (trail 33) just beyond. Turning L and down, the trail comes to a view from the top of a slide at 2.1 mi., descends to the level of the river, and continues to Beaver Meadow Falls at 2.7 mi. These falls of bridal veil-like appearance are well worth the trip alone.

Crossing the brook below the falls, the trail soon comes to a junction. Beaver Meadow Falls Trail (trail 34) leads R to Gothics (2.8 mi.) and Lost Lookout (0.6 mi.). Trail L is to East River Trail and Lake Road (0.5 mi.). Continuing straight ahead, the West River Trail crosses the flat open area known as Beaver Meadow. Following along the base of a steep cliff at 3.2 mi., the trail continues to a junction with the other end of the Lost Lookout Trail (trail 30) at 3.7 mi. and reaches the bridge and dam at the Lower Lake at 3.8 mi.

The trail straight ahead leads to Rainbow Falls, Sawteeth and Gothics. Bridge L leads to East River Trail and Lake Road at 3.8 mi.

Distances: Lake Road to trail to Cathedral Rocks, 0.6 mi.; to Wedge Brook Trail to Lower Wolf Jaw, 2.0 mi.; to Beaver Meadow Falls and Gothics Trail, 2.7 mi.; to Lower Lake bridge and dam, 3.8 mi.; to boathouse, 3.9 mi. (6.3 km).

(29) Cathedral Rocks and Bear Run   Map: F-9

This interesting loop trail offers a short round trip with some interesting rock formations, two views and a pretty little waterfall. The start is on the West River Trail at the bridge at 0.6 mi.; this can also be reached via the East River Trail. Leaving the West River Trail (0 mi.), the trail climbs moderately along the L bank of a small brook heading first W and then NW. The climbing steepens as the trail approaches the first rock face at 0.5 mi. Then swinging L, the trail continues along under a series of cliffs to a larger one on the R at 0.8 mi. This is Cathedral Rocks.

Just beyond Cathedral Rocks is a junction with the trail L leading 0.3 mi. across to the main trail to bypass Bear Run. Bearing R and up at this junction, the trail crosses the property line of the AMR, with the base of a large cliff reached soon after at 1.0 mi. Side trail R leads 300 yds. along the base of the cliff to a narrow slot in the cliff, which is followed up to a panoramic view ranging from Giant on the L to Sawteeth on the R. As the sign at the junction says, "don't miss."

Turning L at the base of the cliff, the trail climbs to a height of land and then descends to another lookout at 1.3 mi. Just beyond this lookout, the trail swings sharp L and descends a narrow shelf through the ledges. Now descending very steeply, it reaches the other end of the bypass trail at 1.4 mi., after which it continues descending steeply along the L bank of Pyramid Brook, past a waterfall, to flatter terrain at 1.5 mi. Now crossing to the R bank of the brook, the trail comes to a junction at 1.5 mi. (Trail R leads 0.2 mi. directly to West River Trail. Continuing L, the trail descends the R bank of Pyramid Brook to the West River Trail at 1.6 mi.

Distances: West River Trail to bypass trail above Cathedral Rocks, 0.8 mi.; to base of cliff at Bear Run, 1.0 mi.; to Pyramid Brook waterfall, 1.5 mi.; to West River Trail, 1.7 mi. (2.7 km).

(30) Lost Lookout　　　　Map: F-10

This trail climbs about 500 ft. onto the side of Armstrong above Beaver Meadow to two exceptional viewpoints of Lower Ausable Lake and the surrounding mountains. The start is at Beaver Meadow Falls, which can be reached by either the East or West River Trail or directly from the Lake Road by the Beaver Meadow Falls Trail to Gothics (see above).

Leaving Beaver Meadow Falls (0 mi.), the trail coincides with the Gothics Trail, climbing a ladder and ascending steeply to a junction at 0.3 mi. Here the Lost Lookout Trail branches L and climbs steadily to the first lookout at 0.6 mi. Leveling off, the trail descends slightly to the second lookout at 0.7 mi. and then begins to descend. There is a lookout to Rainbow Falls on the R at 1.5 mi., after which the trail descends to the West River Trail at 1.7 mi. and, turning R, reaches the bridge and dam at Lower Ausable Lake at 1.7 mi.

Distances: Beaver Meadow Falls to first lookout, 0.6 mi.; to bridge and dam at Lower Ausable Lake, 1.7 mi. (2.7 km).

(31) Rainbow Falls　　　　Map: F-10

This nearly 150-ft.-high waterfall is a sight that should not be missed, whether one makes a trip up the Lake Road just to see the falls or as a side trip while on a longer hike in the area. From the W end of the bridge at the Lower Ausable Lake Dam, follow the Gothics Trail (trail 35) for 0.1 mi. and diverge R for another 0.1 mi. along, and sometimes in, the brook to the base of the falls at 0.2 mi. Distance from Lake Road, 0.3 mi. (0.5 km).

(32) W.A. White Trail to Lower Wolf Jaw   Map: F-9

This trail is named after one of the founders of ATIS and the designer of the Range Trail from Gothics to Haystack. It is a slightly longer route to Lower Wolf Jaw than the Wedge Brook Trail, but it does offer some views on the way up and the grades are generally easier.

Trailhead: Start on Lake Road at watchman's hut, 300 yds. S from the main club building. For information on parking and directions to Lake Road, see introduction to this section. An alternate start via Deer Brook (trail 53) is shorter to the summit of Lower Wolf Jaw when the walk from the parking area is counted, although it precludes a loop via the Wedge Brook Trail.

Leaving the road (0 mi.), the trail starts down a private driveway and descends slightly to the Ausable River where it crosses a bridge to reach a junction on the far side at 0.2 mi. with the West River Trail to Lower Ausable Lake (trail 28). Bearing R, the trail climbs at an easy grade along a side hill to a junction with a lumber road at 0.6 mi. Turning L, the trail follows this road through a lumbered area up to Maghee Clearing at 0.9 mi., where there is a good view of Giant.

Shortly after this view, the trail crests a small hill and descends briefly before climbing to a second crest, which is where the old trail went L. Continuing on, the lumber road climbs easily for a short while and then steeply up to a junction at 1.0 mi. (Trail R leads along lumber road past link trail to Deer Brook Trail (trail 53) and on to a junction with the Deer Brook Trail to Snow Mt., 0.7 mi. from W.A. White Trail. Total distance to the summit of Snow Mt. is 2.2 mi. from Lake Road.)

The W.A. White Trail bears L at this junction and climbs steeply at first and then moderately to the upper edge of the lumbered area at 1.3 mi. The trail now switchbacks up through a cliff band and gains the top of the ridge at 1.4 mi. Climbing the ridge at a moderate grade, the trail reaches a side trail leading 25 yds. to a lookout at 1.6 mi.

Past this junction, the trail again switchbacks to the R and continues at a moderate grade to another ledge 1.9 mi., where there are good views of the Ausable Valley as well as of the surrounding peaks. Then making a short descent, the trail climbs to a higher ledge at 2.0 mi. From here, it descends slightly and then begins an easy climb interspersed with level stretches to the junction with the Hedgehog Trail (trail 18) at 3.0 mi. Trail R with ADK markers leads over Hedgehog Mt. to Rooster Comb and Keene Valley.

Continuing straight ahead, the W.A. White Trail continues to the crest of a ridge and climbs at moderate to easy grades to a slight sag, after which the climbing increases to the top of the Wolf's "Chin" at 4.0 mi. The trail then descends steeply to a col and soon begins an exceedingly steep climb to the summit of Lower Wolf Jaw at 4.6 mi. There are good views from the summit lookout to the N and W.

The trail that continues over the summit leads in 0.3 mi. to the junction with the Wedge Brook Trail (trail 33) and further to the junction with the trail up from Johns Brook at the col between the two Wolf Jaws in 0.5 mi. (trail 4).

Distances: Lake Road to junction with trail to Snow Mt., 1.0 mi.; to junction with Hedgehog Trail, 3.0 mi.; to summit of Lower Wolf Jaw, 4.5 mi. (7.2 km). Ascent from Lake Road, 2825 ft. (860 m). Elevation, 4175 ft. (1273 m). Order of height, 30.

(33) Wedge Brook Trail to Wolf Jaws   Map: F-9

Alexander Wyant, a well-known artist who first came to Keene Valley in 1869, is credited with conferring the name Wolf Jaws, as suggested by the deep col between the two peaks. The spot on Noonmark from which Wyant painted a view of these peaks is supposed to offer the best representation of a wolf's jaw. The Wedge Brook Trail is the shortest route to either Wolf Jaw from the Ausable Club. Combined with the W.A. White Trail, it makes a nice round trip.

This trail branches off the West River Trail (trail 29) at the crossing of Wedge Brook, 2.0 mi. from the Lake Road. Leaving the West River Trail (0 mi.), it climbs fairly steeply at first along the bank of Wedge Brook, but soon leaves the brook on an easier grade and reaches a clearing 1.2 mi. Shortly after this clearing, the grade again becomes steep as the trail climbs the headwall of the ravine with the bare rock slides of Lower Wolf Jaw visible on the R. At 1.6 mi. the cut-off trail to Wolf Jaws Notch branches L, leading 0.3 mi. to the ADK Range Trail (trail 4) at the Notch.

Bearing R at this junction, the Wedge Brook Trail continues climbing to its junction with the ADK Lower Wolf Jaw Trail (trail 5) at 1.9 mi. Turning R and now with ADK markers, the trail climbs steeply to the summit of Lower Wolf Jaw at 2.2 mi., where there are good views to the N and W. Trail straight ahead is the W.A. White Trail (trail 32) leading to St. Huberts and connecting with trails to Hedgehog, Rooster Comb and Keene Valley.

Distances: Lake Road to start of Wedge Brook Trail, 2.0 mi.; to junction with cut-off trail to Wolf Jaws Notch, 3.6 mi.; to summit of Lower Wolf Jaw, 4.2 mi. (6.7 km). Ascent from Lake Road, 2825 ft. (860 m). Elevation, 4175 ft. (1273 m). Order of height, 30.

(34) Gothics from Lake Road   Map: F-9

For the naming of this peak, see description for Gothics via Orebed Brook Trail (trail 8). Also known as the Beaver Meadow Trail, this was the first trail to be cut up Gothics and remains a popular route today.

The trail starts on the Lake Road (trail 25) just past the reservoir 1.8 mi. from the gate. Turning R (W) from the road (0 mi.), the trail climbs at an easy grade to join the East River Trail (trail 26) at 0.5 mi. Swinging L and down at this junction, the trail turns sharp R and down at 0.5 mi. and crosses a bridge to a junction with the West River Trail (trail 28) near the foot of Beaver Meadow Falls at 0.6 mi. Continuing straight across the West River Trail, the Gothics Trail climbs steeply up a ladder and then on at an easier grade to the junction with the trail leading L to Lost Lookout at 0.8 mi. (trail 30).

From this junction, the trail climbs at an easy grade, crossing the AMR boundary line at 1.0 mi. and continuing at an easy to moderate grade past two small streams to a third larger stream at 1.8 mi. Here the trail swings L and begins a steep climb that does not moderate until just before a large balanced rock on the R at 2.5 mi. After this balanced rock, the trail again climbs steeply up past the base of a rock wall to the crest of the ridge at 2.8 mi. From here, the trail begins to work its way across the steep W slope of a shoulder of Armstrong with several good views of Gothics. Three ladders aid the passage across the steep rocks. Beyond this section, the trail comes to a junction with the ADK Range Trail (trail 4) at 3.0 mi. Turning L, the trail crosses a short flat section and then begins a steep climb to the summit of Gothics, reaching it at 3.4 mi.

The view is unobstructed with about 30 major peaks discernible. The boathouse at Lower Ausable Lake can be seen, but to see any of the Upper Lake one must proceed past the summit 0.1 mi. to the ATIS trail over Pyramid and go L on this trail a few yards to a wide ledge with views to the S and W. (The ADK Range Trail continues over the summit and on to the upper Great Range with connecting trails to Johns Brook Lodge and Keene Valley; see Keene Valley Section).

Distances: Lake Road to Beaver Meadow Falls, 0.6 mi.; to ADK Range Trail, 3.0 mi.; to summit of Gothics, 3.4 mi. (5.5 km). From gate to summit, 5.2 mi. (8.3 km). Ascent from Lake Road, 3050 ft. (930 m). Elevation, 4736 ft. (1444 m). Order of height, 10.

(35) Gothics from Lower Ausable Lake via Pyramid   Map: F-10

Known as the Alfred E. Weld Trail, this approach to Gothics was laid out and cut by Jim Goodwin in 1966. It is the shortest route to the summit and offers what may well be the single most spectacular view in the Adirondacks from the summit of Pyramid just below the summit of Gothics. The trail does have some steep climbing approaching the sharp peak of Pyramid.

The trail starts at the W end of the bridge below the dam at the Lower Ausable Lake (0 mi.). It coincides with the Sawteeth and Rainbow Falls Trails at first, but the Sawteeth Trail diverges L in 40 yds. and the Rainbow Falls Trail goes R at 0.1 mi. Now the Gothics Trail begins a steady ascent to a trail R to a lookout over Rainbow Falls at 0.3 mi. Swinging L, the trail climbs for a few yards further before easing off, crossing a brook, and then continuing at a generally easy grade. A few more steep pitches are encountered before a long easy section leads to a crossing of an old, grown-in slide coming down from Sawteeth at 0.9 mi.

Past this slide, the trail continues climbing and crosses a good sized brook at 1.3 mi., after which it becomes steeper and rougher as it ascends to the col between Pyramid and Sawteeth at 1.7 mi. Here there is a junction with the trail L leading 0.5 mi. to Sawteeth (trail 37). Turning R, the Gothics Trail starts at an easy grade, but soon begins climbing steeply and continues so until just short of the summit of Pyramid. Skirting the summit block to the R, the trail reaches the peak of Pyramid at 2.3 mi. The views encompass Gothics and all of the Great Range, seen at such an angle that nearly all of the considerable bare rock on the S side of these peaks is visible and serves as a spectacular foreground for the more distant view.

Turning R at the summit of Pyramid, the trail descends steeply to the bottom of the col at 2.5 mi. and then climbs equally steeply to a ledge on the S side of Gothics at 2.6 mi. A few yards on the level beyond, the trail meets the ADK Range Trail (trail 4). Turning R, the trail reaches the summit of Gothics at 2.7 mi.

Distances: Bridge at Lower Ausable Lake to col between Sawteeth and Pyramid, 1.7 mi.; to summit of Pyramid, 2.3 mi.; to junction with ADK Range Trail, 2.6 mi.; to summit of Gothics, 2.7 mi.; (4.4 km). Ascent from Lower Lake, 2870 ft. (875 M). Elevation, 4736 ft. (1444 m). Order of height, 10.

(36) Sawteeth from Lower Ausable Lake   Map: F-10

The striking serrated profile of this mountain as seen from the Ausable Club suggested the obvious name of Sawteeth to the early inhabitants of the area. It was erroneously labeled "Sawtooth" on the 1953 USGS topographic maps, but that error has been corrected on the 1979 maps.

There are two trails to the summit from Lower Ausable Lake. The older one, sometimes referred to as the "Scenic Trail," follows a wandering course up among the "teeth" and passes many interesting views. The newer trail follows the Gothics Trail to the col between Pyramid and Sawteeth and then ascends directly up the N side. Most hikers make this a loop trip with the descent of the Scenic Trail considered to be the easiest direction.

Leaving the W end of the bridge below the Lower Ausable Lake Dam (0 mi.), the trail diverges L from the Gothics Trail (trail 35) in 40 yds. and follows near the shore of the lake before beginning to climb away from the lake at 0.6 mi. At 1.0 mi. the trail reaches the first spectacular lookout with a boulder on it 250 ft. above the lake, with a second lookout at 1.1 mi. The trail now begins to climb steeply and comes to the base of a rock face at 1.2 mi. Some more steep climbing leads to the third lookout at 1.4 mi. After some easy going, the trail swings R up a gully with a ladder at the top, after which the steep climbing continues to a height of land at 1.8 mi. Lookout Rock, a climb of a few feet up to the R, offers a precipitous view of Lower Ausable Lake 1300 ft. below.

Leaving Lookout Rock, the trail soon begins an easy to moderate climb to a col at 2.2 mi. The trail now swings R and the climbing is very steep in spots as the trail ascends through some ledges and climbs a ladder to reach a lookout (#5) on the L at 2.5 mi. The grade moderates, and after another short steep pitch becomes easy to the SE summit at 2.6 mi. Now descending to a col called Rifle Notch, the trail again climbs steeply out of the notch and then on easier grades to a junction at 3.0 mi. with trail L to Upper Ausable Lake (trail 57). Just beyond this junction a boulder beside the trail indicates the NW summit with a lookout about 20 yds. to the L. There are good views of most of the Great Range from this lookout, with a view of Giant about 20 yds. to the E on the trail toward Gothics.

Distances: Bridge at Lower Lake to Lookout Rock, 1.8 mi.; to NW summit, 3.0 mi (4.8 km). Ascent from Lower Lake, 2275 ft. (693 m). Elevation, 4100 ft. (1250 m). Order of height, 35.

(37) Sawteeth via Pyramid-Gothics Trail   Map: E-10

The Pyramid-Gothics Trail (trail 35) is followed from the bridge to the col at 1.7 mi. Turning L here, the Sawteeth Trail proceeds nearly on the level before beginning to climb at 1.8 mi. Immediately it ascends a steep cleft in the rock face with poor footing, but above this point the climbing becomes easier. It becomes nearly level at 2.1 mi., and reaches the summit at 2.2 mi. The lookout is 20 yds. to the R.

(38) Indian Head   Map: F-10

This rocky peak rises 750 ft. directly above Lower Ausable Lake and offers excellent views of both Ausable lakes, Nipple Top, Colvin, Sawteeth, and much of the Great Range. This trail is also the approach for Fish Hawk Cliffs (trail 39), and approach #1 to Indian Head (see below) is a possible though more difficult start for Colvin and Nipple Top (trails 40 and 41). There are two approaches to this peak, which can be combined to make a nice loop trip including some very pretty walking along Gill Brook. All approaches are marked with ATIS markers.

1. From the top of the hill on the Lake Road just before Lower Ausable Lake, the Indian Head Trail goes L on the flat to a junction with a private trail leading R to the boathouse. Continuing straight through this junction, the trail soon begins climbing a series of switchbacks to a side trail R at 0.3 mi. to a view of Gothics called the "Gothic Window." Continuing up several more switchbacks, the trail ascends a ladder at 0.6 mi. and proceeds under a beautiful mossy cliff for a few yards before climbing steeply to a junction at the crest of the ridge at 0.8 mi. Trail L leads to Gill Brook (alternate #2, below) Trail straight ahead leads to Fish Hawk Cliffs (trail 39).

Turning R at this junction, the trail emerges on the bare ledges at 0.8 mi. Some broader ledges just below offer an even better view and some careful exploration to the R should find a view back down to the boathouse. One can also detour 0.3 mi. along the trail from Gill Brook for a view of Giant.

2. To approach Indian Head from Gill Brook, follow the longer approach to Colvin (trail 40) which leaves the Lake Road (trail 25) 1.8 mi. from the gate. From the Lake Road (0 mi.) follow the Gill Brook Trail past its junction with the shorter link from the Lake Road to a junction at 1.3 mi. Here the route to Indian Head goes R, crosses a small brook, and begins climbing steadily to a junction at 1.7 mi. with a spur trail R to a view. Bearing L, the trail is mostly level to the junction with the trail from the Lower Lake at 2.0 mi.

Distances: Boathouse to Indian Head, 0.8 mi. (1.3 km). Indian Head via Gill Brook Trail and Colvin Trail from Lake Road, 2.0 mi. (3.3 km). Ascent from boathouse, 730 ft. (223 m). Elevation, 2700 ft. (823 m).

(39) Fish Hawk Cliffs   Map: F-10

This slightly lower lookout just beyond Indian Head offers a spectacular view of the cliffs on Indian Head. A trail runs from Indian Head to Fish Hawk Cliffs and then on to the Colvin Trail.

Starting from the trail junction near the top of Indian Head (0 mi.), the trail descends very steeply to a col at 0.1 mi. and then climbs gradually to the ledges on Fish Hawk Cliffs at 0.2 mi. Continuing L, the trail is pretty much on the level to the junction with the Colvin Trail (trail 40) at 0.7 mi. This junction is 0.6 mi. above the junction of the two trails from the Lake Road and 0.7 mi. below the junction with Elk Pass Trail to Nipple Top.

Distances: Indian Head to Fish Hawk Cliffs, 0.2 mi.; to Colvin Trail, 0.7 mi. (1.1 km).

(40) Mt. Colvin from Lake Road

Map: F-9

This mountain was named for Verplanck Colvin in 1873 by Rev. T.L. Cuyler, a member of Colvin's survey party, who thought the peak was nameless. A few years earlier, however, "Old Mountain" Phelps had named it "Sabele" for the Indian credited by some to have discovered the ore at the MacIntyre Iron Works. Colvin was superintendent of the Adirondack Survey and the single most prominent character in Adirondack Mountain history. Besides making the first positive measurement of Mt. Marcy in 1875 with level and rod, he was also largely responsible for the inauguration of the Adirondack Park and State Forest Preserve. It is therefore highly fitting that his name attached to this peak has endured.

There are two approaches to Colvin from the Lake Road. The longer approach turns L from the Lake Road at 1.8 mi., just past the Gothics Trail. This trail follows up the L bank of picturesque Gill Brook with its many waterfalls and small flumes to a junction with the shorter route at 1.2 mi. from the road. Though scenic, this trail is quite rough in spots and requires more time than its distance would indicate. It is, however, worth using this trail in at least one direction when climbing Colvin, Nipple Top, or Indian Head. All of these trails are marked with ATIS markers.

The shorter route branches L from the Lake Road 2.5 mi. past the gate. Leaving the road (0 mi.), the trail climbs at an easy grade to the junction with the Gill Brook Trail at 0.5 mi. Turning R, the trail reaches a junction at 0.7 mi. with the trail R to Indian Head (trail 38). Continuing past this junction, the trail climbs high above Gill Brook and comes to a junction at 1.1 mi. with trail R to Fish Hawk Cliffs and Indian Head (trail 39).

Continuing on, the Colvin Trail climbs with a few steep pitches to a junction at 1.8 mi. with trail L to Elk Pass and Nipple Top (trail 41).

Turning R, the Colvin Trail climbs in a series of alternating steep and flat sections to the top of the ridge and then down to a small sag on the ridge at 2.7 mi. Climbing steeply again, the trail drops into a second sag and then up very steeply to the summit at 2.9 mi. There is a lookout just to the R with splendid views of Lower Ausable Lake, Sawteeth, and the Great Range. About 100 yds. S on the trail to Blake Peak there is another good view of Upper Ausable Lake, Allen Mt., and other peaks. (See trails 55 and 60 for description of trail leading to Blake, and on to the Elk Lake-Marcy Trail.)

Distances: Lake Road via shorter route to Gill Brook Trail, 0.5 mi.; to Indian Head Trail, 0.7 mi.; to Fish Hawk Cliffs Trail, 1.1 mi.; to Nipple Top Trail, 1.8 mi.; to summit of Colvin, 2.9 mi. (4.6 km). Ascent from Lake Road, 2330 ft. (710 m). Elevation, 4057 ft. (1237 m). Order of height, 39.

(41) Nipple Top via Elk Pass   Map: F-10

This peak is named for its characteristic profile when seen from Elk Lake. At one time more fastidious tourists and writers tried to eliminate the anatomical appellation used by the locals by substituting "Dial," a name probably given in 1837 by Prof. Emmons or one of his companions during their approach to climb Mt. Marcy; but with the assistance of Old Mountain Phelps, the current name has survived and the name "Dial" has been transferred to a lower peak to the N. The trail described here is the shortest route to the summit, but one can also ascend Nipple Top via Dial (trail 42), which makes possible a loop trip

The Elk Pass approach begins the same as for Colvin (trail 40) to the junction at 1.8 mi. Bearing L here, the climbing is generally moderate with two short steep sections before leveling off and then descending to a small pond on the L at 2.3 mi. The trail then crosses a small hogback and comes to a side trail leading R to a second pond at 2.4 mi. Now crossing first the outlet to the second pond and then the combined outlet, the trail circles back to the L around the first pond and crosses some wet ground before swinging R and starting up. The grade is moderate at first, but soon steepens and continues up the ridge with alternating steep and easier sections to a junction with the trail from Bear Den and Dial at the crest of the ridge at 3.2 mi.

Turning R, the trail goes over a small knob and reaches the summit at 3.5 mi. The view of Dix and its slides is most impressive, with other good views of Colvin and the Great Range. The view of Elk Lake to the S is partially blocked by scrub growth. Although not a perfect 360-degree view, the impression from the summit is one of solid and all-encompassing wilderness, which caused the Marshall brothers to rate this as having the third best view of all the high peaks.

Distances: Lake Road to departure from Colvins Trail, 1.8 mi.; to Elk Pass, 2.3 mi.; to junction with Bear Den-Dial Trail, 3.3 mi.; to summit of Nipple Top, 3.5 mi. (5.7 km). Ascent from Lake Road, 2760 ft. (841 m). Elevation, 4620 ft. (1408 m). Order of height, 13.

(42) Dial and Nipple Top via Bear Den
Map: F-9

A longer route to Nipple Top leaves the Lake Road (trail 25) 0.7 mi. from the gate and leads 5.9 mi. over Bear Den and Dial to the summit. Called the Henry Goddard Leach Trail, this route is 2.4 mi. longer than the route via Elk Pass, but it makes for a good loop trip.

Leaving the road (0 mi.) and marked with ATIS markers, the trail quickly begins climbing at moderate to steep grades and comes out on the W shoulder of Noonmark at 1.3 mi., having gained 1600 ft. (488 m) from the road. There are some views to the N from this first lookout and better views from a second lookout, reached after a slight descent and gradual ascent to a side trail R at 1.7 mi. Now descending steadily, the trail switchbacks down to the col between Noonmark and Bear Den at 2.0 mi., having lost about 320 ft. (98 m) in altitude from the shoulder of Noonmark.

The trail now climbs out of the col at a mostly moderate grade, with occasional small views back at Noonmark, to the wooded summit of Bear Den at 2.5 mi. Total ascent from road, 2280 ft. (695 m). Elevation, 3423 ft. (1043 m).

Leaving Bear Den, the trail descends to a bare spot at 2.8 mi. with an obscured view of Dial and Nipple Top ahead. Continuing to descend, the trail passes through a col and ascends slightly before dropping again to the main col between Bear Den and Dial at 3.0 mi., having lost 220 ft. (67 m) in altitude. The trail now climbs over one more small bump before beginning the final long climb to the summit of Dial, which is reached at 3.8 mi. A large rock on the R offers good views to the N and W. Total ascent, 3060 ft. (933 m). Elevation, 4020 ft. (1225 m).

This summit has been referred to as North Dial in previous editions of this guidebook, to distinguish it from the next peak to the S on the ridge, which is also 4020 ft. high. North Dial, however, is undoubtedly the peak Old Mountain Phelps had in mind when he conferred the name; and since it has the only view and is the more distinct peak, this peak should simply be called "Dial" and the other, southerly peak considered a part of the Nipple Top ridge.

Leaving Dial, the trail descends to a col at 4.0 mi., and then climbs at easy to moderate grades to a summit ("South Dial") at 4.3 mi. Leaving this summit, the trail descends to a col at 4.4 mi. and climbs again at easy to moderate grades up a fern-covered ridge, reaching a summit with a bare spot at 5.4 mi. Continuing fairly level, the trail dips slightly to the junction with the Elk Pass Trail (trail 41) coming in from the R at 5.6 mi. Continuing straight ahead, the trail climbs over one last bump and reaches the summit of Nipple Top at 5.9 mi.

Distances: Lake Road to S lookout on shoulder of Noonmark, 1.7 mi.; to Bear Den, 2.5 mi.; to Dial, 3.8 mi. (6.1 km); to trail from Elk Pass, 5.6 mi.; to summit of Nipple Top, 5.9 mi.; (9.5 km). Total ascent from Lake Road, 4000 ft. (1219 m). Elevation, 4620 ft. (1408 m). Order of height, 13.

(43) Noonmark via Stimson Trail   Map: F-9

This prominent, pointed peak lies almost directly S of Keene Valley and therefore "marks noon" when the sun is directly over the summit. This trail was scouted by and named for Henry L. Stimson, Secretary of State in President Hoover's cabinet and Secretary of War under Roosevelt.

Trailhead: See introduction to St. Hubert's section for information on parking. From the hiker parking lot it is 0.4 mi. up to the E edge of the golf course where the Noonmark Trail leaves Ausable Club Rd. No parking is permitted on the road near the golf course or on any of the private driveways.

Leaving the road at the golf course (0 mi.), the trail, with ATIS markers, follows up a private driveway. Avoiding a side road R at 0.1 mi., the trail goes straight ahead at 0.2 mi. where the road goes L to a barn. Now a footpath, the trail continues mostly on the level to a small ravine which is crossed at 0.4 mi. Now climbing moderately, the trail reaches a junction at 0.6 mi. with the trail leading through the pass between Noonmark and Round to Dix Mt. (described as part of trail 44).

Bearing R at this junction, the Stimson Trail climbs moderately to steeply with only a few breathers to the base of some ledges at 1.1 mi. Swinging sharp L and up very steeply, the trail emerges on the open ledges at 1.2 mi., where there are views of Keene Valley and the

Ausable Club. The climbing is now easier along a ridge to a lookout at 1.5 mi., from which the summit may be seen. From this point, the grade increases with several more open sections up to a sharp L turn at 1.9 mi. Here the trail enters the woods to avoid some steeper rocks ahead and after dropping down a few feet turns sharp R and ascends steeply back to the open rocks and then on to the summit at 2.1 mi. A trail continues on over the summit and down the SE side to the Dix Trail in 1.0 mi. (trail 44).

From the summit there is an unobstructed view in all directions, dominated by the Great Range to the W, the Dix Range to the S, and Giant to the NE. Both Rainbow Falls and Beaver Meadow Falls may be seen when the leaves are off the trees.

Distances: Ausable Club Road at golf course to junction with Dix Trail, 0.6 mi.; to first ledge, 1.2 mi.; to summit of Noonmark, 2.1 mi. (3.3 km). Ascent from road, 2175 ft. (663 m). Elevation, 3556 ft. (1084 m).

(44) Noonmark from the SE via Felix Adler Trail   Map: F-9

This trail is named for Dr. Felix Adler, a philosopher and founder of the Ethical Culture Society, which sought to combine the common elements of Christian and Jewish faiths. He spent many summers at his home at the start of the Noonmark Trail and was an enthusiastic climber. This trail offers an alternate route to Noonmark; but since it most often descended to make a loop trip when combined with the old Dix Trail, these trails are described in the direction most hikers use them.

Leaving the summit of Noonmark (0 mi.), the trail heads SE and descends steeply a few yds. to a level area and then down the partially open SE ridge of Noonmark. At 0.5 mi. the trail descends more steeply into the taller trees with the grade easing off at 0.8 mi. and the descent continuing to a junction with the Dix Trail at 1.0 mi. Trail R leads 4.5 mi. to Dix Mt. and trail straight ahead across the small brook and leads 2.3 mi. to Rt. 73 via Round Pond (both trail 46). (One can also approach Noonmark from Rt. 73 using this trail, the total distance to the summit being 3.4 mi.)

Turning L, the return route to St. Huberts climbs at an easy grade along the R bank of a brook, then crosses to the L bank at 1.4 mi. Continuing at an easy grade, the trail reaches a junction at the height of land between Noonmark and Round Mt. at 1.6 mi. Trail R lead 0.8 mi. to the summit of Round Mt. (trail 45). From here, the trail begins to descend easily and then swings R away from the old eroded tote road as the descent steepens. Swinging back to the L, the trail crosses the old tote road and soon crosses a brook at 2.0 mi. Now the trail continues a steady, moderate descent with occasional short detours to avoid the most eroded sections of the old tote road. Reaching the junction with the Stimson Trail at 2.7 mi., it is now 0.6 mi. back to the Ausable Club Road at the golf course, making a complete loop trip of 5.3 mi.

Distances: Summit of Noonmark to junction with Dix Trail, 1.0 mi.; to junction with Round Mt. Trail, 1.6 mi.; to junction with Stimson Trail to Noonmark, 2.7 mi. (4.3 km).

(45) Round Mt.   Map: F-9

As distinctively round when seen from Keene Valley as its neighbor Noonmark is pointed, this little peak offers some marvelous views of the cliffs and slides on Giant. One can also find solitude, as this peak is often ignored in favor of its larger neighbors. The S. Burns Weston Trail ascends the NE side of the peak and continues down the W side to join the old Dix Trail, which makes possible an easy round trip.

Trailhead: See introduction to St. Hubert's section for information on parking and driving directions. As of 1992, cars could be parked on the road as far as the start of this trail 0.1 mi. from Rt. 73.

Leaving the road (0 mi.) and marked with ATIS markers, the trail soon becomes steep before leveling off at 0.1 mi. and proceeding along the edge of a high bank with views out through openings in the beautiful hemlock forest high above Rt. 73. At 0.4 mi. there is a good view on the L of Giant and Chapel Pond Pass, after which the trail swings R and away from the edge of the steep bank. The grades are now mostly easy with a few short dips as the trail traverses a side hill.

Crossing a brook and old mossy slide at 1.3 mi., the trail now swings R and up more steeply and comes to an open ledge at 1.4 mi., where there is a good view of Giant. The trail now climbs at a moderate to steep grade to a large ledge with good views at 1.2 mi. The trail enters thicker woods on the flat and after one more short steep pitch emerges onto open rocks at 2.1 mi. Marked with cairns, the trail is now nearly flat along open rocks to the junction with the descent route to the Old Dix Trail branching R at 2.2 mi. The summit is just beyond at 2.3 mi., with views in all directions. Ascent from Ausable Club Road, 1820 ft. (555 m). Elevation, 3100 ft. (945 m).

The descent to the old Dix Trail heads W from the junction near the summit. The trail descends over a series of open ledges and is marked with small cairns. In general the trail heads directly for the summit of Noonmark, bearing R when there seems to be any choice. At the base of this series of ledges, the trail drops steeply into a small valley with a large cliff to the R. Bearing L at the bottom of the valley, the trail crosses a small brook at 2.8 mi., swings R to climb over one last bare spot, and descends to the junction with the Dix Trail (trail 44) at 3.0 mi. Turning R, it reaches the Ausable Club Rd. at the golf course in another 1.6 mi., making a loop trip of 4.6 mi.

Distances: Ausable Club Rd. to summit of Round Mt., 2.3 mi. (3.7 km); to old Dix Trail, 3.0 mi.; to Ausable Club Rd. at golf course via old Dix Trail, 4.6 mi. (7.4 km).

(46) Dix Mt. from Rt. 73   Map: G-9

Dix Mt. was named by Ebenezer Emmons in 1837 for John A. Dix, then Secretary of State for Governor Marcy and later governor himself. He also served as U.S. Senator, Secretary of the Treasury, and a Major General in the Civil War. The first ascent was in 1807, by a surveyor named Rykert, who had the task of running a line that now forms the southern boundary of the town of Keene and passes directly over the summit.

This trail via Round Pond is now the official approach to Dix Mt., from the N. The original route started from the Ausable Club Rd., but this route was only 0.1 mi. shorter, was considerably steeper in spots, and involved over 400 ft. more vertical climb. With the new parking arrangements at the Ausable Club, this old route is now 0.3 mi. longer in addition to its other disadvantages. It is no longer marked as a state trail and is described in this guidebook only as a return route from Noonmark via the Felix Adler Trail (trail 44).

Trailhead: Start on Rt. 73, 1.1 mi. S of the parking area at Chapel Pond and 3.1 mi. N of the junction of Rtes. 9 and 73 in Underwood. The start is marked with a small DEC sign, and there is a small parking area just N of the trailhead. This trail is currently maintained by the Adirondack Forty-Sixers.

From the road (0. mi.) and marked with blue DEC disks, the trail climbs moderately on a traverse across a steep hillside. The grade soon eases, and the trail crosses a height of land and descends to Round Pond just beyond at 0.6 mi. There are some designated campsites to the L near the outlet. Elsewhere, camping is not permitted unless one is at least 150 ft. back from any trail or body of water. Turning R, the trail follows around the N shore of the pond and begins climbing moderately at 1.0 mi. Crossing a brook at 1.2 mi., the trail climbs steadily to a notch at 1.6 mi. Now level or slightly downhill, it crosses a brook at 1.8 mi. and continues across several wet areas to the junction with the old Dix Trail and the Felix Adler Trail at 2.3 mi. Trail R with ATIS markers leads 2.2 mi. to Ausable Club Rd. Trail straight ahead with ATIS markers leads 1.0 mi. to summit of Noonmark (both trail 44).

Turning L, the trail is practically flat to the bank of the N Fork of the Boquet River at 2.7 mi. The trail now follows near the L bank of the river on the flat, but soon swings away from the river through thicker woods and crosses a small brook and then Gravestone Brook on a bridge at 3.7 mi. After the brook, the trail climbs briefly to drier ground and descends to the bank of the Boquet at 4.0 mi., where the outlet to Dial Pond comes in from the R. The trail now continues to the Boquet River Lean-to at 4.2 mi., having gained only 100 ft. since the junction with the old Dix Trail.

Crossing the river on stones, the trail swings R and follows up near the R bank on a steadily increasing grade. Reaching a fair-sized tributary at 5.1 mi., the trail follows up the R bank of this brook on a steady, moderate grade and crosses it at 5.2 mi. The trail now crosses and recrosses several other brooks and arrives at the base of a large slide at 5.8 mi. Crossing the base of the slide, the trail swings L and begins the real climbing to the summit, gaining approximately 1600 ft. (500 m) in a little over a mile. Paralleling the slide until 5.8 mi., the trail swings away and begins an unrelenting steep climb, with rough footing in spots, to a junction at the top of the ridge at 6.4 mi. with the Hunters Pass Trail from Elk Lake (trail 119).

Turning L, the climbing continues steady but not quite as steep along the ridge to the summit crest at 6.7 mi. From this point, hikers should use care to remain on the marked trail so as not to damage the fragile alpine vegetation (see Introduction). The going is now nearly level, past one rock on the L with a U.S. Coast and Geodetic Survey marker, and on to the summit with an old survey bolt at 6.8 mi. This bolt was placed by Verplanck Colvin in 1873 as part of his Adirondack Survey. The view is unobstructed in all directions with Elk Lake seen to the SW, Lake Champlain and the Green Mts. to the E, and the Great Range to the NW. A trail marked with yellow DEC disks continues over the summit to the Beckhorn and then on to Elk Lake (trail 120).

Distances: Rt. 73 to Round Pond, 0.6 mi.; to junction with old Dix Trail, 2.3 mi.; to Boquet River Lean-to, 4.2 mi.; to Hunters Pass Trail from Elk Lake, 6.4 mi.; to summit of Dix, 6.8 mi. (11.0 km). Ascent from Rt. 73, 3200 ft. (975 m). Elevation, 4857 ft. (1480 m). Order of height, 6.

(47) Giant via Roaring Brook Trail
Map: F-9

The full name for Giant Mt., Giant of the Valley, is the name given this peak by early residents in Pleasant Valley on the E side of the mountain. From the low valley of the Boquet River, Giant does appear as a massive mountain with many ridges and subsidiary peaks towering 4000 ft. above the valley. The first ascent of Giant (and the first of any 4000-ft. peak) was in 1797, by a surveyor named Charles Brodhead, who had the task of surveying the boundaries of the Old Military Tract, which was to be divided up as compensation for soldiers who had fought in the Revolduntiary War. Brodhead had to fight his way up the E face and directly down the W face, a route that has probably never been repeated since. The first trail was cut in 1866 via Hopkins, with the Roaring Brook Trail cut soon after in 1873 and later improved enough to be passable by horses to within 300 ft. of the summit. This early use accounts for the somewhat more moderate grades and the series of switchbacks as the trail approaches the crest of the ridge. Recent (1989) trail work by the ADK on behalf of the ATIS has greatly improved the footing on the trail from the crossing of Roaring Brook to the view at 2.3 mi. The switchbacks above, however, have deteriorated to the point that the footing is very poor in spots and only a complete reroute is likely to improve the rest of the trail.

Trailhead: Begin at a small parking area on Rt. 73, 3.3 mi S of the High Peaks sign in Keene Valley and 5.6 mi. N of the junction of Rtes. 9 and 73 in Underwood.

From the end of the parking lot (0 mi.), the ATIS-marked trail begins on the level to a junction at 0.1 mi. with a trail leading R to the base of Roaring Brook Falls. Bearing L, the trail begins a moderate climb to a crest at 0.3 mi., after which it dips and continues at an easier grade to a junction at 0.5 mi. (Trail R leads 80 yds. to the top of Roaring Brook Falls, where there are views of Noonmark and the lower Great Range. Approach this view with caution; there have been several unfortunate accidents at this spot in recent years.)

Bearing L, the grade soon moderates to a junction with an unmarked spur trail leading L just short of the R bank of Roaring Brook at 1.0 mi. Trail L leads 40 yds. to a campsite and a nearly grown-up view of the slides on Giant. In 1963 there were massive slides on all sides of Giant, and the rush of water down the W side widened the bed of Roaring Brook to nearly 200 yds. in spots. All the trees growing near the brook and now obscuring what was once a very spectacular view have grown up since then.

Continuing past this junction, the trail crosses Roaring Brook, and comes to a junction on the far side at 1.1 mi. with a trail leading R to the Nubble and Washbowl (trails 49 and 50). Turning L, the trail ascends an easy to moderate grade, crosses two brooks, and comes to a short side trail leading L to some open rocks in the brook at 1.4 mi. Now the trail begins to pull away from the brook at a mostly steady, moderate grade and soon begins a series of switchbacks along the crest of a broad ridge. At 2.3 mi. a side trail R leads to a good view and a welcome chance for a breather. Continuing to climb via switchbacks, at 2.9 mi. the trail reaches a junction at the top of the main SW ridge of Giant with the Giant Ridge Trail leading R 2.2 mi. to Chapel Pond (trail 48).

Turning L, the grade is more moderate to a small summit and a spectacular view of the slides at 3.0 mi. Now flat for a short way, the trail begins climbing again at 3.2 mi. and after another short flat stretch climbs steeply to some open rock at 3.4 mi. and the junction with East Trail from New Russia and Rocky Peak (trail 112). From here, easy grades lead to the open summit at 3.6 mi. The views range from the Ausable Club directly below to the W with the Great Range beyond, to Lake Champlain and the Green Mts. to the E. In all, 39 major peaks can be seen.

Distances: Rt. 73 to top of Roaring Brook Falls, 0.5 mi.; to junction with trail to Nubble and Washbowl, 1.1 mi.; to junction with Ridge Trail, 2.9 mi.; to junction with East Trail, 3.4 mi.; to summit of Giant, 3.6 mi. (5.7 km). Ascent from Rt. 73, 3375 ft. (1029 m). Elevation, 4627 ft. (1410 m). Order of height, 12.

(48) Giant via Ridge Trail   Map: G-9

This slightly shorter route to Giant was completed in 1954 and offers the easiest access to the Giant's Washbowl and Nubble, as well as a route to the summit with many views from the long, open ridge.

Trailhead: Start on Rt 73, 4.8 mi. S of the High Peaks sign in Keene Valley and 4.1 mi. N of the junction of Rtes. 9 and 73 in Underwood. Parking is available for several cars at the trailhead with more available 0.2 mi. to the N at Chapel Pond. Given the busy nature of this road, all cars should be parked so that both sets of tires are off of the paved shoulder. The trail is marked with ATIS markers.

From the road (0 mi.), the trail crosses a small brook to the trail register and soon begins climbing. Taking a sharp L across a small stream in 150 yds., the trail recrosses the stream in another 100 yds. and climbs steeply to a short flat section. Soon after the end of this flat area, the trail turns sharp L at 0.3 mi. (trail straight ahead leads to a spring at the base of a small cliff) in the first of several switchbacks leading up a steep slope. (Stay on marked trail since cutting switchbacks causes erosion and defeats the purpose of creating them.) The grade eases at 0.5 mi., but there are a few more steep sections as the trail crosses an old stream bed and climbs to an open lookout at 0.7 mi. directly above Chapel Pond. The trail now makes a slight descent to a junction at the S end of the Giant's Washbowl at 0.7 mi. Trail L skirts the SW side of the pond and leads 1.0 mi. to the Roaring Brook Trail (trail 50).

The Ridge Trail bears R at this junction and crosses the outlet of the Washbowl on a bridge necessitated by recent (1990) beaver activity. Just past the end of the bridge the trail swings sharp R with a designated campsite on the R just beyond. (No camping is permitted along the shore of the Washbowl.) Past the campsite the trail climbs moderately to a junction at 0.9 mi. (Trail L leads down 0.2 mi. to N side of Washbowl, but the connection to the Roaring Brook Trail is closed due to high water.) Continuing straight ahead, the Ridge Trail reaches another junction at 1.0 mi. with the summit of Nubble (trail 49).

Bearing R, the Ridge Trail climbs steadily through conifers to a sharp line of demarcation between the large conifers and smaller poplars and birches at 1.1 mi. This marks the furthest extent of the 1913 forest fire, which burned off much of the ridge above and created the views that make this trail so attractive. Here the climbing becomes steep up to the first ledge at 1.2 mi. The trail swings R to gain this ledge, then back L, and traverses above a large boulder on the ledge to reach a gully just beyond. Now turning R and up steeply, the trail gains a higher ledge at 1.3 mi. There are good views of both

Washbowl and Chapel Pond further below; and by walking 40 yds. to the R (S), one can catch a glimpse of the Giant's Dipper. Turning sharp L at two cairns, the trail leaves this ledge and continues at an easier grade over other bare ledges.

Dipping to a small col at 1.4 mi., the trail climbs a few steep pitches and emerges at the base of a long climb across a large open face. At 1.7 mi., near the top of this open area, is a junction. (Trail R goes up and over the top of a small bump with more views and is 100 yds. longer than the trail L.) Bearing L, the trail slabs across the N side of the ridge and in 110 yds. reaches the junction with the longer trail over the bump. After a short flat section in a col, the trail climbs again through another smaller bare section to easier climbing at 2.0 mi. Soon starting up again, it reaches a short side trail L to a ledge with a view to the N at 2.1 mi., after which the climbing is mostly easy to the junction with the Roaring Brook Trail at 2.2 mi. From here the description to the summit is the same as that for the Roaring Brook Trail (trail 47).

Distances: Rt. 73 to Washbowl, 0.7 mi.; to side trail to Nubble, 1.0 mi.; to Roaring Brook Trail, 2.2 mi.; to East Trail, 2.8 mi.; to summit of Giant Mt., 3.0 mi. (4.7 km). Ascent from Rt. 73, 3050 ft. (930 m). Elevation, 4627 ft. (1410 m). Order of height, 12.

(49) Giant's Nubble   Map: G-9

This small, rocky knob at the end of the SW ridge of Giant offers some interesting views of St. Huberts and the slides on Giant's W face. There are two approaches, with the one branching from the Ridge Trail being the easiest. Approaching via the Roaring Brook Trail, however, one can make an interesting loop of 4.7 mi. taking in Roaring Brook Falls, the Giant's Washbowl and the Nubble.

1. From the junction 1.0 mi. up the Ridge Trail (0 mi.), the trail crosses a small brook and climbs a short, steep pitch followed by more moderate climbing to a view of the Washbowl at 0.1 mi. Dipping across a small sag, the trail comes to better views to the S at 0.3 mi., after which the trail is flat and then climbs steeply up to a junction at 0.4 mi. (Trail R leads to Roaring Brook Trail; see below.) The trail now proceeds along a nearly flat open ridge to the summit of the Nubble at 0.5 mi.

Distances: From Chapel Pond via Ridge Trail: to junction with Nubble Trail, 1.0 mi.; to summit of Nubble, 1.5 mi. (2.5 km). Ascent from Chapel Pond, 1150 ft. (350 m).

2. From the junction (0 mi.) on the Roaring Brook Trail at 1.1 mi. just after crossing Roaring Brook, the trail starts on the flat. It begins climbing soon after crossing a small stream and reaches a junction at 0.2 mi. with a trail R to Washbowl (trail 50). Turning L, the Nubble trail climbs moderately, crossing a stream at 0.3 mi., and another at 0.5 mi., before reaching a junction at 0.8 mi. (Trail L leads to Ridge Trail and Washbowl; see above.) Turning R, the trail swings R and onto a nearly flat open ridge to the summit of the Nubble at 0.9 mi.

Distances: From Rt. 73 via Roaring Brook Trail to junction with Nubble and Washbowl Trail, 1.1 mi.; to summit of Nubble, 2.0 mi. (3.1 km). Ascent from road, 1480 ft. (451 m). Elevation, 2760 ft. (841 m).

(50) Giant's Washbowl from Roaring Brook Trail   Map: G-9

This alternate approach to Giant's Washbowl leaves the Roaring Brook Trail (trail 47) 1.1 mi. from the parking lot on Rt. 73. Turning R at the junction (0 mi.), the trail soon crosses a small stream and then climbs to a junction at 0.2 mi. with trail L to Nubble (trail 49). Bearing R, the trail continues to climb at a moderate grade until it eases at 0.5 mi. and reaches a height of land below the Nubble at 0.5 mi. Now descending at an easy grade, it reaches a second junction at 0.8 mi. at the NW shore of the Giant's Washbowl. (Trail L which formerly led to Ridge Trail is now closed due to high water.) Continuing along the shore of the pond, the trail reaches a junction with the Ridge Trail (trail 48) at 1.0 mi. This point is 0.7 mi. above Rt. 73 at Chapel Pond and 0.3 mi. below the turn-off for the Nubble Trail.

Distances: Parking lot on Rt. 73 to turn-off from Roaring Brook Trail, 1.1 mi.; to junction with Ridge Trail at Washbowl, 2.1 mi. (3.4 km).

(51) Mossy Cascade Trail to Hopkins   Map: F-9

With the direct approach to Hopkins from Keene Valley closed (as of 1992), the Mossy Cascade Trail is probably the best approach. Hopkins was named for Rev. Erastus Hopkins of Troy, New York, who later served several terms in the Massachusetts legislature while a resident of Northampton. It was he who suggested to Old Mountain Phelps the name "Resagone," meaning the "king's great saw," for the mountain we now call Sawteeth.

Trailhead: Start on Rt. 73 just S of the steel-sided bridge over the East Branch of the Ausable River 2.0 mi. S of Keene Valley.

From the road (0 mi.) and marked with ATIS markers, the trail follows along above the R bank of the river to a house on the L at 0.4 mi. Swinging R onto a tote road at the house, the trail immediately swings L onto an older road and then in another 100 yds. bears R at another junction. The trail now veers around from NE to SE while remaining mostly on flat going. At 0.5 mi. the trail leaves the tote road, going L to the L bank of Mossy Cascade Brook, which is followed to a junction at 0.7 mi. (Side trail L leads to the base of Mossy Cascade in 200 yds.) Bearing R, the trail now climbs steeply to the top of a steep bank above Mossy Cascade to the edge of a recent clearing for a private camp on the R at 1.0 mi. Just past this camp the trail crosses the brook and climbs away from the brook with several steep pitches. It crosses a yellow-blazed property line at 1.1 mi. and comes to a lookout on the L at 1.5 mi.

Past this lookout, the trail descends to a col, then climbs to another ledge with a view at 1.7 mi., and continues to climb through an open forest along an interesting monolithic ridge of granite. The grade moderates at 2.2 mi. and the trail comes to a junction at 2.3 mi. with the Ranney Trail with ADK markers from Keene Valley (trail 24). Now the trail continues up into a ravine between Hopkins and Green and arrives at a junction in a col at 3.0 mi. with trail R leading 3.0 mi. over a shoulder of Green Mt. to the summit of Giant (trail 52). Turning L, the trail climbs very steeply for a few yards, and then eases off along bare slabs to the summit of Hopkins at 3.2 mi. There are many blueberries and the views are unobstructed in all directions except NE, with 22 major peaks discernible. (Trail with ADK markers continues over the summit to Spread Eagle and Keene Valley; but due to landowner problems the trail is no longer marked all the way to Keene Valley. See description of trail 22 for more information.)

Distances: Rt. 73 to Mossy Cascade, 0.8 mi.; to junction with Ranney Trail, 2.3 mi.; to junction with trail to Giant, 3.0 mi.; to summit of Hopkins, 3.2 mi (5.1 km). Ascent from Rt. 73, 2120 ft. (646 m). Elevation, 3183 ft. (970 m).

(52) Giant from Hopkins via Green Mt.   Map: G-8

Owing to its length and the lack of any views along the way, this is not a popular route to the summit of Giant, but it does offer pleasant walking through some virgin forests and makes for an interesting way to return from Giant to St. Huberts or Keene Valley.

Leaving the junction with the Mossy Cascade Trail (trail 51) in the Hopkins-Green col (0 mi.), the trail climbs a short steep pitch and then continues at moderate grades to the crest of a shoulder of Green Mt. at 0.4 mi. The trail now descends to a col at 0.5 mi., after which it slabs along a side hill on the level and enters a swampy area with lush moss at 0.7 mi. After some more flat going, the trail descends and crosses a tributary to Putnam Brook (also called Beede Brook) at 1.1 mi. After climbing out of this small valley, the trail continues the easy to moderate descent and joins an old tote road just before crossing the main branch of Putnam Brook at 1.7 mi. and coming to a junction in the col between Green Mt. and Giant shortly after. (In descending this trail, hikers should watch for the sharp R turn off the tote road 0.2 mi. below the junction in the Giant-Green col.) The trail coming in from the L is the North Trail to Giant (trail 111) which leads 6.1 mi. to Rt. 9N. From here, the route is marked with red DEC disks.

Turning R at the junction, the trail begins climbing steeply out of the col and at 1.9 mi. there is a sharp switchback to the L to negotiate a small cliff band. From here the grade continues steep for a few yards, but slowly eases until it levels off at 2.5 mi. Descending slightly, the trail resumes its climb and arrives at a ledge on the R at 2.8 mi., soon after which it levels out and crosses other ledges to the summit at 3.0 mi. (ATIS trail continues over the summit and down to St. Huberts via Ridge Trail, or Roaring Brook Trail, trails 47 and 48.)

Distances: Rt. 73 via Mossy Cascade Trail to Hopkins-Green col, 3.0 mi.; to junction with North Trail, 4.7 mi.; to summit of Giant, 6.0 mi. (9.7 km). Ascent from Rt. 73, 3500 ft. (1067 m). Elevation, 4627 ft. (1410 m). Order of height, 12.

(53) Snow Mt.　　　　　　　　Map: F-8

This 2360-ft. (719-m) peak NW of St. Huberts offers some splendid views of the surrounding peaks as well as acres of good blueberries. There are three possible approaches, but the most popular is via Deer Brook, as described here. In addition to being the shortest, the Deer Brook approach offers a short side trip to a waterfall and an alternative hike through a narrow flume. (Recent maintenance has improved the walking in the flume somewhat and it is now a more attractive alternative because the regular trail is now almost entirely on a private gravel driveway.)

The W.A. White Trail approach is over a mile longer if one counts the walk from the Ausable Club parking area to the start of the trail and it is now described only as a spur trail from the W.A. White Trail (trail 32). The approach from the N via the Rooster Comb from Rt. 73 (Sachs) Trail (trail 19) is 0.3 mi. longer than Deer Brook. With all these trails there are a multitude of loop trips possible, combining Snow, Rooster Comb, and any of these approaches. This trail is also a good approach to the W.A. White Trail to Lower Wolf Jaw and Hedgehog.

Trailhead: Start on Rt. 73, 0.1 mi. N of the steel-sided bridge over the Ausable River, 1.9 mi. S of the High Peaks sign in the center of Keene Valley. The start is marked with green ATIS signs and ATIS markers.

Leaving the highway (0 mi.), the trail heads up the R bank of Deer Brook to a junction at a private driveway at 0.1 mi. (Trail straight ahead leads 0.5 mi. up the ravine of Deer Brook. It is scenic but somewhat more difficult to walk, crossing Deer Brook several times before rejoining the main trail.) Turning L on the driveway, the main trail immediately joins a gravel road (private—no public traffic or parking) that climbs at a moderate grade past a house on the L followed by a view of Noonmark to a driveway R at 0.3 mi. Here the trail follows a newer road before going straight into the woods at a sharp L turn in the road at 0.6 mi. Now on an old lumber road, the trail reaches a four-way intersection at 0.7 mi. where the trail up the Deer Brook ravine comes in from the R. (Trail L is the connection to the W.A. White Trail and leads along an orange-blazed property line to a fresh logging road and then R and up to a junction at a wider logging road, 0.2 mi. after leaving the Deer Brook Trail. Turning L, the W.A. White Trail, trail 32, is reached at 0.3 mi.; see above.)

Continuing straight through this junction, the Deer Brook Trail comes to another junction at the R bank of Deer Brook at 0.8 mi. (Trail L leads 90 yds. to the base of a pretty little falls.) Turning R, the trail crosses Deer Brook and follows a tote road at a moderate grade which eases off just before a junction at 1.3 mi. (Trail L is the approach from the Ausable Club via W.A. White Trail; trail 32.) Turning R, the trail continues on the flat in a beautiful, open valley to a junction at 1.4 mi. (Trail straight ahead is the approach from the N. It leads mostly on the level for 0.4 mi. to a junction with the Sachs Rooster Comb Trail (trail 19) which leads down to Keene Valley or up to Rooster Comb.

Turning R, the Snow Trail proceeds across a side hill for a little over 100 yds. and then turns R and ascends steeply to the first ledge at 1.6 mi. with a spectacular view of the cliffs on Rooster Comb. The trail now re-enters the woods and climbs to a second ledge. The summit is just beyond at 1.7 mi. The best views are on ledges just down the SE side.

Distances: Rt. 73 to re-entry of trail up Deer Brook ravine, 0.7 mi.; to junction with trail from Ausable Club, 1.3 mi.; to junction with trail to Sachs Rooster Comb Trail, 1.4 mi.; to summit of Snow, 1.7 mi. (2.8 km). Ascent from Rt. 73, 1360 ft. (414 m).

Upper Ausable Lake Area

Following the sale of the higher land by the Adirondack Mountain Reserve (AMR) to the State of New York in 1978, most of the trails approaching the shores and along the shores of Upper Ausable Lake have been closed to the public. As before, camping, fishing, and hunting on any of the private lands near this lake are prohibited, but there are several through trunk line trails that are still open to the public and which offer some interesting and rugged hiking. All access to the Upper Ausable Lake area is by foot over the summits of 4000-ft. peaks, as there is no trail the shores of Lower Ausable Lake; bushwhacking is prohibited, no boats are available for rent by the public; and portable boats brought in by the public are not permitted on Lower Ausable Lake. Hiking in this area is therefore a serious undertaking, requiring careful planning to insure that one can complete one's planned trip or arrive before nightfall at a campsite above the private land boundary.

These restrictions are designed to protect the private camp owners on the lake, who in the past have complained of illegal camping on their land, break-ins, and even some instances of burglary. Their wishes and privacy should obviously be respected. There is a Warden's Camp at the N end of Upper Ausable Lake, from which the area is patrolled. During the summer months, the Warden's Camp has radio communication with the Ausable Club in St. Huberts.

There are many interesting trips available to the public in this region, provided one is willing to do a lot of climbing and descending. Camping is allowed on state land, generally above the 2500-ft. level (see map that accompanies this guidebook for exact state/private land boundaries), although there are not yet any designated campsites on state land in this area. One must therefore be careful that in establishing new campsites the regulations regarding distances from streams and trails are obeyed and that exceptional care is taken in building fires, since much of the forest floor in this area is covered with a deep layer of duff which can burn as easily as wood. (See information on camping in the Introduction.)

Summary of Approaches to Upper Ausable Lake:

The "easiest" approach to this area is from St. Huberts over the summit of either Sawteeth or Colvin. A loop trip over both these summits makes an interesting but rugged day trip totaling 11.1 mi. (17.9 km) and 4500 ft. (1370 m) of climb and descent. (See descriptions for: Sawteeth via Pyramid-Gothics Trail, Sawteeth from Warden's Camp, Carry Trail, Mt. Colvin from the Carry, Colvin from Lake Road and Gill Brook, Fish Hawk Cliffs and Indian Head.) This round trip distance assumes one uses the bus service to the Lower Ausable Lake. Add another 7.0 mi. if the bus is not used.

A considerably more difficult approach for backpackers is a possible loop trip from Keene Valley over Marcy, down the Elk Lake-Marcy Trail, and returning to St. Huberts along Pinnacle Ridge to Colvin and down to the Lake Road. Total distance for this loop is 27.1 mi. (43.6 km). Total ascent and descent is approximately 7200 ft. (2200 m). See descriptions for: Mt. Marcy via Phelps Trail (Keene Valley section), Elk Lake-Marcy Trail (Southern section), Blake and Colvin via Pinnacle Ridge (St. Huberts section), and Colvin from Lake Road and Gill Brook (St. Huberts section).

Other approaches and loop trips are possible using these and other trails described in full below.

(54) Carry Trail   Map: E-10

This trail runs 1.0 mi. from the boat sheds at the S end of Lower Ausable Lake to the Warden's Camp at the N end of Upper Ausable

Lake. It follows close to the bank of the Ausable River, on the flat for most of its distance. It is paralleled by a tractor trail running along further up the slope away from the river. There is a small spring beside the trail at approximately the half-way point. A few yards from the boat sheds on Lower Ausable Lake is a junction with the trail to Mt. Colvin and Blake Peak. At the Warden's Camp is a junction with the trails leading to Sawteeth, Haystack and Marcy via Bartlett Ridge.

(55) Mt. Colvin from Carry Trail   Map: E-10

The trail climbs steeply up the valley between Colvin and Blake to the top of the ridge where it connects with the trail to Blake, Pinnacle and the Elk Lake-Marcy Trail. For the history of the naming of Mt. Colvin see description for Colvin from Lake Road and Gill Brook (trail 40).

From the junction with the Carry Trail (0 mi.), the trail heads E on the flat on a road, but in a few yards bears R off the road and crosses the Ausable River on a bridge at 0.1 mi. The climbing starts almost immediately at the far side of the bridge, with the trail following the R bank of a small brook and then crossing it at 0.3 mi. and beginning a steep climb. The climbing soon eases a bit but remains steady. The trail climbs high above the brook and then back to brook level at 0.5 mi., where the brook forks. This area offers some possible campsites.

The trail follows but soon crosses the L fork and continues a steady grade with a few steeper pitches until the grade finally moderates shortly before the junction in the col between Colvin and Blake at 1.1 mi. Trail R leads 0.6 mi. to summit of Blake Peak, 3.2 mi. to Pinnacle, and 4.6 mi. to Elk Lake-Marcy Trail (trails 56 and 60). Turning L (onto trail 40), the Colvin Trail climbs steeply, the grade moderating at 1.3 mi., after which the trail crosses a ridge and dips slightly before continuing at relatively easy grades up the S ridge of the mountain. There is a lookout on the L, a few yards before the summit, with views of Upper Ausable Lake, Allen and other peaks. The actual summit is reached at 1.9 mi., where there are good views. (Trail 40 continues over the summit and down to Lake Road and St. Huberts.

Distances: Carry Trail to junction with Blake Trail, 1.1 mi.; to summit of Colvin, 1.9 mi. (3.1 km). Ascent from Carry Trail, 2100 ft. (640 m). Elevation, 4057 ft. (1237 m). Order of height, 39.

(56) Blake Peak   Map: E-10

Blake Peak was named for Mills Blake, who was Verplanck Colvin's chief assistant during the Adirondack Survey, and his closest personal friend. The two worked and lived together for forty-eight years until Colvin died in 1920, so it is therefore fitting that the peak adjacent to Colvin bears Blake's name. Blake can be approached from St. Huberts over Colvin following the trail from the Lake Road and Gill Brook to Colvin's summit (trail 40) and then the trail described immediately above down to the col between Colvin and Blake.

Leaving the junction in the col (0 mi.), the trail climbs a short, steep pitch, moderates, and then begins a very steep pitch at 0.2 mi. Reaching the crest of a ridge at 0.5 mi., the trail climbs mostly easily to the summit at 0.6 mi., where there are views through the trees to Elk Lake.

Distances: From Lake Road to junction at Colvin-Blake Col, 3.7 mi.; to summit of Blake, 4.2 mi. (6.8 km). Total ascent from Lake Road, 2800 ft. (850 m). Elevation, 3960 ft. (1270 m). Order of height among the original 46 peaks, 43.

(57) Sawteeth from Warden's Camp

Map: E-10

From the Warden's Camp at the N end of Upper Ausable Lake (0 mi.), this trail heads NW across a meadow, bearing R at a junction with the Lake Trail (closed to the public) and coming to another junction at 0.2 mi. with trail straight ahead to Haystack and Marcy via Bartlett Ridge (trail 58). Turning R, the trail crosses Shanty Brook on rocks and briefly follows up the L bank, but soon swings away from the brook on an easy grade. Crossing a brook at 0.9 mi., the trail comes to a junction with the Tammy Stowe Trail at 1.0 mi. (This approximately 1-mi. loop from the Sawteeth Trail climbs, steeply at times, to the crest of a ridge where there are views of Upper Ausable Lake and some of the upper Great Range. It rejoins the Sawteeth Trail approximately 0.5 mi. above its lower end.)

Continuing straight ahead, the trail begins to climb more steeply, crossing several more small brooks and coming to the upper end of the Tammy Stowe Trail at 1.5 mi. The trail soon dips to cross a brook which is a possible campsite, being above the private land. (This is the first brook encountered on the descent from Sawteeth.) After one more short climb and a dip past this brook, the trail begins to climb steeply up the S ridge of Sawteeth with occasional views out through the trees. After several alternating steep pitches and more moderate sections, the trail reaches a small summit at 2.7 mi., and in 20 more yds. joins the trail from Lower Ausable Lake (trail 36). Turning L, the trail comes to the summit of Sawteeth at 2.8 mi. Trail continues over the summit and on to Gothics or down to Lower Ausable Lake (trail 35).

Distances: Warden's Camp to junction with Haystack and Marcy Trail, 0.2 mi.; to junction with Tammy Stowe Trail, 1.0 mi.; to summit of Sawteeth, 2.8 mi. (4.5 km). Ascent from Warden's Camp, 2110 ft. (643 m). Elevation, 4100 ft. (1250 m). Order of height, 35.

(58) Haystack and Marcy via Bartlett Ridge from Warden's Camp

Map: E-10

This trail leads to the top of Bartlett Ridge, from which one may climb Haystack or descend into Panther Gorge and ascend Marcy from there via the Elk Lake-Marcy Trail.

From the Warden's Camp (0 mi.), the trail goes NW through a field, bearing R at a junction with the Lake Trail (now closed to the public) and arriving at a junction at 0.2 mi. (Trail R leads to Sawteeth, trail 57.) Continuing straight ahead, the trail climbs at an easy to moderate grade, crossing several small brooks to a junction with the Sage's Folly Trail (now closed to the public) at 0.9 mi. Past this junction, the moderate grade continues to another junction at 1.5 mi., with trail R leading via Haystack Brook to the Range Trail between Haystack and Basin (trail 59).

Turning L, the trail proceeds mostly on the flat around the end of a ridge to a junction at 1.7 mi. with the Crystal Brook Trail (now closed to the public). Bearing R, the trail soon crosses Crystal Brook and begins a steep, rough climb to the crest of Bartlett Ridge at 2.4 mi. Now the grade eases and the trail crosses two brooks and many wet areas before reaching the junction with the trail to Panther Gorge and Marcy at 2.7 mi. [Trail L leads steeply down the W side of Bartlett Ridge to the Elk Lake-Marcy Trail at the Panther Gorge Lean-to, 3.5 mi. from the Warden's Camp, having lost 600 vertical ft. from the top of Bartlett Ridge. From here it is another 1.8 mi. to the summit of Marcy, making it 5.3 mi. (8.5 km) and a total of approximately 4000 ft. (1219 m) of climbing from the Warden's Camp to the summit of Marcy.]

Turning R, the Haystack Trail begins one of the steepest climbs in the mountains up the S side of the peak. (It is strongly recommended that backpackers not attempt this trail even though it is part of a seemingly attractive loop trip taking in the lean-to and campsites at Panther Gorge. It is unremittingly steep with numerous small ledges posing the danger of a serious fall — especially for less experienced backpackers.) The trail is quite eroded in spots, with almost no respite to timberline at 3.2 mi. From here, the trail is marked with cairns and care is needed to follow it as it winds up through several ledges and finally to the R (E) side of the summit ridge to surmount the final large ledge. The summit is reached at 3.5 mi. The trail continues 0.6 mi. to the Range Trail and on to the Johns Brook Valley and Keene Valley (trails 9 and 10).

Distances: Warden's Camp to junction with Haystack Brook Trail, 1.5 mi.; to Bartlett Ridge and junction with Marcy Trail, 2.7 mi.; to summit of Haystack, 3.5 mi. (5.6 km). Ascent from Warden's Camp, 3070 ft. (935 m). Elevation, 4960 ft. (1512 m). Order of height, 3.

(59) Haystack and Great Range via Haystack Brook Trail   Map: E-10

This trail leads to the Range Trail at the former site of Sno-Bird Lean-to between Haystack and Basin. The grade is easy for much of the way, but it finishes with some very steep climbing and several ladders which can be quite difficult when backpacking. There are several possible campsites along this trail, as it is on state land from just past the junction with the Bartlett Ridge Trail.

From the Warden's Camp (0 mi.), follow the Bartlett Ridge Trail (trail 58) to the junction at 1.5 mi. Turning R here, the trail is mostly flat to a crossing of an old slide track and brook at 2.1 mi. Continuing at an easy grade along the lower slopes of Haystack, the trail comes near the R bank of Haystack Brook at 2.7 mi. From here the trail gets progressively steeper to the first ladder at 2.9 mi. There are several more ladders with short breathers in between before the

Haystack Brook Trail reaches a junction with the Range Trail (trail 8) at 3.4 mi. (Trail R leads to JBL via Shorey Short Cut and Slant Rock, 4.7 mi., or to JBL via Basin and Saddleback, 5.1 mi. Trail L leads up to Haystack, 1.0 mi.).

Distances: Warden's Camp to junction with Bartlett Ridge Trail, 1.5 mi.; to junction with Range Trail, 3.4 mi.; to summit of Haystack, 4.4 mi. (7.0 km). Ascent from Warden's Camp, 3070 ft. (935 m). Elevation, 4960 ft. (1512 m). Order of height, 3.

(60) Blake Peak and Mt. Colvin via Pinnacle Ridge from Elk Lake-Marcy Trail   Map: E-11

The Pinnacle Ridge leading to Blake and Colvin does not offer any striking 360-degree views, but it is a beautiful series of seldom-visited peaks covered with virgin forests of spruce and balsam underlain with moss-covered rocks. The best views are from Colvin, a peak S of Blake, and the Pinnacle; but there are other narrower views including vistas of the Ausable Lakes, Elk Lake and the mountains beyond.

Since 1978, when the AMR sold its higher lands to the State of New York, this entire ridge has been public land; a short connection between the existing trails on the ridge and the Elk Lake-Marcy Trail was constructed to assist public access. Hikers should be aware, however, that the lower portions of the three trails leading to the shores of Upper Ausable Lake are closed to the public from the point where these trails reach the private land boundary. There is no water on this ridge, but there are possible campsites on the new access trail from the Elk Lake-Marcy Trail, and one could find a possible campsite by descending about 0.3 mi. from the col between Colvin and Blake. This trail is described from S to N since that is the direction in which it is hiked in the suggested loop trip in the introduction to the Upper Ausable Lake Area.

This approach to Blake and Colvin begins on the Elk Lake-Marcy Trail (trail 118) 6.0 mi. from the summit of Marcy and 5.0 mi. from Elk Lake. This junction is also 0.2 mi. E of the log bridge over the inlet to Upper Ausable Lake. From the junction (0 mi.), the trail heads NW on the flat, crossing two brooks and following a series of shelves through a beautiful hardwood forest. After climbing a short bit, the trail winds among rocks with a view of Haystack through the trees at 0.4 mi. and continues on to a brook with a small waterfall at 0.7 mi., where there are some possible campsites. Crossing the brook, the trail climbs moderately with a few steep pitches to a junction at 1.0 mi. (Trail L is original Pinnacle Trail now closed to the public.)

Turning R, the trail climbs moderately to steeply to a junction just below the summit of the Pinnacle at 1.6 mi. (Spur trail R climbs at first steeply and then more easily to the summit of Pinnacle in 0.2 mi., where there is a spectacular view of Elk Lake and the Dix Range.) Turning L, the trail descends briefly to a col and then begins climbing over another summit and down to another col at 2.2 mi. Shortly above this col the trail comes to a junction with the Otis Ledge Trail (now closed to the public) at 2.2 mi. Climbing again past this junction, the trail goes over another summit and drops steeply to another col at 2.5 mi. Now the trail climbs quite steeply, but eases off at 2.7 mi. and soon comes to a side trail R leading to a good view of Elk Lake. Dropping steeply from this summit, the trail comes to a junction at a col at 2.9 mi. (Trail L, now closed to the public, leads to Cy Beede Ledge and Upper Lake.)

Continuing on the level for a short stretch, the trail soon begins to climb, steeply at times, to a lookout on the R at 3.2 mi. The climbing is now easier and the trail passes between two large boulders just before reaching a summit at 3.6 mi. Shortly beyond this summit, the trail passes Lookout Rock on the L, from which there are good views of Upper Ausable Lake. The trail now descends gradually to a col and begins to climb Blake, crossing a minor summit at 4.0 mi. and reaching the true summit less than 100 yards later. Total ascent from Elk Lake-Marcy Trail, approximately 2800 ft. (850 m). Elevation, 3960 ft. (1207 m).

See trail 56 for history of the naming of Blake as well as complete description of trail from the summit down to the col between Blake and Colvin and then up the S side of Colvin to the summit at 5.4 mi. Trail from the summit leads down to the Lake Road and St. Huberts.

Distances: Elk Lake-Marcy Trail to Pinnacle, 1.8 mi.; to summit of Blake, 4.0 mi.; to summit of Colvin, 5.4 mi. (8.6 km). Total ascent, approximately 3400 ft. (1050 m). Elevation, 4057 ft. (1237 m). Order of height, 39.

Mt. Colden

Heart Lake Section

This popular hiking center is reached by turning S from Rt. 73, 4 mi. SE of Lake Placid Village. There is a sign for the Adirondak Loj as well as a large DEC sign, "Trails to the High Peaks."[1] The first mile of the road is open, offering views of many of the peaks that can be reached from Heart Lake. At 3.8 mi. a dirt road marked with DEC signs goes L to South Meadow. Across a bridge and up a hill, another DEC sign indicates the start of the Indian Pass Trail at 4.7 mi. (no parking permitted here), with a small entrance booth just beyond at 4.8 mi. A daily parking fee, paid here, is charged both to help maintain this public facility and to support ADK's trail maintenance and education programs. Past the entrance booth, turn L for the parking lot and the High Peaks Information Center (HPIC). (Road R leads to Adirondak Loj, where overnight accommodations and meals are available; see Introduction.) At the HPIC, maps, guidebooks, and information are available as well as snacks, limited camping supplies, showers, and a dry area for packing up.

Heart Lake and the surrounding property are owned by the Adirondack Mountain Club and maintained for the benefit of the hiking public as well as members of the club. Heart Lake is the start for the shortest approach to Marcy as well as many other trails. All of the 61 miles of trails described in this section are maintained by the DEC, except for the Mt. Jo trails.

---

[1] "Adirondak Loj" is spelled as it is because its builder was Melvil Dewey, champion of "simplified spelling." Dewey was founder of the Lake Placid Club, which acquired the Loj property around 1900. As noted below, the original Adirondack Lodge was built by Henry Van Hoevenberg; it was destroyed in a forest fire in 1903. The Adirondack Mountain Club now owns the property and its facilities.

Trails in winter: The Heart Lake section has more trails suitable for skiing than either the St. Huberts or Keene Valley sections, but a majority are still suitable only for snowshoe travel unless specifically noted as ski routes. Crampons will likely be needed either for the open summits or on any steep trails after a thaw/freeze cycle. Additional precautions and equipment such as a face mask may be needed above timberline.

On many of these heavily-used trails, posted DEC signs dictate the wearing of snowshoes or skis when there is snow on the trails. Do not ignore these signs because the result is "postholes" which are dangerous to other trail users.

Trying to select the best trails or loop trips in this region is difficult, since almost every destination is both attractive and popular, but below are some of the better possibilities this area offers.

Short Hikes:

Mt. Jo—2.3-mi. round trip. Superior views of the High Peaks and Heart Lake for very little overall effort. See description for Mt. Jo.

Rocky Falls—4.8-mi. round trip. An easy walk along the start of the Indian Pass Trail to an attractive little series of waterfalls and large pool for swimming. See description for Indian Pass Trail.

See also—Table of Short Hikes in Appendix III.

Moderate Hikes:

Phelps Mt.—8.8-mi. round trip. A wonderful close-up view of Marcy and other peaks without too much steep climbing. See description for Van Hoevenberg Trail to Marcy and Phelps Mt.

Avalanche Lake—10-mi. round trip. A relatively flat hike through Avalanche Pass and on to the S end of the lake with spectacular cliffs on both sides. See description for Van Hoevenberg Trail to Marcy and Avalanche Pass Trail.

Harder Hikes:

Mt. Colden with return via Avalanche Pass—13.8-mi. round trip. This loop takes in the summit of Mt. Colden with its view of Marcy, Algonquin, Avalanche Lake and Lake Colden, with a return through the spectacular Avalanche Pass. See descriptions for Van Hoevenberg Trail to Marcy, Avalanche Pass Trail, Lake Arnold Trail, L. Morgan Porter Trail to Mt. Colden, Mt. Colden from Lake Colden, and return on Avalanche Pass Trail.

Wallface Ponds—13.7-mi. round trip. A relatively flat walk to several remote and very interesting ponds with a view along the way of the MacIntyre Range that is a photographer's dream. See descriptions for Indian Pass Trail and Scott and Wallface Ponds.

(61) Mt. Marcy via Van Hoevenberg Trail   Map: D-8

This is one of the oldest and by far the most popular route to Mt. Marcy, as it is the shortest route by over 1.5 mi. It was laid out by Henry Van Hoevenberg, builder of the original Adirondack Lodge, in the 1880s. The trail has been rerouted several times over the years as heavy use caused erosion, but the reroutes generally follow the original line which manages to ascend to the summit at a relatively easy grade. Marcy is the only major peak (save Whiteface via the highway) that can readily be skied by advanced skiers, and sections of the Van Hoevenberg Trail were widened in the 1930s to make skiing easier.

In the past few years, ADK and DEC trail crews have done extensive work on this trail and have stemmed the steady deterioration caused by erosion. The trail is in better overall shape than it was ten years ago. Log and board bridges now cross many of the mud "wallows" referred to in earlier editions of this guidebook; and in many cases unattractive wide muddy sections have recovered to become grassy areas with only a narrow path through the center. The hope is that this level of trail maintenance will continue on these trails and spread to other badly deteriorated trails.

The trail begins at the end of the parking lot at the Adirondak Loj's High Peaks Information Center. Leaving the trail register (0 mi.), it proceeds on the level, and then descends to a bridge over Algonquin Brook at 0.4 mi. At the far side of the bridge, the trail turns sharp R while a ski route continues straight ahead. The trail now climbs away from the brook, passes several other ski trail junctions, and reaches a junction at 1.0 mi., where the Algonquin Peak Trail (trail 64) with yellow markers goes straight ahead. The original route of the Van Hoevenberg Trail comes in from the R.

Turning L, the trail proceeds mostly on the flat, with a few short climbs, to the L bank of Marcy Brook at 1.9 mi. Swinging R, it climbs two short pitches, levels off, and then drops slightly to Marcy Dam at 2.3 mi. The trail crosses the dam, from which there are views of Phelps, Colden, and Algonquin, and comes to the trail register at the far end, (Yellow trail L is the South Meadow Truck Road, trail 78, leading 2.6 mi. to South Meadow.) The Marcy Dam Interior Outpost is 50 yds. straight ahead from the trail register. There are seven lean-tos and numerous designated campsites at this popular camping area. Three lean-tos are located on the E side of the small pond (also referred to as Marcy Dam), two more are located at the S or upper end, and two more are on the W side. A trail circles Marcy Dam giving access to these lean-tos and campsites. Be aware that in this area camping is permitted only at designated areas. Also realize that firewood is very scarce in this area, which makes a camping stove highly advisable. (As noted in the introduction, future regulations for this area may prohibit fires, making a camping stove mandatory. Two or three of the lean-tos may also be removed with a similar number of designated campsites created in the area E of Marcy Dam towards Phelps Brook. The rationale for these two changes is to disperse camping pressure and to emphasize wilderness self-reliance by not providing as many lean-tos.)

Turning R at the trail register, the Van Hoevenberg Trail comes, in just over 100 yds., to a junction with the Avalanche Pass Trail (trail

68), which leads R with yellow markers. Bearing L at this junction, the trail climbs gradually to the L bank of Phelps Brook at 2.5 mi. (Bridge on L crossing the brook is the high-water route. Turn R at far end of bridge to rejoin main trail in 125 yds.) Bearing R, the trail continues up the L bank of Phelps Brook to a crossing at 2.6 mi., with the high-water route rejoining the trail at the far side. Now climbing at a steady, easy to moderate grade along the R bank of the brook, the trail comes to a junction at 3.2 mi. with red trail L leading 1.2 mi. to summit of Phelps (trail 62).

Bearing R, the trail continues at the same easy grade to a bridge over Phelps Brook at 3.5 mi., after which the trail climbs steeply to a four-way junction at 3.6 mi. The trails going straight ahead and L at this point are two variations of the ski route which take a slightly longer course from here to Indian Falls. The Van Hoevenberg Trail turns sharp R and climbs at a steady, moderate grade with some steeper pitches until finally easing off at 4.1 mi. Now crossing several wet areas, the trail climbs again at an easy grade to the junction at the upper end of the ski route at 4.4 mi., where it turns R and quickly arrives at a height of land just before Indian Falls. From this point there is a view of Marcy straight ahead. The only designated camping areas in the Indian Falls vicinity are just L of this height of land.

Just past this height of land, the trail comes to the R bank of Marcy Brook, which it crosses (no bridge) at 4.4 mi. Fifty yds. to the R and down from this point is the top of Indian Falls, with a spectacular view of the MacIntyre Range from the flat, open rocks. Just beyond the brook crossing, the trail comes to a junction with the yellow trail leading R in 0.8 mi. to the Lake Arnold Trail (trail 63). Turning L at this junction, the trail climbs at an easy to moderate grade to a level spot at 5.0 mi., drops down slightly, and then begins climbing steeply at 5.2 mi. At 5.4 mi., the grade begins to ease off as the trail approaches the top of a ridge where there are views of

Marcy. Continuing along the ridge with only a few short rises, the trail comes to a junction at 6.2 mi. Yellow trail L is the Hopkins Trail to Keene Valley (trail 2).

Bearing R and slightly down, the trail passes the former site of the Hopkins Lean-to in 200 yds. and then climbs to the former site of Plateau Lean-to at 6.5 mi., with the summit dome of Marcy in full view. Dipping briefly across a small stream, the trail then climbs through thick scrub to the junction with the red-marked Phelps Trail (trail 11) which comes in from the L at 6.8 mi.

Swinging R, the trail makes a short climb to some bare rocks and then dips across a wet area before climbing up to the first rocky shoulder of Marcy at 7.0 mi. Briefly leveling off, the trail now climbs over mostly bare rock and is marked with cairns and yellow paint blazes. Use care when following the trail, especially in poor weather. Proceeding up the bare rocks, the trail reaches the smaller E summit and flattens out for a few yards before coming to the true summit at 7.8 mi. The alpine vegetation on the upper half-mile of the summit area is fragile. For more information on how to protect it, see Introduction. From the summit, the yellow trail leading to Lake Colden and Elk Lake (trails 118 and 121) continues down the SW slope. (See "Mt. Marcy" in Introduction for information on history and view.)

Trail in winter: This trail can be skied to Marcy Dam with six inches of cover, but heavy foot traffic often makes the surface less than ideal. Beyond Marcy Dam the trail becomes steeper and is definitely for experienced skiers only, although for those capable of handling the descent, Marcy is one of the classic ski mountaineering trips in the East.

Distances: Adirondak Loj to Marcy Dam, 2.3 mi.; to Indian Falls, 4.4 mi.; to Hopkins Trail, 6.2 mi.; to Phelps Trail, 6.8 mi.; to summit of Marcy, 7.4 mi. (11.9 km). Ascent 3166 ft. (965 m). Elevation, 5344 ft. (1628 m). Order of height, 1.

(62) Phelps Mt.   Map: D-9

Phelps is named for Orson Schofield Phelps, better known as Old Mountain"Phelps, who cut the first trail up Marcy and over the years guided many parties to its summit. It is thus fitting that this peak whose view is so dominated by Mt. Marcy is named after Phelps, even though he probably never climbed the peak himself. Phelps is the easiest high peak to climb from the Marcy Dam area, and is thus a good alternative for Marcy-bound parties who find themselves short of time.

The red-marked trail turns L from the Van Hoevenberg Trail to Marcy (trail 61) at a point 1.0 mi. from Marcy Dam or 3.2 mi. from Adirondak Loj. The trail immediately climbs away from the Van Hoevenberg Trail on a moderate grade and continues with occasional steeper pitches to the first open rock at 1.1 mi. The red markers are now supplemented by yellow paint blazes as the trail soon comes to a second rocky outcrop with views of Marcy Dam. From here, the trail is mostly flat to large open ledges at the summit at 1.2 mi.

Distances: Adirondak Loj to start of Phelps Trail, 3.2 mi.; to summit of Phelps, 4.4 mi. (7.10 km). Ascent from Adirondak Loj, 1982 ft. (604 m). Elevation, 4161 ft. (1268 m.). Order of height, 32.

Unmaintained Trail to Table Top

(See Peaks Without Maintained Trails in Introduction)

There are two distinct routes up Table Top. Both leave the Van Hoevenberg Trail to Marcy Trail (trail 61) at Indian Falls. The most used follows virtually on a compass line from Indian Falls, hitting several areas of blowdown and many false summits before finally arriving at the summit. A harder approach to find (but generally easier to climb) goes approximately 0.3 mi. up the R bank of Marcy Brook before veering to the NE. This emerges on the summit plateau just W of the summit.

(63) Indian Falls-Lake Arnold Crossover   Map: D-9

From the Van Hoevenberg Trail to Marcy (trail 61) at Indian Falls, 4.5 mi. from Adirondak Loj, a trail with yellow markers branches R and connects with the blue trail to Lake Arnold and Feldspar Brook from Avalanche Camp (trail 73). Although formerly extremely rough and wet, the ADK trail crew rehabilitated this trail extensively in 1992 so that it now provides a good connection between the popular camping areas at Indian Falls and Lake Colden without a traverse of Marcy or a descent to Marcy Dam.

Leaving the junction (0 mi.) just above the brook crossing at Indian Falls, the trail descends for 75 yds. to a good view of Indian Falls from below. In another few yards, the trail swings L and away from the original route of the Van Hoevenberg Trail, climbs briefly, and then begins a rough descent to a sharp L turn at 0.6 mi. Now more of a stream than a trail, it climbs gradually, crosses an extensive wet area, and reaches the R bank of a stream. Following the R bank for a few yards, the trail crosses on the rocks to the junction with the Lake Arnold Trail at 0.8 mi. (Turn R for Avalanche Camp, 1.0 mi.; L for Lake Arnold, 0.5 mi.)

Distance: Indian Falls to Lake Arnold Trail, 0.8 mi. (1.3 km).

The MacIntyre Range[1]

The series of peaks known as the MacIntyre Mts., or the MacIntyre Range, rises loftily against the sky S of Heart Lake. Named in honor of Archibald McIntyre, the dominating figure in the Tahawus Iron Works enterprise that bore his name, this is one of the noblest

---

[1]The spelling of MacIntyre conforms to the USGS topographic map which has been approved by the U.S. Board of Geographic Names. It is used throughout this guidebook to be consistent, but the man for whom the range is named spelled his name McIntyre.

groups of peaks in the Adirondacks. Standing apart from all surrounding peaks, the range extends for about 8 miles, running NE and SW. Its steep NW slopes form one side of Indian Pass and the SE spur helps to form the spectacular cliffs of Avalanche Pass.

The most northerly major peak is Wright Peak, 4580 ft., named after Governor Silas Wright. A lesser peak NE of Wright is called Whale's Tail because of its shape when viewed from Marcy Dam. The NE shoulder of Wright, adjacent to Whale's Tail, is sometimes referred to as the "Whale" and offers some interesting views for those willing to make the short bushwhack up to this point from the ski trail in Whale's Tail Notch (trail 67).

To the SW of Wright is Algonquin Peak, 5114 ft., the highest peak in the range and the second highest in the Adirondacks. Algonquin has also been called Mt. MacIntyre and is still referred to as such on a few DEC trail signs. SW of Algonquin stands Boundary Peak, so named because it is supposed to have marked the boundary between the Algonquin and Iroquois Indian tribes. In reality, it stands on the southern boundary of the Old Military Tract which was originally surveyed in 1797 by a Charles Brodhead, who thus lays claim to the first ascent in the MacIntyre Range—forty years before Ebenezer Emmons first climbed Algonquin in 1837. Although high enough to count as one of the 46 high peaks, Boundary is considered to be merely a prominence on the ridge to Iroquois.

At 4840 ft., Iroquois is the second highest peak in the range and the eighth highest in the Adirondacks. Its rocky summit offers many fine views, particularly the view of Wallface Mt. in Indian Pass.

Farther to the SW and separated from Iroquois by a deep valley is Mt. Marshall. Colvin first named this peak in honor of Governor DeWitt Clinton of Erie Canal fame. Colvin at first attached the name to the peak we now call Iroquois, but later transferred it to this southernmost peak of the MacIntrye Range. For some time this peak was also called Herbert in honor of Herbert Clark, the Marshall family's guide and one of the original three forty-sixers. After Robert Marshall's death in 1939, the Adirondack Forty-Sixers successfully petitioned the New York State Board of Geographic Names to officially name this peak Marshall. Even though the Board accepted this name, it was labeled Clinton on the 1954 USGS maps. The 1978 USGS Ampersand Lake 15 by 7.5 minute metric series sheet, however, does show this peak as Mt. Marshall.

Robert Marshall, with his brother George, drew up the original list of the 46 peaks and with Herb Clark became the first to climb them all. Marshall was a noted forester, explorer, author and conservationist. The naming of the 950,000-acre Bob Marshall Wilderness Area in western Montana is a tribute to his efforts; various groups have proposed that an expanded Five Ponds Wilderness area of over 400,000 acres in the western Adirondacks also be named for Bob Marshall.

(64) Algonquin from Heart Lake   Map: D-9

From the Adirondak Loj's High Peaks Information Center, take the Van Hoevenberg Trail (trail 61) to the trail junction at 1.0 mi. Here the trail to Algonquin continues straight ahead. (Trail L leads to Marcy Dam.) Continuing at a generally easy grade with a few steeper pitches, the trail reaches the junction with the Whale's Tail Notch Ski Trail (trail 67) at 1.4 mi. Bearing R and up at this junction, the trail climbs at a steady, moderate grade along the lower portion of the old Wright Peak Ski Trail. Crossing several small streams as it climbs, the trail veers R from the old ski trail at 2.3 mi. and in 50 yds. joins the route of the original trail from Heart Lake which comes in from the R. The trail soon climbs a steep rock step, after which markers point L and up to a designated campsite. The trail then comes to a beautiful cascade on the L at 2.4 mi.

After this waterfall, the trail climbs a short, steep pitch, levels out for a bit, and then climbs again steeply to a flat area at 2.9 mi. with a small rock cobble on the R. Turning L and up, it climbs over one steep rock step, after which the grade eases a bit across a side hill before the trail reaches the junction with the 0.4 mi spur trail to Wright (trail 65) at 3.1 mi.

Bearing R at this junction, the Algonquin Trail begins to climb steeply, going up over several sections of smooth rock and leveling out just before reaching timberline at 3.6 mi. From timberline the trail is marked with cairns and yellow paint blazes. Hikers should use care and stay on the marked trail so as to avoid damaging the fragile alpine vegetation.

In the past few years several groups, most notably the Adirondack 46ers, have done much to restore the areas near Algonquin's summit which had become denuded of their natural vegetation. The techniques for sowing grass seed in this harsh climate were developed by Dr. E.H. Ketchledge of the College of Environmental Science and Forestry at Syracuse, and they have proved successful enough to warrant their use on other summits as well. These restoration efforts have improved the summit's appearance noticeably, but this fine effort can easily be negated by the carelessness of individual hikers. (See Introduction for more on alpine vegetation.)

On the summit, the trail meets the Lake Colden Trail (trail 71) coming up the SW slope and similarly marked with cairns and yellow paint blazes. The view from the summit is spectacular and expansive, highlighted by the view of Mt. Colden with its many sides and famous dike, or cleft, as well as by the view of Lake Colden and Flowed Lands at the foot of the mountain. The further view encompasses most of the high peaks to the E and S, with many lakes visible to the W and N. On the descent, hikers should pay close attention to the markers, especially in poor weather. The route down generally traverses slightly to the R across the fall line to reach the trail at timberline.

Distances: Adirondak Loj via blue trail to junction with yellow trail for Algonquin, 1.0 mi.; to blue trail to Wright Peak, 3.1 mi.; to summit of Algonquin, 4.0 mi. (6.4 km). Ascent, 2936 ft. (895 m). Elevation, 5114 ft. (1559 m). Order of height, 2.

(65) Wright Peak   Map: D-9

The blue-marked trail to Wright Peak diverges L from the yellow trail to Algonquin 3.1 mi. from Adirondak Loj. Leaving the trail junction (0 mi.), the trail climbs steadily to timberline at 0.2 mi., after which the route is marked with cairns up the bare rock ridge. Soon after timberline the grade eases, with the summit reached at 0.4 mi.

A bronze plaque on a large vertical rock face just N of the summit memorializes four airmen who lost their lives in the crash of a B-47 bomber at that spot in 1962. Some parts of the ill-fated aircraft are still scattered around the area close to the top of the mountain.

Distances: Adirondak Loj to blue trail for Wright Peak, 3.1 mi.; to summit of Wright Peak, 3.5 mi. (5.7 km). Ascent from Adirondak Loj, 2400 ft. (732 m). Elevation, 4580 ft. (1396 m). Order of height, 16.

(66) Boundary and
Iroquois Peaks   Map: D-10

Although not an official trail, there is a reasonably well-defined route from the col between Algonquin and Boundary along the mostly open ridge to Iroquois. The trail is marked with cairns in the open areas, but there are no other signs or markers. In 1975, the Adirondack 46ers improved this trail somewhat, mainly to establish a route around a unique alpine bog on Boundary, in order to prevent the bog from being trampled. No significant maintenance has been done since, but the route has remained reasonably well-defined.

The trail leaves the Lake Colden Trail to Algonquin (trail 71) 0.4 mi. below the Algonquin summit, at a large cairn at timberline. The "herd path" for Iroquois goes straight ahead, while the marked trail for Lake Colden swings L and down.

Leaving the col (0 mi.), the route climbs quickly to the first summit of Boundary, dips down and bypasses the above-mentioned bog on the R, and comes to the summit of Boundary at 0.2 mi. The route now descends over open rock, enters the woods for a few hundred yards, and finally climbs steeply up and slightly L to the summit of Iroquois at 0.7 mi. from the Algonquin Trail.

Distances: Algonquin summit to start of "herd path," 0.4 mi.; to summit of Iroquois, 1.0 mi. (1.7 km). Elevation, 4840 ft. (1475 m). Order of height, 8.

(67) Whale's Tail Notch Ski Trail   Map: D-9

This trail leads from Marcy Dam over a notch NE of Wright to a point on the Algonquin Trail. The trail is quite rough and is not maintained for summer travel. It does offer a 0.5 mi. shorter approach to the Algonquin Trail for those camped at Marcy Dam, but this saving in distance is not great when compared to the rough footing and 380-ft. vertical climb through Whale's Tail Notch. The trail is thus described from Marcy Dam to the Algonquin Trail, instead of as an alternate approach to Marcy Dam, as in earlier editions of this guidebook.

The start of the Whale's Tail Notch Ski Trail is at the top of a slight rise a few yards from the W end of Marcy Dam on the Van

Hoevenberg Trail (no sign). Leaving this junction (0 mi.), proceed past the first lean-to to a trail R at approximately 100 yds. from the Van Hoevenberg Trail. (Trail straight ahead leads around Marcy Dam to other lean-tos and campsites.) Turning R, the trail proceeds mostly on the level through an open forest before starting to climb at 0.3 mi. The climb is steady and becomes steeper near the height of land. Easing off at 0.6 mi., the trail reaches the actual top of the pass at 0.8 mi., having gained approximately 380 ft. from Marcy Dam. Now starting down a slightly easier grade than that just ascended, and going in and out of a small brook, the trail reaches the Algonquin Trail (trail 64) at 1.3 mi.

Trail in winter: As the name implies, this was cut as a ski trail and is therefore a bit wider than most hiking trails. The Marcy Dam side is steeper and more of a challenge to ski down, while the other side has been badly eroded over the years and requires at least a foot of snow to be skiable. Skied in either direction, it is recommended only for advanced skiers.

Distance: Marcy Dam to Algonquin Trail, 1.3 mi. (2.1 km).

(68) Avalanche Pass to Lake Colden   Map: D-9

The trail through Avalanche Pass is probably the most spectacular route in the Adirondacks. Sheer rock walls rise directly out of the water on both sides of Avalanche Lake, and the trail is forced to wind among large boulders and even cross two catwalks set into the rock face in order to negotiate this impressive piece of terrain. This is the most popular approach to Lake Colden and is much used. Backpackers should be aware, however, that this is a very rough trail in spots, and should allow plenty of time so as not to have to rush.

Many parties, for instance, find that it takes an hour to cover the one-mile section from the top of the pass to the lower end of Avalanche Lake.

The Avalanche Pass Trail diverges R from the Van Hoevenberg Trail to Marcy (trail 61) at Marcy Dam just over 100 yds. past the trail register and right in front of a lean-to. Marked with yellow DEC disks, the trail proceeds along the flat for 200 yds., where a trail leads R and over a bridge to additional lean-tos and campsites. Bearing L and still on the flat, the trail soon comes to the R bank of Marcy Brook, which it now follows. At 0.4 mi. the trail swings away from the brook and soon crosses two small bridges. At the second bridge, an obscure trail leads R to Kagel Lean-to. Continuing up a gradual climb, the trail passes Marcy Brook Lean-to on the R at 0.8 mi. and then crosses Marcy Brook on a bridge just before the two lean-tos at Avalanche Camp at 1.1 mi. At the second lean-to there is a trail junction with the blue trail L to Lake Arnold and Feldspar Brook (trail 73).

Continuing R, the Avalanche Pass Trail crosses a wet area and begins to climb steeply with several log stairs. At 1.2 mi. the trail swings sharp L, and continues climbing as it comes to a junction where the ski trail crosses at 1.3 mi. (This ski trail follows a slightly longer route down from the top of the pass and eventually joins the Lake Arnold Trail just above Avalanche Camp. It is extremely rough and not suited for summer travel.) Continuing straight ahead, the trail swings R at 1.4 mi., where the ski trail again crosses, and then continues on to the top of the pass at 1.6 mi. Here, at the height of land, a small waterfall descends a cliff during wet seasons and splits, with one part flowing N to the St. Lawrence River and the other flowing S to the Hudson.

The trail now descends toward Avalanche Lake, which it reaches at 2.1 mi. The precipitous slopes of Mt. Colden rise on the left, while the even steeper slopes of Avalanche (Caribou) Mt. rise on the R. The trail proceeds along the R side and is quite rugged, but interesting—passing over ledges, around huge boulders, and across crevices aided by ladders and bridges. At two places the cliffs rise directly out of the water, and only bridges bolted into the cliff make the passage possible. These structures are known as "Hitch-up Matildas" after a young lady of that name who was carried across this section on the back of her guide. As the water became deeper, her sister on the shore exhorted her to "hitch-up," and the whole scene was recorded by an artist for *Harper's* magazine, whose drawing of the scene made this spot famous.

From the second such bridge at 2.5 mi., there is an impressive view directly up the slide of Colden, with the Trap Dike just to the left. The largest slides date from 1869 and 1942. The deep cleft of the Trap Dike was caused by the differential erosion of the gabbro dike intruded into the native anorthosite granite.

The trail reaches the foot of the lake at 2.6 mi., crosses the outlet, and follows down the L bank. There is a trail L 200 yds. past the outlet, which leads in 125 yds. to a designated campsite. Continuing down, the trail reaches a junction near the former site of Caribou Lean-to at 2.9 mi. The blue trail R leads around the NW shore of Lake Colden (trail 69) to the Interior Outpost and then on to the dam at the outlet; see below. Bearing L, the yellow trail leads to the E shore of Lake Colden and then along the shore to the junction with the red trail leading L to Mt. Colden (trail 70) at 3.4 mi. Continuing on, the trail reaches the register at the junction with the red trail to Marcy (trail 121) at 3.8 mi. Trail R leads 200 yds. to a bridge and dam at the outlet, from which the red trail continues on to Flowed Lands and Lake Sanford. The far side of the dam is also the end of the blue trail around the NW shore of Lake Colden.

There are now six lean-tos at Lake Colden, but there were once as many as thirteen. This reduction in numbers is an attempt to reduce the physical deterioration of this popular camping area by offering fewer attractions for campers. There are, however, many designated tenting sites in the area. One of the lean-tos is visible from the junction of the Avalanche Pass Trail and the red trail to Marcy, but this lean-to was scheduled to be torn down during the summer of 1992 and replaced with a structure located E and uphill from the trail register. Three others are located on the L(E) bank of the Opalescent River below the Lake Colden outlet. This can be reached by crossing the Opalescent (use suspension bridge just upstream on the Marcy Trail in high water) and following the trail down the L bank. The other two lean-tos are located on a point on the S shore of Lake Colden and are reached by crossing the dam and turning R for 175 yds. There are designated camping areas at many spots along both banks of the Opalescent River. In general, they are back away from the river on the opposite side of the trail running along the river.

Trail in winter: The ski through Avalanche Pass and across the lakes is a classic tour and available to any strong intermediate skier. It is not uncommon to see more than 100 skiers on this trail when conditions are good. To be skiable, Avalanche Pass needs at least one foot, and preferably more, of snow. Crossing Avalanche Lake when it is windy can present problems similar to being above timberline, making goggles and a face mask potentially necessary.

Distances: Marcy Dam to Avalanche Camps, 1.1 mi.; to Avalanche Lake, 2.1 mi.; to trail around NW shore of Lake Colden, 2.9 mi.; to junction with Marcy Trail at Lake Colden, 3.8 mi. (6.2 km). (6.1 mi. from Heart Lake.)

(69) Trail around Northwest Shore of Lake Colden   Map: D-10

Starting at the trail junction 0.3 mi. from the foot of Avalanche Lake or 2.9 mi. from Marcy Dam, this trail connects with the Algonquin Trail, Lake Colden Interior Outpost, and the Algonquin

Pass Trail to Indian Pass. Leaving the junction (0 mi.), follow blue markers across a brook and past a trail L leading to the the former site of Caribou Lean-to. Bearing R, the trail continues on the level to the L bank of a stream and the junction with the yellow trail leading R 2.1 mi. to the summit of Algonquin (trail 71). Continuing L across the bridge, the trail reaches a trail register at 0.6 mi. (Side trail L leads 150 yds. to the Lake Colden Interior Outpost.) Continuing R, the trail immediately comes to the junction with the yellow trail leading straight ahead 3.3 mi. to the Indian Pass Trail (trail 72). The blue trail turns sharp L, crosses Cold Brook, and swings L and back to Lake Colden. Near the S end of the lake there are now three designated campsites (marked with yellow campsite disks) up and to the R of the trail. Rounding the S end of the lake, the trail passes Beaver Point Lean-to on the L at 0.9 mi. and West Lean-to (named in honor of Clinton West, a ranger at Lake Colden for many years) 50 yds. later. (This lean-to has also been called Cedar Point.) Now the trail swing R and comes to the dam at the outlet and junction with trail 121 at 1.0 mi., ending the blue markers. Red trail straight ahead leads to Flowed Lands and Upper Works. Trail L crosses the dam and leads to Marcy and the other lean-tos and campsites described above.

Distances: Junction with yellow trail to Interior Outpost, 0.6 mi.; to dam at outlet, 1.0 mi (1.7 km). (6.3 mi. from Heart Lake.)

(70) Mt. Colden from Lake Colden   Map: D-10

Though seemingly dwarfed by its neighbors Marcy and Algonquin, Mt. Colden is perhaps even more interesting with the extensive slides and unique large dike on its W side. Forming the SE rampart of Avalanche Pass, Colden offers an unforgettable view practically straight down from its summit to the inky depths of Avalanche Lake.

Colden was named for David C. Colden, one of the proprietors of the McIntyre Iron Works. Professor Ebenezer Emmons later tried to name it Mt. McMartin in honor of another leader in the McIntyre Iron Works, but the first name has endured. The trail from Lake Colden is very rough and steep with the approach from Lake Arnold generally preferred. Ascending from Lake Arnold with a descent via this trail and a return via Avalanche Pass, however, makes for one of the most spectacular and interesting circuits in the mountains.

The trail starts on the E side of Lake Colden, 0.4 mi. NE from Lake Colden Outlet and 5.8 mi. from Adirondak Loj (trail 68). Leaving the yellow trail (0 mi.), the red trail immediately climbs several steep long log steps but then eases off as it continues at a steady grade through a thick spruce forest. At 0.6 mi. the trail swings L and up a ladder and begins a nearly unrelenting steep climb—much of it over trail washed right down to bare rock. Finally moderating at 1.3 mi., the trail passes under two huge boulders and soon comes to a ladder leading up a small cliff to a flat area above. Veering L, the trail emerges onto open rock and then veers back R and up a bare rock step to the top of the ridge just below the summit. When descending this section, follow the markers very carefully, as it is easy to lose the trail and there is only one possible route to the ladder that makes it possible to get past the cliffs.

After a short level stretch on the ridge, the trail climbs a final rock step and arrives at a large open area just S of the actual summit. Extensive reseeding has recently been done on the "lawn" just S of the balanced boulder. Step or sit only on the bare rock to avoid undoing this restoration. Here is the best view of Lake Colden and Flowed Lands, but just beyond at a large balanced boulder on the L is a view of Avalanche Lake and the "Hitch-up Matildas" (see trail 68) with the actual summit just beyond at 1.6 mi. Here the Lake Colden Trail (trail 70) meets the L Morgan Porter Trail (trail 74) which leads 1.4 mi. to Lake Arnold.

Distances: Lake Colden to summit of Mt. Colden, 1.6 mi. (2.6 km). Ascent from Lake Colden, 1950 ft. (594 m). Elevation, 4714 ft. (1437 m). Order of height, 11.

(71) Algonquin Peak from Lake Colden   Map: D-10

This trail leads 2.1 mi. from the trail on the NW shore of Lake Colden to the summit of Algonquin. (See above for additional information on Algonquin and the MacIntyre Range.) The trail climbs 2350 ft. from Lake Colden to the summit, which makes this one of the most continuously steep climbs in the mountains. Although actually a slightly shorter route between Lake Colden and Heart Lake, this trail up and over Algonquin is not recommended for backpackers in either direction.

The trail begins 0.2 mi. NE of the Lake Colden Interior Outpost at a bridge on the trail around the NW shore of Lake Colden (trail 69), 0.4 mi. from its junction with the Avalanche Pass Trail (trail 68). Leaving this junction (0 mi.), the yellow-marked trail climbs moderately at first along the L bank of the stream. Reaching the top of a cataract at 0.2 mi., the grade soon eases and the first stream crossing is reached at 0.3 mi. The trail crosses and recrosses the brook several times, finally returning to the L bank at 0.5 mi. Shortly after, the grade again steepens, and the trail reaches the foot of a waterfall at 0.6 mi. Jogging R to get around the falls, the trail then enters the stream bed and climbs the sloping ledges next to the stream, where there are some fine views of the slides of Mt. Colden.

The trail leaves the brook at 0.7 mi. and continues steeply up the L bank, with only occasional slight breathers. At 0.9 mi. the trail again crosses the brook and winds among the boulders on the R bank, returning to the L bank just before it reaches a big pool at 1.0 mi. The trail now climbs away from the brook on a very rough section, on a steady, steep grade. Coming back to the stream a few hundred yards later, it again leaves the stream before finally crossing to the R bank for the last time. There is a very steep pitch up over some large roots before the trail settles down to being merely steep to timberline, just above the col between Boundary and Algonquin, which is reached at 1.7 mi. An unmarked trail leads L to Boundary and Iroquois peaks (trail 66). Following cairns and yellow paint blazes, the trail reaches the summit of Algonquin at 2.1 mi., where it meets the trail from Heart Lake. (See trail 64 for description of trail from Heart Lake as well as cautions on staying on marked trail to preserve the alpine vegetation.)

Distances: Trail junction with blue trail around NW shore of Lake Colden to waterfall, 0.6 mi.; to trail to Boundary and Iroquois, 1.7 mi.; to summit of Algonquin, 2.1 mi. (3.4 km). Ascent from Lake Colden, 2350 ft. (716 m). Elevation, 5114 ft. (1559 m). Order of height, 2.

(72) Trail from Lake Colden to Indian Pass Trail   Map: D-10

Cut in 1965, this trail leads from the trail on the NW shore of Lake Colden (trail 69) near the Interior Outpost, through Algonquin Pass between Iroquois and Marshall, to a point on the Indian Pass Trail (trail 75) 0.9 mi. from Scott Clearing and 1.1 mi. from Summit Rock in Indian Pass. This trail is quite steep and rough in spots, which make for slow going—especially with backpacks—but it is a useful connection for those wishing to combine a trip through Indian Pass with a stay at Lake Colden.

Marked with yellow markers, this trail starts just NE of the bridge over Cold Brook on the blue trail around the NW shore of Lake Colden (trail 69). This point is 0.6 mi. from the Avalanche Pass Trail junction and 0.4 mi. from Lake Colden's outlet.

Leaving the junction (0 mi.), the trail begins at an easy grade along the L bank of Cold Brook. Crossing two small tributaries as it begins to climb, the trail then crosses Cold Brook at 0.3 mi., just below the junction of the two branches of Cold Brook. The trail now climbs steeply along the banks of, and sometimes in, the S branch of Cold Brook until crossing it for the last time at 0.7 mi. and climbing away from the brook onto a shoulder of Iroquois. Several more steep pitches lead to easier grades if not smoother footing at 1.0 mi. as the trail begins to slab across the shoulder of Iroquois. At 1.4 mi. the trail drops slightly and then climbs to the top of Algonquin Pass at 1.5 mi., having climbed approximately 1100 ft. from Lake Colden.

The trail is now level through the grassy col, but soon begins to descend easy to moderate grades, becoming steeper at 2.2 mi. After crossing two branches of a large brook coming from the L, the trail veers away from the brook into an adjacent valley, and descends to the R bank of another large brook at 2.5 mi. The trail then joins an old tote road, veers away from the brook, and then returns to cross it at 2.7 mi.

Passing a very steep falls in the brook, the trail crosses to the R bank at 2.8 mi., recrosses at 3.0 mi., and climbs briefly before dropping down to a junction with the red-marked Indian Pass Trail (trail 75) at 3.3 mi. Trail L leads 1.1 mi. to Summit Rock in Indian Pass. Trail R leads 1.1 mi. to Scott Clearing Lean-to.

Distances: Start of trail at Lake Colden to Algonquin Pass, 1.5 mi.; to Indian Pass Trail, 3.3 mi. (5.3 km).

Unmaintained Trails to Marshall

(See Peaks Without Maintained Trails in Introduction)

For the history and naming of this peak, see above for introduction to MacIntyre Range. The most popular route leaves the Lake Colden-to-Indian Pass Trail (trail 72) just NW of the height of land between

Marshall and Iroquois, climbing over one intermediate peak before dropping down across the head of Herbert Brook and then on to the summit. A currently less used but far prettier approach is from Flowed Lands via Herbert Brook—an unofficial but very appropriate name recognizing Herbert Clark, the Marshall's friend and guide. This brook crosses the red trail 0.7 mi. NE of the Calamity lean-tos and 0.3 mi. from the Lake Colden dam. An obvious herd path leads up its easterly bank through the blowdown. Avoid following a tributary entering from the R (going up) about 0.5 mi. up the brook. Open rock slides make the ascent attractive for part of the way. At the head of the brook near the col, head SW for Marshall, staying close to the ridge line.

(73) Avalanche Camp to Lake Arnold and Feldspar Brook   Map: D-9

Once characterized by a very rough ascent from Avalanche Camp to Lake Arnold followed by an equally undesireable swampy finish to Feldspar Brook, this trail has received a good deal of attention from both ADK and DEC trail crews in recent years. Their efforts have now made this direct route to the upper Opalescent River valley more appealing.

The Lake Arnold trail begins at Avalanche Camp, 1.1 mi. from Marcy Dam on the yellow-marked Avalanche Pass Trail (trail 68). Marked with blue markers, the Lake Arnold trail diverges L at a signpost (0 mi.) next to the upper lean-to. Beginning on a gradual grade, in 250 yds. the Lake Arnold Trail turns sharp L and crosses a small brook on a bridge. (Trail straight ahead is the ski route through Avalanche Pass.) The Lake Arnold Trail now begins climbing along an old tote road high above Marcy Brook. At 1.1 mi. the trail reaches a junction with a yellow-marked trail L leading 0.8 mi. to Indian Falls (trail 63).

From this junction, the trail bears R and crosses a stream in 75 yds. Swinging R after the brook, the trail continues to climb along the R bank of the brook. At 1.4 mi. the trail forks, with the L fork staying on the old tote road and bypassing the former Lake Arnold Lean-to site. This route, however, is only 50 yds. shorter than the R fork, which is now the most used. Bearing R, the trail comes to Lake Arnold and the former lean-to site at 1.5 mi. Yellow trail R is the L. Morgan Porter Trail (trail 74) leading 1.4 mi. to Mt. Colden. Although the lean-to has been removed, this remains a designated campsite.

Crossing the outlet to Lake Arnold, the trail soon joins the direct route and swings R toward Lake Arnold Pass, which is reached at 1.8 mi., having gained 1200 ft. from Avalanche Camp. The trail now descends steeply along a small brook before easing off at 2.1 mi. Continuing a moderate descent, the trail passes the bottom of a large, new (1990) slide on Mt. Colden just before reaching the R bank of the Opalescent River at 2.8 mi. Crossing the river on stones, the trail veers away from the L bank, crosses some wet areas on broad bridges, and returns to the bank of the Opalescent River opposite Feldspar Lean-to at 3.1 mi. (This lean-to was scheduled to be torn down in the summer of 1992 and rebuilt further back from the river.) In another 60 yds. the trail crosses Feldspar Brook and comes to a junction with the yellow-marked Marcy Trail from Lake Colden (trail 121) at 3.2 mi. (Turn L for Marcy, 2.4 mi.; R for Lake Colden Dam, 2.2 mi.)

Distances: Avalanche Camp to Indian Falls Crossover Trail, 1.0 mi.; to Lake Arnold 1.5 mi.; to junction with Marcy Trail, 3.2 mi. (5.1 km).

(74) Mt. Colden from Lake Arnold via L. Morgan Porter Trail   Map: D-10

This approach to Mt. Colden from Lake Arnold replaces the now-abandoned trail that formerly turned off 0.7 mi. S of Lake Arnold on the trail to Feldspar Brook. Rudy Strobel laid out this trail in 1966, and it was cut by ADK with the approval of DEC, which now maintains it. It has officially been named the L. Morgan Porter Trail in memory of the man who produced the sixth and seventh editions of this guidebook.

The trail starts at Lake Arnold at the former lean-to site (0 mi.). Marked with yellow markers, the trail bears R and soon begins climbing. The climbing is not steady, with steep pitches alternating with nearly flat areas. At 0.7 mi., the climbing becomes steeper, and at 1.0 mi. the trail emerges on the bare N summit of Colden, from which there are some interesting views. The trail veers L and quickly descends back into the timber. (This spot is not well marked and should be noted for the return trip.) Dropping into a small sag, the trail climbs over another small bump and then drops to the col at the base of the main peak at 1.1 mi., where the abandoned trail enters on the L. From here the trail climbs steadily to the summit at 1.4 mi., where it meets the route from Lake Colden. (See trail 70 for trail description and notes on the view.)

Distances: Lake Arnold to summit of Colden, 1.4 mi. (2.2 km); from Heart Lake, 6.3 mi. (10.2 km). Ascent from Heart Lake, 2535 ft. (772 m). Elevation, 4714 ft. (1437 m). Order of height, 11.

(75) Indian Pass from Heart Lake
Map: D-8

Indian Pass is a stupendous gorge between Wallface Mt. and the MacIntyre Range. The Pass is over a mile in length, and its sheer NW wall rises nearly 1000 ft., which makes it one of the highest cliffs in the East, rivaled only by Cannon Cliff in Franconia Notch in the White Mountains. At places, the bottom of the gorge is an almost impossible tangle of boulders that have fallen off the cliff over the ages. There are several places where ice and snow remain throughout the year deep in caves that never see the light of day. The trail passes above this rock jumble on the SE side of the pass, but nevertheless the going is often difficult.

The trail begins on the W side of Adirondak Loj Road just before the parking lot at the High Peaks Information Center. Because parking on the road is prohibited, hikers must park in the lot, return to the road and turn R, going a few yards on the road to get to the start. Leaving the road (0 mi.) and marked by red markers, the trail proceeds to an old road next to Heart Lake at 0.1 mi. The trail turns sharp R, passing the trail R to Mt. Jo (trail 77) 50 yds. later. Continuing straight ahead along the lake, the trail comes to a register at 0.4 mi., where all hikers should register.

At 0.5 mi. the Old Nye Ski Trail diverges R, but the Indian Pass Trail bears L and down past the end of Heart Lake and then up to the property line and Westside Ski Trail at 0.6 mi. The trail now goes gently up and down through a mature open forest, crossing a brook on a bridge at 1.6 mi. and then a second larger brook without a bridge at 2.1 mi. Just beyond this second brook is a junction with the first of two trails leading to Rocky Falls. (Trail R leads 100 yds. to the bank of Indian Pass Brook and then up R bank to a crossing to a lean-to above the upper part of Rocky Falls at approximately 300 yds. from the Indian Pass Trail. The falls are not high, but there is a good swimming hole below the lower falls. The side trail then continues steeply up to rejoin the Indian Pass Trail in another 150 yds.)

Bearing L at this junction, the Indian Pass Trail soon begins a steep climb of 150 yds, easing off just before the second junction of the side trail to Rocky Falls at 2.4 mi. Now mostly on the flat and with some extensive wet areas, the trail crosses a large stream at 2.6 mi., climbs for a few yards, and then continues with short rises and falls to another stream at 3.6 mi. Crossing this stream and another one shortly after, the trail comes to Scott Clearing Lean-to at 3.8 mi. From the lean-to bear R, cross another small stream, and climb gradually to Scott's Dam at 4.1 mi. and the junction with the Wallface Ponds Trail (trail 76) leading R 2.8 mi. to Scott and Wallface Ponds. Scott Clearing is the site of a former lumber camp, and the high rock dam was used to control the flow of water in Indian Pass Brook for driving logs. Turning L at the junction, there are two choices. One is to use the old low-water route that runs up the gravel bars next to Indian Pass Brook. Beaver dams or recent rains may make this route impractical, but it does save quite a bit of climbing on the high-water route. Continuing on the marked trail (high-water route), follow up the L bank of a large brook before veering up and R to a height of land and on to rejoin the low-water route at 4.5 mi.

Turning L and crossing two brooks, the trail comes to a junction with the trail over Algonquin Pass from Lake Colden (trail 72) at 4.9 mi. (Trail L leads 3.3 mi. to Lake Colden.) At 5.0 mi. the trail crosses Indian Pass Brook diagonally and shortly after recrosses it to the R bank. Now beginning a very steep, rough climb, the trail ascends into the pass. There is a short level stretch at 5.5 mi., where the first views of the cliff on Wallface are possible. The actual height of land is marked by a sign at 5.5 mi., but most hikers continue on to Summit Rock at 6.0 mi. where there is the most spectacular view of the cliff. From Summit Rock it is 4.4 mi. to the Upper Works via trail 125.

Trail in winter: With at least a foot of snow, this trail is skiable as far as the start of the steep climbing at just over 5 mi.

Distances: Adirondak Loj to Rocky Falls, 2.1 mi.; to Scott Clearing Lean-to, 3.8 mi.; to trail to Scott and Wallface Ponds, 4.1 mi.; to trail to Lake Colden, 4.9 mi.; to Summit Rock, 6.0 mi. (9.7 km).

Unmaintained Trail to Street and Nye

(See Peaks Without Maintained Trails in Introduction)

Colvin named the first peak in honor of Alfred Billings Street, New York State law Librarian and author of the book *The Indian Pass*. The latter peak bears the name of William B. Nye, the North Elba guide best known for having carried Matilda across Hitch-Up-Matilda ford on Avalanche Lake.

Leaving the Indian Pass Trail (trail 75) at the W corner of Heart Lake, follow the remains of the old Nye Ski Trail due W and down to Indian Pass Brook. Follow down the R bank of Indian Pass Brook to a sharp turn where the brook turns from W back to N just above the first tributary entering from the L (W). Cross Indian Pass Brook just below this sharp turn and follow the herd paths as they skirt the S side of some fresh beaver activity and begin along the S (R) bank of the tributary.

Soon the established path crosses the tributary and heads up a basin on the E side of Nye. (This is the basin in which the USGS map shows a stream even though the brook coming down from between Street and Nye is of equal size but not shown.) The herd path then leads to a col on the ridge S of this basin. It then turns W and climbs steeply to the S end of the summit ridge of Nye. Turn R (N) and proceed over two intermediate bumps to the summit of Nye. Turn L and follow a confusing maze of herd paths generally SW and down to an open vlei just W of the crest of the ridge running between Nye and Street before ascending to the summit of Street.

A beautiful but longer approach to Street and Nye lies up the valley above Wanika Falls, reached from Lake Placid via the Northville-Placid Trail (trail 99). From Wanika Falls, follow the larger, more easterly branch of Wanika Falls Brook (the headwaters of the Chubb River) and stick to the flanks of Nye in the brook's upper reaches.

(76) Scott and Wallface Ponds

Map: C-9

Starting at Scott's Dam on the Indian Pass Trail, this trail climbs W to a series of remote and seldom-visited ponds. There are possible campsites at both Scott and Wallface ponds as well as a spectacularly framed view of the MacIntyre Range from one of the upper Scott Ponds. This area offers unexcelled opportunities for solitude in a very pretty setting, and is thus highly recommended as a place to camp for a night or more. The only thing lacking from these ponds is fish: because of the pond's altitude, they were apparently among the first to be affected by acid precipitation.

Leaving the Indian Pass Trail (trail 75) at the stone dam (0 mi.), the trail goes R (W) and crosses Indian Pass Brook just below the old spillway. Climbing the steep bank on the far side, the trail joins an old tote road and begins a steady, moderate climb to a flat area at 0.5 mi. Dropping slightly, the trail crosses a small stream and climbs again to a height of land at 1.1 mi. The trail now drops slightly, flattens out, and then drops more steeply to a trail sign at 1.5 mi. with Scott Pond visible beyond. Just past this sign, a side trail goes R and steeply down 30 yds. to a possible campsite at the inlet. The trail now drops down to the old dam at the outlet and bears L and down the L bank a few yards to a crossing at 1.6 mi. The trail now goes steeply up the R bank and swings back R to the other side of the old dam. (It may be possible to cross the dam itself in low water.)

The trail now skirts the shore but quickly veers away to the L. (There are more possible campsites on this shore beyond the point where the trail leaves the shore.) Climbing to an open area, the trail crosses it, skirts a second open swampy area on the L and then climbs, steeply at times, to a ridge at 2.2 mi. Dropping now, the trail passes a small pond on the L at 2.3 mi., and then swings R and down to a large open area with a small pond at one end at 2.4 mi.

Here is an outstanding view of the MacIntyre Range perfectly framed by the valley at the end of the pond. Bearing L, the trail enters the woods and climbs to an extremely wet area. There are now (thanks to volunteers from the Adirondack 46ers) just enough logs and bridges to make this section passable to Wallface Pond at 2.8 mi. From the shore of this attractive large pond there are views of MacNaughton. A vague trail leads L 150 yds. from this spot to an attractive point.

Distances: Scott's Dam to Scott Pond, 1.5 mi.; to Wallface Pond, 2.8 mi. (4.5 km). (6.9 mi. from Heart Lake.)

(77) Mt. Jo   Map: D-8

On the N shore of Heart Lake is Mt. Jo, a small but steep and rocky peak rising 710 ft. above the lake. It was named in 1877 by Henry Van Hoevenberg in honor of his fiancee, Josephine Schofield. There are two routes to its summit, both of which begin from the Indian Pass Trail. From the parking lot at the High Peaks Information Center at the end of Adirondak Loj Road, return to the road and turn R 100 yds. to the trail signs at the start of the Indian Pass Trail. (Note: parking is not permitted on this section of the road.)

Leaving the road (0 mi.), the trail proceeds on the flat to a road next to Heart Lake. Turn R 30 yds., find the sign for Mt. Jo, turn R again and climb moderately up to a junction where the Long Trail and Short Trail split at 0.3 mi. The Long Trail goes L and is 0.3 mi. longer, but less strenuous. Taking the Long Trail, proceed along a side hill practically on the level before turning R and up at 0.6 mi. Climbing over some rocks, the trail turns sharp L and then starts swinging back to the R to a trail junction at 0.7 mi. (Trail L with blue paint blazes leads to the W property line which can be followed back down to the Old Nye Ski Trail and thence back to Heart Lake.)

The Mt. Jo Trail bears R and climbs to a lookout on the R at 0.9 mi., and at 1.0 mi. The Short Trail enters on the R. Just after this junction, a side trail leads L and up a rock step to the W summit. Continuing to the R on the flat to the base of the summit rocks, the trail reaches the summit at 1.1 mi. From the summit the views are impressive, reaching from Cascade to Marcy to Algonquin to Indian Pass, making this one of the best views for the least effort in the Adirondacks.

The Short Trail which diverges R at the junction at 0.3 mi. climbs through some boulders and then up a gully to a sharp L turn at 0.6 mi. The trail ascends to a good view at 0.7 mi. and then joins the Long Trail at 0.7 mi. Turn R to reach the summit at 0.9 mi.

Distances: Adirondak Loj Road to junction of Short and Long Trails, 0.3 mi.; to summit via Long Trail, 1.1 mi. (1.6 km); to summit via Short Trail, 0.9 mi. (1.4 km). Elevation, 2876 ft.

South Meadow

South Meadow is a clearing that can be reached by auto from Adirondak Loj Road. There are many primitive but attractive campsites along the road (look for camping markers) and at the end of the road, which is also the start for the Klondike Notch Trail and the South Meadow Truck Trail to Marcy Dam. The dirt road, which is marked with DEC trail signs, starts 3.8 mi. S of Rt. 73 on Adirondak Loj Road and 1.0 mi. N of Adirondak Loj. It leads 0.9 mi. to a fork, with the R fork leading to the Truck Trail and the L fork leading to the best camping areas and the start of the Klondike Notch Trail (trail 12).

(78) South Meadow to Marcy Dam   Map: D-8

This fire truck trail is a graded gravel road offering an alternative route to Marcy Dam that is only about 0.3 mi. longer than the approach from Heart Lake. It was constructed by the Civilian Conservation Corps in the 1930s. Because this area is now classified as wilderness, even DEC vehicles are prohibited from using this road except in the event of an emergency. This route can be especially recommended during the raspberry season.

From the junction 0.9 mi. from Adirondak Loj Road (see above), bear R and down to a small parking area at a bar gate and trail register. Leaving the gate (0 mi.), the road crosses South Meadow Brook and proceeds along the flat to a junction with the Mr. Van Ski Trail (trail 80) at 0.3 mi. The road now begins a short climb, and after several more ascents and descents crosses a large brook at 1.6 mi. At 2.0 mi. the road dips down to the R, crosses another large brook, and climbs back before dropping down two pitches to the R bank of Marcy Brook at 2.3 mi. The road now continues straight up a gradual grade along the brook to the Van Hoevenberg Trail (trail 61) at Marcy Dam at 2.6 mi.

Trail in winter: As a gravel road, this is a favorite ski tour from early in the season to late and is the the preferred access for skiers to Mt. Marcy and Avalanche Pass. If South Meadow Rd. is plowed, there will be a generous parking area at the end of the road, 200 yds. beyond the side road leading to the gate at the start of the truck trail. An easy trail leads directly from this large parking area to the gate.

Distance: Parking area at trail register to Marcy Dam, 2.6 mi. (4.2 km).

(79) Mt. Van Hoevenberg from South Meadow Road   Map: D-8

Mt. Van Hoevenberg is a low mountain rising above South Meadow and offering a spectacular view of the high peaks and Lake Placid. Originally called South Mt., its name was changed in 1932 when the

Olympic Bobsled Run was built on its north side. Hiking over the mountain and down the N side offers the unique opportunity to see the Olympic Bobsled and Luge runs as well as enjoy the fine view.

The trail starts from the South Meadow Road 0.3 mi. from the Adirondak Loj Road and is marked with blue DEC disks. Starting on an old road blocked by a bar gate, the trail proceeds on the level until it dips down to cross a wet area at 0.9 mi. After climbing a bit and dipping again to cross a small stream, the trail begins climbing steadily, first L across the slope and then R and under some small cliffs before arriving at a height of land at 1.6 mi.

From here, the trail climbs the W ridge of Mt. Van Hoevenberg to the first open ledges at 2.1 mi., where there are views of Marcy, Algonquin, and Lake Placid. These first ledges offer perhaps the best views, but the trail continues on to the summit ledge at 2.2 mi., with a view further to the E including Porter and Giant.

To continue down the N side, turn sharp L at the summit ledge. The trail soon begins descending through thick woods and joins the upper end of an old road at 2.3 mi. This point was the original start of the Bobsled Run when it was 1.5 mi. long. The run was shortened to 1 mi. in length in 1936 because greater speeds by technically superior sleds had made the longer run unsafe. (The run was again shortened, to 1,500 meters, in 1990 for the same reason.) There are occasional traces of the old run L. Passing through a small clearing at the end of a newer gravel road, the trail comes to the upper end of the Bobsled Run at 2.8 mi.

Turning L, the trail follows the spectator walkway down the R side of the Bobsled Run, coming to the famous Shady Curve at 3.3 mi. and a small grandstand at Zig-Zag Curves at 3.6 mi., with the Luge Run visible to the R. The trail reaches the foot of the run at 3.8 mi. The parking lot on the other side of the gate is at the end of the access road that branches off from Rt. 73 3.0 mi. E of the Adirondak Loj Road. One could start the climb from the Bobsled Run side of Mt. Van Hoevenberg, but there is a fee charged ($1.00 to $2.50 in 1992 depending on the services offered that day) to enter through the gate at the base of the run.

Distances: South Meadow Road to summit of Mt. Van Hoevenberg, 2.2 mi. (3.5 km). To foot of Bobsled Run, 3.8 mi. (6.1 km). Ascent, 740 ft. (225 m). Elevation, 2860 ft. (872 m).

(80) The Mr. Van Ski Trail   Map: D-8

The Mr. Van Ski Trail was named after Henry Van Hoevenberg, builder of the original Adirondack Lodge. It provides a useful connection between the ski trails around Adirondak Loj and the cross-country center at Mt. Van Hoevenberg. It is used mostly by skiers, since the first section of the trail between Adirondak Loj and the South Meadow Truck Trail crosses several beaver flows that make the trail wet at any time, and nearly impassable after heavy rains. It is described from Adirondak Loj to Mt. Van Hoevenberg because that is the easiest direction in which to ski it. Those who follow this trail in reverse direction should be aware that finding one's way through the complex of cross-country trails to Hi-Notch can be confusing. (See notes at the end of this description.)

Starting at the parking lot at the High Peaks Information Center at Adirondak Loj, the Mr. Van Trail proceeds along the Marcy Trail for 175 yds. to a junction where the Mr. Van Trail goes sharp L. Proceeding through a thick spruce forest on the level, the trail passes a junction with the "Easy Side" ski trail and begins to descend gradually to Marcy Brook, which it reaches at 0.7 mi. Crossing the brook on a bridge, the trail continues across the generally open alder swamp, with views of Colden and Algonquin, to the first of two beaver dams at 1.0 mi. Crossing these dams, the trail reaches the South Meadow Truck Trail (trail 78) at 1.3 mi.

Crossing the truck trail, the Mr. Van Trail continues mostly on the flat to a point near the base of a new (1979) slide coming down off a shoulder at Phelps at 1.9 mi. Just beyond this point, the trail reaches the Klondike Trail (trail 12) and turns R for approximately 250 yds. along the Klondike Trail. Diverging L at 2.1 mi., the trail soon crosses Klondike Brook and continues with short ups and downs along a side hill to the Mr. Van Lean-to at 3.6 mi. Immediately crossing South Meadow Brook on a bridge, the trail crosses some flat, swampy ground before beginning a steady, moderate climb to Hi-Notch, which it reaches at 4.7 mi.

Hi-Notch is the edge of the Mt. Van Hoevenberg Cross-Country Area, and the Mr. Van Trail now follows wide, graded ski trails. Bearing L, the trail descends to a sharp L turn, passes straight through the first junction, continues to descend to a second junction (#35), and then descends gradually to a junction (#36) at 5.3 mi. Here skiers should follow the "Stadium" signs to the L to maintain one-way traffic, but hikers can save some distance by bearing R and down. Continue straight through the next junction (#4) and finally arrive at the bottom of the descent at 5.6 mi. at a small open area. From here, bear L on a very wide trail leading to the Cross-Country Stadium. The parking lot is at the far end of the stadium at 6.0 mi. This parking lot is 200 yds. from the entrance to the Bobsled Run and the end of the access road which leaves Rt. 73 3.0 mi. E of the Adirondak Loj Road.

Following this trail from the Mt. Van Hoevenberg end, in summer especially, is considerably more difficult, but by heading generally uphill and SE one should be able to arrive at Hi-Notch where the Mr. Van Trail leaves the developed cross-country trail system.

Distances: Adirondak Loj to South Meadow Truck Trail, 1.3 mi.; to Mr. Van Lean-to, 3.6 mi.; to Mt. Van Hoevenberg Cross-Country Area, 6.0 mi. (9.6 km).

Northern Section

This section includes those trails formerly included in the Saranac Lake and Lake Placid sections of previous editions of this guidebook, plus those trails W of the East Branch of the Ausable River formerly included in the Cascade-Keene-Hurricane section. There is also a description of the Northville-Lake Placid Trail from Averyville Rd. to Duck Hole which was formerly included in a separate section on the N-P Trail. This region is dominated by Whiteface Mt., but there are many other excellent summits and ponds, most of them relatively uncrowded.

Both Saranac Lake and Lake Placid have been popular resort areas for many years, and little needs to be added here about Lake Placid's role in hosting the 1932 and 1980 Winter Olympics. To provide hiking opportunities for the early visitors to the Lake Placid area, the Adirondack Camp and Trail Club, initiated by Henry Van Hoevenberg in 1910, began to construct a system of formally marked and regularly maintained trails with shelters available along them. This system allowed far greater numbers of people to hike in the mountains, because getting lost was less of a problem and an overnight pack could be considerably lighter. Although no one can claim that Henry Van Hoevenberg "invented" such facilities for hikers, in this area at least he is the one who deserves the credit for starting the current system of trails and shelters (now maintained by the DEC) that most hikers take for granted.

This northern region offers a great variety of hikes, particularly easy to moderate ones, and many of them should be more popular than they are. Below are a few recommended hikes.

Short Hikes:

Owls Head—1.1-mi. round trip. A near-perfect little hike for children, with views starting almost immediately, plenty of blueberries, and a great view from the summit.

Baker Mt.—1.7-mi. round trip. The same could be said about Baker as about Owls Head, except that one must wait a little longer for the first view.

See also—Table of Short Hikes in Appendix III.

Moderate Hikes:

Pitchoff Mt.—4.9-mi. point to point. A wonderful hike along a long, rocky ridge with two possible shorter destinations.

Ampersand Mt.—5.4-mi. round trip. The truly commanding view from this bald summit is good enough to make one forget the very steep spots on the way up.

Harder Hikes:

Whiteface via Whiteface Landing and Connery Pond Trail—7.0-mi. round-trip hiking distance plus 6-mi. round-trip paddling. Surely the most civilized way to do this very civilized peak is to paddle from the boat launching site at the S end of Lake Placid to Whiteface Landing and then ascend the peak. Great views from both the lake and summit. See general description of Whiteface for paddling information and Whiteface Mt. from Connery Pond Trail for hiking description.

Whiteface Mt.

Standing alone over 10 mi. to the N of any other 4000-ft. peak, Whiteface and its lower companion, Esther, are an important sight from any viewpoint. Equally impressive are the views from the summit. Lake Placid and its heavily wooded island are directly below, with the rest of the high peaks arrayed beyond, while to the N and E Lake Champlain and Mount Royal in Canada are visible. Even with the intrusions of the summit buildings and the accompanying throngs of tourists, there is still a magnificent wilderness view from this summit.

Geologically, Whiteface is unique in that its anorthosite granite welled up from the earth from a separate source from the rest of the high peaks. More recently, geologically, mountain glaciers clung to its higher slopes long enough in the aftermath of the last ice age to create the most distinct alpine features to be found on any Adirondack peak. On the N, W, and E faces of Whiteface are well-defined bowl-shaped cirque valleys with sharp aretes separating the cirques. The walkway from the top of the highway ascends the sharpest of these aretes, while the Wilmington Trail ascends another.

Whiteface has also seen more development than any other high peak; it now has a paved two-lane highway, a major ski area, and a complete summit weather observatory. Beginning in Wilmington, the Memorial Highway is a toll road leading to within 300 vertical feet of the summit. From here there is an elevator to the summit as well as an improved stone walkway up the spectacular NW arete. The summit observatory provides weather information for local and national forecasters as well as providing a base for atmospheric research on such phenomena as acid precipitation.

Opened in 1956, the present Whiteface Mt. Ski Center replaced the original, smaller development on Marble Mt. Expanded several times since 1956, the ski center was the site for the alpine events at the 1980 Winter Olympics.

There are two hiking trails to the summit of Whiteface. One ascends steeply from Connery Pond and Lake Placid, with another coming from Wilmington. An only slightly harder, and in many ways more scenic approach, is via boat to Whiteface landing on Lake Placid and then up the peak via the Connery Pond Trail. There is a boat launching site at the S end of Lake Placid located on Mirror Lake Dr., 0.6 mi. N from the Hilton Hotel at the end of Main St. As of 1992 there were no canoes available for rent on Lake Placid, but several locations on Mirror Lake in downtown Lake Placid do rent canoes. One can also inquire at the marina adjacent to the state boat launching site about chartering a boat, but prices are likely to be prohibitive, except for a large group.

Trails in winter: Unless otherwise noted, the trails in this section are too steep or rough to be suitable for anything but snowshoeing. Steeper trails may require crampons, and the exposed summits of Cascade or Whiteface may require a face mask and goggles in windy conditions. The Jackrabbit Ski Trail, begun in 1986, traverses this section. Mention is made when this trail follows any of the summer hiking routes. This trail is not, however, a continuous summer hiking trail as it crosses several golf courses and a number of wet areas along its 24-mile route between Keene and Saranac Lake.

(81) Whiteface Mt. via Connery Pond and Whiteface Landing

Map: D-5

Trailhead: This trail starts on Rt. 86, 3.1 mi. E from its junction with Rt. 73 in Lake Placid and 0.2 mi. W of the bridge over the West Branch of the Ausable River. From the small DEC sign on the highway, turn down a narrow dirt road marked with red DEC disks. Drive down the road and bear L at 0.5 mi. to a parking area marked with signs about 70 yds. farther. (Trail R at this point is a newly-established fishing access point to Connery Pond.)

From the parking lot (0 mi.) continue on the road, bearing L after 130 yds. to avoid a private residence. The trail now skirts the NW shore of Connery Pond on an old road, before it bears away from the pond and climbs to a junction with another road at 0.4 mi., where the Connery Pond Trail bears L and down to a bar gate. This is the start of an old truck trail used to salvage timber in the aftermath of the 1950 hurricane.

From the gate the road is at first on the level, but slowly begins climbing to a height of land at 1.4 mi., after which it gently descends to a junction at 2.5 mi. (Trail L leads 110 yds. to Whiteface Landing on Lake Placid. Trail straight ahead is a now-abandoned Shore Owners Association trail around N side of Lake Placid; see explanation between trails 96 and 97.) Turning R, the trail climbs gently to a straight section of old road at 3.1 mi., with Whiteface in view directly ahead. The trail now drops down to the L to cross Whiteface Brook, which it recrosses three times before arriving at Whiteface Lean-to above the L bank of the brook at 3.6 mi.

Turning L here, the grade steepens as the trail climbs above the L bank, bearing away from the brook at about 4.5 mi. The grades are now easy to moderate for a short stretch, but soon the grade becomes mostly steep to a short breather where there is a view to the S at 5.6 mi. Reaching timberline at 5.8 mi., the trail is now marked with yellow paint blazes and climbs steeply over numerous ledges to the S summit. The actual summit is a few yards farther at 6.0 mi.

Trail in winter: Suitable for skiing for novices as far as Whiteface Landing. In most conditions the recommended parking is at Rt. 86, making for a 6-mi. round trip to Whiteface landing.

Distances: Parking area at Connery Pond to junction at Whiteface landing, 2.5 mi.; to Whiteface Lean-to, 3.6 mi.; to summit of Whiteface, 6.0 mi. (9.7 km). Ascent from Connery Pond, 3232 ft. (985 m). Elevation, 4867 ft. (1483 m). Order of height, 5.

(82) Whiteface Mt. via Wilmington Trail   Map: E-3

Trailhead: This trail branches L from the Whiteface Memorial Highway 0.6 mi. from Rt. 86 in Wilmington on a dirt road marked with a small DEC sign. At the Town of Wilmington Reservoir 0.2 mi. up this road there is a parking area on the R, just before a sign that promises that any car parked beyond will be towed.

From the parking area (0 mi.), bear L and cross the brook below the dam on a good bridge and then turn R and up the R bank of the brook. The trail slowly veers away from the brook, crossing an old road at 0.3 mi. Continuing to veer L, the trail soon heads S along a side hill practically on the level through an open maple and oak forest.

Finally, reaching the S side of a ridge, the trail turns R at 1.4 mi. and begins a steady, steep climb which continues to the summit of Marble Mt. at 2.2 mi. Here the unofficial route from the base of the old Marble Mt. Ski Area comes in from the R. The summit rocks on Marble Mt. can be reached by an overgrown trail which branches L a few feet from this junction. It is 150 yds. to the top of the former T-bar lift, where there are views to the S and E.

Continuing on the level with a view of Esther straight ahead, the trail soon begins to climb and comes to a steep stretch of bare rock at 2.4 mi. The trail bears L a few feet up this rock, but there are good views of Esther, the Wilmington Range, and to the N and E, by continuing straight ahead on the rock for 75 yds. (It is easy to miss the sharp L turn at the lower edge of these rocks.) After turning L, the trail climbs with alternating steep and level pitches to a flat area at an old toboggan shelter on the L at 3.3 mi. with a good view of Whiteface straight ahead.

The entire plateau ahead was once covered with a network of ski trails, including one to the summit of Esther, and there are many old signs along this section of trail marking the former (and now indiscernible) junctions with these trails. At the upper end of this plateau there was a series of two small rope tows leading up to the Wilmington Turn on the Memorial Highway. In the days before snowmaking was common at ski areas, these rope tows were a high altitude back-up in the event that the snow was insufficient at lower Marble Mt.—an occurrence much more frequent than the Lake Placid Chamber of Commerce would have cared to admit. Skiers were trucked up the road and at the end of the day had the option of skiing back down the highway or descending via a ski trail that followed very closely the route of the current hiking trail.

From this first view of Whiteface, the trail drops gently to the junction at 3.4 mi. with the unmarked trail leading right to Esther (see below). The trail now continues generally down until crosses a wet area on several log bridges at 4.0 mi., after which it is flat for a short ways before climbing again. Now the trail goes steeply up an old ski tow line before diverging L and coming to the base of the wall of Wilmington Turn, which is skirted on the L over large boulders to the Memorial Highway at 4.8 mi. The trail now climbs the steep ledge to the L and proceeds through small trees to timberline at 4.9 mi. The final climb along the arete is spectacular, with fresh slides visible down to the L and the top of the Whiteface Ski Center chairlift further to the L. Veering L of the summit buildings, the trail arrives at the summit at 5.2 mi.

Distances: Parking area at Wilmington reservoir to summit of Marble Mt., 2.2 mi.; to unmarked trail to Esther Mt., 3.4 mi.; to summit of Whiteface, 5.2 mi. (8.3 km). Ascent from parking area, 3620 ft. (1103 m). Elevation, 4867 ft. (1483). Order of height, 5.

(83) Old Marble Mt. Ski Area Approach to Wilmington Trail   Map: E-3

An unofficial and unmarked variation to the Wilmington Trail starts at the Atmospheric Sciences Research Center 2.4 mi. up the Whiteface Highway. Hikers should drive around the turn-around and park on the R on the exit road at an old road. Head down this road a few yards, turn L, and descend to a radio tower at the base of the old T-bar line which is followed almost to the top of Marble Mt. The route turns R just before the top and in a few yards joins the Wilmington Trail. This route has no official signs or markers (save perhaps a sign directing hikers where to park) and the turn off the Wilmington Trail can be hard to find on the descent.

Unmaintained Trail to Esther

(see Peaks Without Maintained Trails in Introduction)

This major peak N of Whiteface has in the past been listed as a peak with a trail in the Lake Placid section of this guidebook. However, the ski trails once cut to its summit are now so overgrown that they are somewhat difficult to follow—showing that nature "reclaims its own" rapidly when humans do not interfere by maintaining trails.

This most northern of the major Adirondack peaks was named for Esther McComb, who in 1839 at the age of 15, while trying to climb Whiteface from the N, became lost and made the first recorded ascent of this mountain instead. A tablet to her memory was placed on the summit by the Forty-Sixers in 1939.

Take the Wilmington-Whiteface Trail (trail 82) to the junction at 3.4 mi. where the latter trail begins to flank the sides of the hump known as Lookout Mountain. Leaving the red-marked trail where an old illegible sign points NW, a herd path to Esther ascends to the summit of Lookout Mountain at 0.4 mi. where a ski lodge once stood. From here, the route to Esther descends into a col at 0.7 mi. and continues N along the ridge to Esther's summit at 1.3 mi. from the Whiteface Trail.

(84) Cooper Kiln Pond Trail   Map: E-3

This is an interesting walk through a notch between the Stephenson and Wilmington ranges to a seldom-visited pond with a lean-to. This pond has also been called Cooper "Kill" Pond on the USGS maps, but the name on the DEC signs is used here. The route is probably more often skied than hiked because it offers an exceptional downhill run of nearly 2000 ft. and a net drop of over 1000 ft.

Trailhead: Start on the Franklin Falls Road, found by driving 2.8 mi. up the Whiteface Memorial Highway from Rt. 86 in Wilmington and then turning R just before the toll house. There is a DEC sign on the R 0.7 mi. from the Memorial Highway.

Leaving the road (0 mi.), the trail climbs briefly, turns L and proceeds on the flat on a good road. At 0.2 mi. the trail bears R and begins a gentle climb to an open area at 0.3 mi. The climbing continues easy to moderate with some eroded sections to a bridge over a small brook at 1.6 mi. Here the climbing steepens a bit before easing off near a height of land at 1.8 mi.

Beginning to descend at 2.2 mi., the trail reaches the outlet to Cooper Kiln Pond at 2.7 mi., with the lean-to (mis-located on the 1978 USGS map) just beyond the outlet. The pond itself is approximately 1/4 mi. long, with some large rocks that make nice picnic spots near the E shore. Swimming is possible but hardly ideal from these rocks, and fishing is problematical, given the size and altitude of the pond; but this is a picturesque spot far from the populated trade routes, and solitude is just about guaranteed.

To continue past the pond, turn sharp R at the lean-to and descend to a crossing of the outlet at 2.8 mi. The trail ascends a short, steep bank and turns L onto an overgrown tote road that has been marked as a snowmobile trail. Following this old road, the trail crosses the outlet again at 3.3 mi. and two additional times, ending up on the L bank at 3.7 mi., where it veers L away from the brook and comes to a good jeep trail at 3.9 mi. Joining another jeep trail coming in from the L at 4.2 mi., the route (still marked with snowmobile trail markers) turns R and down. Passing several other side roads, the grade slowly flattens out as the trail crosses a large stream at 5.4 mi. and levels out shortly thereafter. The trail reaches Bonnieview Rd. in Wilmington at 5.9 mi. This point is 3.2 mi. N of Rt. 86 in the center of Wilmington and 2.9 mi. S of the Silver Lake Road leading W from Ausable Forks.

Trailhead in winter: At least a foot of snow is desirable before trying to ski this route, and the terrain is suitable only for "adventurous" intermediate skiers or better.

Distances: Franklin Falls Rd. to Cooper Kiln Pond Lean-to, 2.7 mi. (4.4 km); to Bonnieview Rd., 5.9 mi. (9.5 km).

(85) Catamount Mt.   Map: E-2

Catamount is one of the most spectacular small peaks in the Adirondacks. Much of the mountain's steep S side is bare as a result of first cutting for charcoal and later burning. The trail is not marked or maintained, but it remains relatively easy to follow. Be careful, however, on the many open ledges, as the old paint blazes are fading and the cairns are few.

Trailhead: The start is now a few hundred yards N of the original tote road start in order to keep this route entirely on state land. From Rt. 86 in the center of Wilmington, go up the Whiteface Memorial Highway for 2.8 mi. and turn R on the Franklin Falls Rd., which is followed for 3.3 mi. to another R turn. Follow this road 0.8 mi. and turn R again onto Forestdale Rd., from which the mountain is soon visible. At 2.2 mi. down this road, on a short straight stretch at the bottom of a small hill, there is a vague path marked by some old orange surveyor's tape. This is the start of the trail. (This point is also 6.2 mi. S of the Silver Lake Rd. running W from Ausable Forks.)

Leaving the road (0 mi.), the narrow trail is level to a well-marked property corner post at 0.3 mi. After this corner the trail follows an orange painted property line straight across an old field. At the far end of the old field, at 0.6 mi., do not follow the orange property line, but instead turn R and enter the woods at the far corner of the field. The trail soon begins to climb steeply before dipping briefly to cross a small brook at 0.8 mi. The trail now climbs at moderate to steep grades over several ledges to a balanced boulder at 1.3 mi. Soon thereafter, a steep rock scramble up the S summit begins, ending with a nearly vertical chimney in the rock. Reaching the S summit at 1.5 mi., the trail dips slightly through thick trees to the col and then climbs to the summit at 1.8 mi. The views from the summit are expansive and dominated by Whiteface Mt., Taylor

Pond and Silver Lake. In season, the blueberries are almost as good as the views.

Distance: Road to summit of Catamount, 1.8 mi. (2.9 km). Ascent from road, 1542 ft. (466 m). Elevation, 3168 ft. (966 m).

(86) Silver Lake Mt.   (Page map)

This peak is located about 10 mi. N of Whiteface on the road running from Ausable Forks to Silver Lake and Clayburg. The attractions of this peak are the rocky ledges on the summit, which offer wonderful views of Whiteface, Silver Lake and Taylor Pond, as well as the many blueberries in season.

Trailhead: The start is 0.8 mi. E of Silver Lake at a point where the power and telephone lines cross the road. There is a DEC sign at the entrance to a grassy road.

Leaving the road (0 mi.), the trail is level for a few yards before climbing moderately to an open area at 0.3 mi., where the grade eases a bit. From here there are frequent red DEC markers. Soon after this open area, the grade again becomes moderate, with a lookout on the L at 0.5 mi. and another at 0.7 mi. where the trail turns sharp R just before reaching two angular boulders on the ledge. From here, the trail climbs steeply up a ridge with ever-expanding views to the summit at 0.9 mi. A vague trail continues over the summit, but this fades out within 0.3 mi. before reaching the first col on the ridge. For the adventurous, however, there are many more ledges on this more than 2-mi. ridge.

Distance: Road to summit of Silver Lake Mt., 0.9 mi. (1.5 km). Ascent from road, 900 ft. (275 m). Elevation, 2374 ft. (724 m).

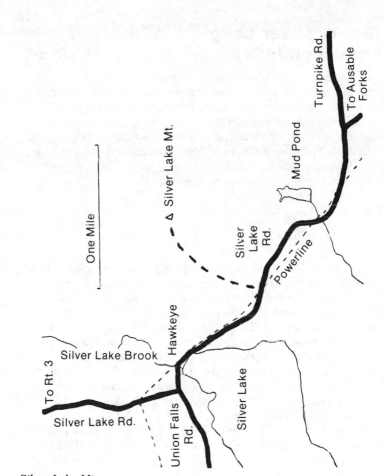

Silver Lake Mt.
Base map is Redford quadrangle, 7.5 min. series, 1968.

(86-A) Silver Lake
Snowmobile Trail   Map: E-1

Although used mostly in winter by snowmobiles, this trail provides some pleasant walking and access to the bushwhack route up Douglass Mt. and its fine views of Taylor Pond, Silver Lake, and Whiteface Mt. One can also use this trail to reach the state-owned shoreline of Silver Lake, but the distance is too great to provide boat access. In the future, some of the badly overgrown roads connecting this trail with the Taylor Pond Trail (trail 103) may be cleared to make for a number of possible excursions in this area. Distances are estimated.

Trailhead: Start on a private road directly across from the Silver Lake Mt. trailhead (see trail 86). Foot travel, but no public vehicular traffic, is permitted on this road.

From Silver Lake Road (0 mi.) the private road is mostly flat to a junction at 0.5 mi. with an old jeep road going straight ahead. Turn R to another junction at about 1.0 mi. Here the trail goes sharp L and up to another old road at 1.2 mi. Turning L, the trail generally slabs a side hill to a junction with an overgrown road going L at 1.8 mi. (This road leads over the N shoulder of Douglass Mt. to Taylor Pond and provides the best route up Douglass Mt.) Continuing on, the trail passes two roads leading R to the state-owned shoreline on Silver Lake before swinging to the SE and reaching a junction at 3.0 mi. (Overgrown road L leads S of Douglass Mt. to Taylor Pond.)

Turning R and swinging to the W, the trail is flat or slightly down to a junction with a jeep road leading R at 4.3 mi. Bearing L, the trail reaches another junction at 4.7 mi. Turning R here on a newer trail, it reaches the E shore of Union Falls Pond (actually a large artificial lake) at 5.3 mi.

Trail in winter: This route receives moderate to heavy snowmobile use, making it less than ideal as a ski tour although the terrain makes for generally easy skiing. In winter one can make this a point-to-point trip by crossing the ice and following the continuation of the snowmobile trail up to the road on the W shore of Union Falls Pond.

Distance: Silver Lake Road to Union Falls Pond, 5.3 mi.

(87) Owen, Copperas and Winch Ponds   Map: E-5

This scenic trio of ponds offers some very pleasant walking with little climbing, good views, and ample opportunities for swimming, picnicking, and camping in the lean-to on Copperas Pond. Their easy accessibility makes these ponds some of the most popular destinations in the Lake Placid area.

Trailheads: There are two starts from Rt. 86 in Wilmington Notch, approximately 1 mi. apart. Both approaches are marked with small DEC signs. The easier approach is the southerly one, located 5 mi. from the junction with Rt. 73 in Lake Placid and 3.9 mi. S of the entrance to Whiteface Mt. Ski Center.

Leaving the road (0 mi.) at the southerly approach, the blue-marked trail leads gradually up near the R bank of Owen Pond Brook and comes to the NW corner of Owen Pond at 0.6 mi. The trail follows the shore to the NE corner at 0.7 mi., where it veers away to the L as it climbs a few easy grades and then a steeper one at 1.0 mi. Swinging R at the top of this grade, the trail soon descends and reaches a former lean-to site on the shore of Copperas Pond at 1.3 mi. From here there is an excellent view of Whiteface Mt.

Passing behind the lean-to, the trail immediately crosses the outlet and continues along the shore to a junction at 1.4 mi., where the yellow-marked trail to Winch Pond turns R. (This trail climbs a short pitch, after which there are several gradual ups and downs to Winch Pond at 1.9 mi.) Continuing straight ahead, the blue trail follows the shore to a junction at 1.6 mi. (Trail straight ahead leads 0.1 mi. along the shoreline to the Copperas Lean-to.) The blue trail now turns R and climbs to a height of land, and descends to a junction at 1.8 mi. (Red trail R leads 0.5 mi. to Winch Pond. Using this approach to Winch Pond from the N end of the blue trail, it is 0.7 mi. from the highway to the pond.) The blue trail now continues down, becoming rocky and eroded in spots, and reaches the highway at 2.0 mi.

Trail in winter: Although this trail is rough and needs a foot or more of snow, Copperas Pond is a worthwhile destination. The steep hill between Copperas and Owen ponds can be avoided by a bushwhack through open woods near the outlet to Copperas Pond.

Distances: Highway at S approach to Owen Pond, 0.6 mi.; to Copperas Pond (S shore), 1.3 mi. (2.1 km); to Winch Pond, 1.9 mi. Highway at N approach to Copperas Pond (N shore), 0.5 mi.; to Winch Pond, 0.7 mi.

The Sentinel Range

Running for nearly 10 miles NE and SW between the valleys of the East and West Branches of the Ausable River, the Sentinel Range is the major feature of the 23,000-acre Sentinel Wilderness Area. The three major peaks, Stewart, Kilburn and Sentinel, lack significant views and thus have seen little hiker traffic over the years. The best views are from 3893-ft. Mt. Kilburn, which can best be approached from the North Notch Trail. Stewart and Sentinel offer some views in the winter when the snow pack raises hikers above the level of the smaller balsams and permits some interesting views out through the numerous blowdown areas. The only real rocky peak with a view is a 2080-ft. eastern shoulder of Sentinel called Cobble Mt., which offers views of the valley of the E Branch of the Ausable as well as of Cascade and other peaks. Cobble Mt. has no trail, but can be approached from Bartlett Rd. running between Keene and Upper Jay.

For those wishing to explore the central part of the Sentinel Range, there are two trails that penetrate from the western edge of the area. These trails are all that is left of the ski trail system constructed for the 1932 Olympics, which once went through North Notch and South Notch and connected near Keene to form a long loop. The maintained portions of both these trails are still skiable, and the adventurous skier can try a traverse of either of these notches when the snowpack is deep enough.

(88) North Notch   Map D-6

The North Notch Trail is currently maintained for 2.7 mi., stopping approximately 0.5 mi. below the top of the notch. The grades are easy to moderate throughout.

Trailhead: The start is on River Rd. near Lake Placid, 1.0 mi. S of Rt. 86 and 3.0 mi. N of Rt. 73. There is a sizeable turnout on the E side of the road at a small iron bridge over a small brook.

Leaving the road (0 mi.) and marked with red DEC disks, the trail follows an old tote road along the R bank of the brook for 100 yds. before turning sharp L and up away from the tote road to avoid a large swampy area. Gaining higher ground, the trail swings sharp R and parallels the brook before dipping to cross it on a bridge at 0.4 mi. Soon climbing to higher ground again, the trail swings L and rejoins the tote road beyond the swamp at 0.8 mi., just after recrossing the stream.

Turning R the trail begins to climb at an easy grade. Crossing a small stream at 1.4 mi., it encounters a short, flat, wet area before resuming a steady gradual to moderate climb which eases off at 2.3 mi. Shortly afterwards, the trail crosses another small stream and climbs in gradual stages to the sign announcing the end of the maintained trail at 2.7 mi., at the R bank of a sizeable brook.

Distance: River Rd. to end of maintained trail, 2.7 mi. (4.3 km). Ascent from River Rd., 1200 ft. (365 m).

(89) South Notch   Map: D-6

The South Notch Trail leads 2.8 mi. to an old and barely serviceable lean-to located approximately 0.5 mi. below the top of South Notch. The grades are easy to moderate throughout. Although this trail offers some very pleasant walking, particularly the 0.8-mi. section next to a pretty brook with moss-covered rocks, the upper part is overgrown and difficult to follow.

Trailhead: The trail starts on River Rd. near Lake Placid, 2.0 mi. N of Rt. 73 and 2.0 mi. S of Rt. 86. The start is also 1.0 mi. S of the North Notch Trail and just N of the entrance to St. Francis Academy (Camelot), an Episcopal church-run boys' home. There is a sign marking the chained-off road.

Marked with red DEC disks, the trail leaves River Rd. (0 mi.) on a flat, grassy road in an open field and passes two bridges on the R. At the second bridge, the trail swings L and up and climbs to a private lean-to on the L at 0.3 mi. Now nearly on the flat, the trail enters state land at 0.4 mi. and soon reaches the R bank of a brook, which it follows closely for over 0.8 mi., crossing the brook three times on bridges in varying states of disrepair.

After the third crossing at 1.4 mi., the trail climbs away from the brook and swings sharp R approximately 150 ft. after leaving the brook. The trail now climbs at a steady, moderate grade until another sharp R at 2.3 mi. Now on the level on a side hill, the trail crosses a height of land at 2.4 mi. and drops slightly before resuming a gradual climb to the South Notch Lean-to at 2.8 mi.

Distance: River Rd. to South Notch Lean-to, 2.8 mi. (4.4 km). Ascent from River Rd. 1100 ft. (335 m).

(90) Cascade Mt. from Cascade Lakes   Map: E-8

As the easiest of all the 4000-ft. peaks to ascend, this bald summit attracts many hikers in all seasons to enjoy its marvelous views of the other peaks and the Champlain Valley. Once called Long Pond Mt., Cascade is named for the steep falls which tumbles down between the two Cascade Lakes. The current trail follows a route laid out in 1974 by the Algonquin Chapter of ADK to replace the old trail, which was steep and badly eroded. It follows the SW ridge on generally moderate grades with only a few steeper pitches, making this a very enjoyable hike.

Trailhead: The trail starts on Rt. 73, 6.8 mi. from Keene and 4.5 mi. from Adirondak Loj Road, and is marked with red DEC disks.

Parking can be a problem on popular weekends at this trailhead, especially given the heavy traffic on Rt. 73. Park as efficiently as possible and be prepared to use one of the wider turnouts either E or W of the trail-head where one can get completely off the road. Parking on the road directly across from the Cascade trailhead is not recommended owing to the potential hazard created by cars parked on both sides of the road.

Leaving the highway (0 mi.), the trail descends for 30 yds. and then begins an easy climb. Swinging R and leveling out, the trail crosses a small brook at 0.4 mi. and resumes an easy climb until it steepens at 0.7 mi. It continues steep to moderate to the top of the ridge at 1.2 mi. Now on the crest of the ridge, there are several moderate climbs alternating with flatter sections until a short, steep climb brings the trail to a ledge with a good view at 1.8 mi. Now the grade eases, and the trail reaches a junction with the trail to Porter Mt. at 2.1 mi. (see below). Bearing L, the trail soon reaches the base of the open rocks and ascends along the R side of the open rocks to the summit at 2.4 mi.

Distances: Highway to Porter Trail junction, 2.1 mi.; to summit of Cascade, 2.4 mi. (3.8 km). Ascent, 1940 ft. (591 m). Elevation, 4098 ft. (1249 m). Order of height, 36.

(91) Porter Mt.   Map: E-8

Once called West Mt., Porter is named for Dr. Noah Porter, President of Yale University from 1871 to 1886, who was a summer resident of Keene Valley and who made the first recorded ascent of the peak in 1875 with guide Ed Phelps. Although Porter does not have a bald summit, it offers 360-degree views and is a worthwhile side trip from Cascade. Two other trails ascend the peak from the Keene Valley side.

Leaving the junction near the summit of Cascade (0 mi.), the trail descends to the col at 0.2 mi. and then climbs moderately to steeply to a large boulder at 0.6 mi. and then at easy grades along the ridge to the summit at 0.7 mi. (Trail with ADK markers continues straight ahead, leading either to the Keene Valley Airport at 4.5 mi. or to the Garden at 3.8 mi.; see trails 16 and 17).

Distances: Highway to trail junction, 2.1 mi.; to summit of Porter, 2.8 mi. (4.5 km). Ascent from highway, 1960 ft. (597 m). Elevation, 4059 ft. (1237 m). Order of height, 38.

(92) Pitchoff Mt.   Map: E-7

This bare ridge N of the Cascade Lakes offers exceptional views and as described below is a nice traverse. There are also several worthwhile intermediate destinations that make excellent up-and-back trips. The two ends of this trail are separated by 2.7 mi. on Rt. 73, so two cars are advisable, but one also can hike just to the broad ledge with the balanced boulders at 1.6 mi. or to the summit at 2.0 mi. In season there are blueberries on all the ledges along this ridge.

Trailhead: The W end of the trail starts just down and across the road from the Cascade trailhead (see above for trailhead description and parking considerations).

Leaving the highway (0 mi.) and marked with red DEC disks, it climbs some steps to the R of a retaining wall and enters the woods on a moderate climb. Soon swinging R, the trail levels off and after some short ups and downs comes to a lookout on the R at 0.8 mi. About 70 yds. farther there is a better lookout with views of the Cascade Lakes directly below, as well as of Marcy and other peaks.

Descending to a small saddle, the trail now climbs several steep pitches before angling L across a steep hillside below the base of some cliffs and then swings R and up to a junction at the top of the ridge at 1.5 mi. (Trail R leads 0.1 mi. on the level to the broad ledge with the balanced rocks.) Continuing L, the trail climbs at first easily and then encounters a few steep pitches before reaching the summit of Pitchoff at 2.0 mi. (3.2 km). Elevation, 3600 ft. (1097 m). Ascent from highway, 1440 ft. (439 m).

From this first summit, the trail continues along the crest of the ridge, passing over three lesser summits at 2.2 mi., 2.6 mi., and 3.0 mi. From the fourth summit the trail makes a longer descent to a lower col at 3.6 mi., after which it climbs steeply up rocks to the fifth and final summit at 3.6 mi.

Straight ahead, the trail begins to descend steeply to the woods, where it doubles back to the R under the fifth peak and soon begins a steep descent, which lessens as the trail begins to follow down the L bank of a brook. Crossing the brook at 4.6 mi., the trail recrosses the brook 60 yds. later and continues an easy descent to the highway at 4.9 mi. This point is just below a small bridge 4.1 mi. from Keene and 2.7 mi. from the starting point.

Distances: Highway to balanced rocks, 1.6 mi.; to summit of Pitchoff, 2.0 mi.; to fifth summit, 3.6 mi.; to end of trail at highway, 4.9 mi. (7.9 km).

(93) Owls Head   Map: E-7

This little rocky peak has long been a popular climb and has probably been the first climb for many, many junior hikers. The start has changed considerably in recent years, but it is now easy and access is seemingly assured. Remember, however, that this is private land practically all the way to the summit.

Trailhead: The start is on Rt. 73, 3.2 mi. above Keene and 3.6 mi. from the Cascade Mt. trailhead. Turn off Rt. 73 at a sign for Owls Head Acres and follow the gravel road for 0.2 mi. up to a turnout on the L, where the road makes a sharp R. There is a small green sign marking the start of the trail. There are no other markers on this trail.

From the parking area (0 mi.), the trail climbs moderately through open woods to the crest of a ridge, where it joins the original route at 0.1 mi. Turning L, the trail quickly reaches the first ledge and continues on to a second and larger ledge at 0.3 mi. Flattening out above the second ledge, the trail soon resumes the climb and reaches a third ledge at 0.3 mi. Above this ledge, the trail flattens again before scrambling up the L side of the summit rocks and reaching the summit at 0.6 mi. There are views of Cascade, Pitchoff, Giant, and Hurricane, with views to the N and E found by walking around the summit.

Distance: Parking area to summit of Owls Head, 0.6 mi. (0.9 km). Ascent from parking area, 460 ft. (410 m). Elevation, 2120 ft. (646 m).

(94) Old Mountain Road   Maps: E-7 & E-6

This trail follows the route of the original road from Keene Valley to Lake Placid through a wild, rugged notch with high cliffs rising to the E and many signs of beaver activity along the way. Recent research has determined that if the incident related in the famous poem "Allen's Bearfight Up In Keene" actually happened, it would have happened on this road and not on the "Tight Nipping" road between Porter and Big Slide as suggested by the Adirondack historian Alfred Donaldson. Hikers must still guess, however, which of the several large boulders is the one referred to by the lines, "Against the rock with giant strength / He held her out at his arm's length. / 'Oh God!' he cried in deep despair, / 'If you don't help me, don't help the bear.'"

Since 1986 this route has been part of the Jackrabbit Ski Trail and has received both regular maintenance and many improvements such as bridges and drainage to make for much easier walking than before. Since it is a ski trail, however, the beaver ponds are potential obstacles to summer travel as long as the beavers remain active. The route is marked with occasional red "Jackrabbit Trail" markers. The trail is described from W to E, but up-and-back trips from either end are equally enjoyable.

Trailheads: The Lake Placid trailhead is at the end of a dirt road which leaves Rt. 73 2.3 mi. E of Adirondak Loj Road and 0.7 mi. W of the entrance to the Mt. Van Hoevenberg Recreation Area. This road is passable for 1.0 mi., where there is parking for a few cars. The Keene trailhead is at the end of Alstead Hill Rd., which branches N off Rt. 73 0.9 mi. W of the center of Keene. This road swings L at the Bark Eater Inn, after which it is straight uphill to the end of the road 3.0 mi. from Rt. 73.

From the parking area at the Lake Placid trailhead (0 mi.) the trail is mostly level, passing some large boulders on the L and then coming to a large sloping rock on the R at 0.7 mi. One can scramble to the top of this "summit in a valley" for a view of the cliffs and the notch ahead. About 150 yds. beyond, the trail comes to a beaver dam and pond with a vague trail skirting the L shore until the original road is rejoined and the summit of the pass reached at 1.0 mi.

Now descending, the trail crosses a sidehill at 1.1 mi. with a view through the trees down the valley and then past an old beaver pond on the L to a large beaver pond on the R. The trail descends a short, steep pitch to a beaver pond blocking the road at 1.4 mi. Bushwhack R around this pond and continue the descent crossing several small brooks before arriving at a large beaver meadow at the bottom of the hill at 2.5 mi. The descent is now easy to the end of Alstead Hill Rd. at 3.5 mi.

Trail In winter: As part of the Jackrabbit Trail, this trail is frequently skied. The first mile at the Lake Placid end is not plowed, making this a 4.5-mi. ski trip. Parking on Rt. 73 is also a problem because this is a dangerous corner, but skiers may park at Cascade Ski Touring Center just to the W on Rt. 73 and ski back 1.5 mi. via the Jackrabbit Trail. As of 1992, the touring center did not require skiers just transiting the Jackrabbit Trail to buy a trail pass, but did ask for a nominal parking fee.

Distance: Parking area to end of Alstead Hill Rd., 3.5 mi. (5.6 km).

(95) Cobble Hill   Map: D-6

This small, rocky knob rising directly above the village of Lake Placid offers interesting views of the village as well as of the high peaks farther away. The trail is not marked and the start is not easy to find, but it is worth the effort required to find one's way through a developed section of Lake Placid to the start.

Trailhead: From the stoplight at the junction of Rts.73 and 86, proceed NE on Rt. 86 past the golf course to the second L at 1.1 mi. This is Cobble Hill Rd., which is followed up the hill for 0.3 mi. to a gravel drive leading R. Go down this drive for 0.1 mi. to a grassy area on the L. At the upper edge of this grassy area (where cars may be parked) there are several large white pines with small orange paint spots on them. In this obviously suburban setting it should go without saying that this is private land. Hikers are now welcome to pass through, but this permission is contingent upon each hiker respecting the owner's property to the utmost.

Leaving the parking area (0 mi.), the trail goes up through the large pines and past a private home on the L. At 0.1 mi. the trail begins climbing steeply, with one trail soon coming in from the L and another at 0.2 mi. Bearing R at this second junction, the trail reaches the base of a steep, open ledge at 0.3 mi., with the easiest route of ascent on the R. At the top of the ledge is an excellent view of Lake Placid (village and lake) as well as Mirror Lake. Just past the top of the ledge, there are some concrete foundations which are the remains of an old chairlift that was part of an attempt to develop this peak as a ski area in the early 1960s. Bearing R at another junction, the trail reaches the summit at 0.4 mi. Just beyond the summit are ledges with good views to the S and E with glimpses of Whiteface possible to the N. On the descent, there are no signs or markers, but bearing L at every turn will reverse the route back to the parking area.

Distance: Parking area to summit of Cobble Hill, 0.4 mi. (0.7 km). Ascent, 460 ft. (140 m). Elevation, 2343 ft. (714 m).

The Peninsula Nature Trails

This series of three loops offering a total of about two miles of trail is located on the Brewster Peninsula on the S shore of Lake Placid. There is a sign for these trails on Saranac Ave. (Rt. 86) at the Howard Johnson's, 0.5 mi. W of Main St. Drive 0.5 mi. from Saranac Ave. to a gate on the L. A descriptive pamphlet on these trails is available from the Lake Placid Commerce and Visitor's Bureau.

(96) McKenzie Mt. from Whiteface Inn   Map: C-5

This is the shortest approach to this 3861-ft. peak which rises impressively above the W shore of Lake Placid. Though mostly wooded, the summit has two ledges which combine to offer a complete 360-degree view with Lake Placid. Algonquin, the Seward Range, and the Saranac Lakes being most prominent. One can make this a loop trip by descending the old Shore Owners Association trail, which returns past Bartlett Pond to the W shore of Lake Placid approximately 0.5 mi. up the lake from the starting point. The Shore Owners Association trail is recommended as a descent route only; because it is very difficult to find going up because it is no longer maintained and the markers are left from 20 years ago when it was last cared for.

Trailhead: The start is on the Whiteface Inn Rd., which begins 1.3 mi. W of the Village of Lake Placid on Rt. 86. Turn N on this road. The unmarked trailhead is a dirt road on the L, 1.4 mi. from Rt. 86 just past the Olympic Resort condominiums.

Leaving Whiteface Inn Rd. (0 mi.) there is an old vehicle barrier and then a cross country ski trail (part of Whiteface Inn is Nordic Center) going L; 40 yds. beyond, another ski trail goes R just as the old road begins a steady climb. At 0.3 mi. another ski trail goes R and 150 yds. later a road goes L and down to a small pond and dam. The steady climb continues until 0.7 mi. before easing off with the McKenzie Trail bearing L and continuing at an easy grade to Placid Lean-to on the R at 1.5 mi., with a brook crossing just beyond.

Past the lean-to, the trail descends gently to a junction at 1.9 mi., with the trail from Rt. 86 near Ray Brook coming in from the L. (The Jackrabbit Trail continues straight ahead to McKenzie Pond and McKenzie Pond Rd. near Saranac Lake in approximately 3.5 mi. The trail crosses a wetland near the W end and is not maintained for summer travel.) Turning sharp R at this junction, the trail is now marked with red DEC disks and an occasional ADK marker. The trail climbs moderately at first and even levels off for a brief stretch, but it soon begins a steep to very steep climb, gaining over 1000 ft. in just over half a mile. The steep climbing ends at a side trail R to a view to the S at 2.6 mi.

Soon crossing the first summit, the trail descends and then climbs to pass just below the second summit at 2.8 mi. Dipping and climbing again, the trail arrives at the third summit at 3.0 mi., with views to the N and W from a ledge just L of the trail. The trail continues to the fourth summit at 3.2 mi., and then descends steeply before beginning the final climb to the true summit. Climbing over a ledge at 3.5 mi., the trail levels out near the summit with a trail L a few yards farther leading to a spectacular "balcony" over the NW Adirondacks, with views as far E as Marcy as well. This is the best and most unique view from McKenzie, but just beyond at the true summit at 3.6 mi. there is a good 180-degree view encompassing Whiteface, Lake Placid, and many of the high peaks. This is the end of the red DEC markers and the officially maintained trail.

For those wishing to make a loop trip, it is possible to descend via the old Shore Owners Association trail. Continuing on over the summit, the trail descends steeply to a junction at 3.7 mi. with the former trail along the ridge to Moose Mt. (No trace of the trail exists beyond 0.3 mi. on the 2-mi ridge.) Turning R and descending steeply, the trail comes to Bartlett Pond at 4.3 mi. Because the pond is now enlarged by beavers, the trail must detour L through some thick terrain, but it turns R after crossing the outlet and joins the original route at 4.4 mi. Now following basically down the R bank of the outlet, the trail is at times on a shelf high above the brook, but returns to the R bank of the brook and comes to signs marking a junction with the now nonexistent Twin Brook Trail to Moose Mt. at 5.6 mi.

Continuing along the brook, the trail passes an old dam at 5.9 mi. and soon reaches a road and turns R. Approaching the shore of Lake Placid, the trail turns sharp R at a junction with the Lake Trail at 6.3 mi. and follows this trail on the level past several private camps. As the signs indicate, hikers "pass at their own risk and at the owner's pleasure," and courtesy dictates that one refrain from leaving the trail even to see the view from the end of a dock. The Lake Trail reaches Whiteface Inn at 6.9 mi., from which it is a short climb up through the buildings to the paved road leading back to the starting point.

Distances: Whiteface Inn Rd. to junction with trail from Rt. 86 near Ray Brook, 1.9 mi.; to summit of McKenzie, 3.6 mi. (5.7 km). Ascent, 1940 ft. (591 m). Elevation, 3861 ft. (1177 m).

Shore Owners Association Trails

At one time the Lake Placid Shore Owners Association maintained an extensive system of trails along the shores of Lake Placid and on to the mountains above. Maintenance continued long enough to clear away much of the damage left by the 1950 hurricane, but since then no trail save the Lake Trail has seen much maintenance. The three approaches to Moose Mt. have almost completely vanished except for a few signs and markers, although these trails seem to continue to show up on maps, including the 1978 USGS maps.

The Lake Trail is easily followable along the W shore as far as Undercliff, but beyond that is obscure in spots as it circles the N side of the lake to Whiteface Landing. The Lake Trail on the E side is plain at Whiteface Landing, but access at the McLenathan Bay end is blocked by many new camps. The trail up Eagle Eyrie from the N end of the Lake was improved a few years ago and is now followable, but the view from the top, while interesting, includes only the E portion of Lake Placid and a few of the high peaks.

Moose Mt.

The three approaches to Moose Mt. have almost completely vanished except for a few signs and markers, although these trails seem to continue to show up on maps, including the 1978 USGS map. This nearly 4000-ft. peak offers good views in all directions provided one is willing to explore a bit to find the various lookouts.

The original route of the Twin Brooks Trail (see trail 96) appears to be the most used of the possible routes up Moose Mt. There is occasional surveyor's tape and a discontinuous series of herdpaths. The trail to Loch Bonnie on the NE side is difficult to find close to the lake, but as one approaches this interesting little body of water, it becomes plainer. By skirting the N shore of Loch Bonnie one can pick up the vague traces of the old trail at the far W end; with difficulty this trail can be followed to the summit.

(97) Haystack Mt. from Rt. 86 Near Ray Brook   Map: C-6

This approach to Haystack and McKenzie mts. formerly started behind the DEC Headquarters in Ray Brook, but recent access problems over a piece of private land have necessitated the cutting of a new approach, which was finished in the fall of 1984. The new approach is approximately 0.9 mi. longer than the previous route, but it follows easy grades throughout and even takes in an additional view. Even with the additional distance of this new approach, Haystack (not to be confused with the 4960-ft. peak of the same name) still offers a very rewarding view for relatively little effort.

Trailhead: *The new trail begins at a turnout on Rt. 86, 1.6 mi. E of DEC Headquarters in Ray Brook and 1.4 mi. W of the junction with Old Military Rd. The trail is marked with a DEC sign and blue DEC markers.*

From the highway (0 mi.) the trail crosses a small knoll and dips to cross a small wet area after 100 yds., before swinging L and beginning a gradual climb to a crest at 0.3 mi. in an open hardwood forest. Dipping slightly, the trail climbs gradually to a second crest and soon crosses a stream at 0.5 mi. Swinging L after crossing the stream, the trail slabs gently upward along the base of low ledges until it begins an equally gentle descent at 1.1 mi. Following down a small ridge, the trail comes to a small open area at 1.5 mi., with some views to the SW. After a short, moderate descent, the trail swings to the R and continues to descend gently to a small brook at 1.8 mi., where the old route comes in from the L.

Now following an old road, the trail is practically level for a few hundred yards before beginning a gradual to moderate climb along the L bank of Little Ray Brook. Passing some old foundations on the R at 2.2 mi., the trail reaches a junction at 2.4 mi. with a red-marked trail to the R to McKenzie Mt. (trail 98). Bearing L and still with blue markers, the Haystack Trail crosses a small brook in 25 yds. and then Little Ray Brook just below an old dam in another 50 yds. From this dam the trail begins to climb a series of steep pitches interspersed with short stretches of easier going. At 3.0 mi. the trail begins the final pitch, going up a steep gully to the L of some cliffs to emerge on the first ledge at 3.2 mi. After a slight dip, the trail continues to the summit at 3.3 mi., where there are good views from Whiteface to Marcy, Algonquin, the Seward Range, and many of the larger lakes to the W.

Distances: Rt. 86 to junction with trail to McKenzie Mt.; 2.4 mi.; to summit of Haystack Mt., 3.3 mi. (5.3 km). Ascent, 1240 ft. (377 m). Elevation, 2878 ft. (877 m).

(98) McKenzie Mt. from Rt. 86 Near Ray Brook   Map: C-5

This route follows the Haystack Mt. Trail to the junction at 2.4 mi. (see above). Bearing R at the junction, the McKenzie Trail, with red markers, continues to follow the old road at gradual to moderate grades. Crossing a brook near the foundations of an old camp at 2.6 mi., the trail continues to climb until it crosses the headwaters of Little Ray Brook at 3.4 mi. From this brook, the grade moderates but the trail becomes quite wet to the junction with the yellow-marked trail from Whiteface Inn at 3.6 mi. (trail 96). Continuing straight ahead with red markers, the trail leads to the summit in another 1.6 m.

Distances: Rt. 86 to junction with Haystack Mt. Trail, 2.4 mi.; to junction with Whiteface Inn Trail, 3.6 mi.; to summit of McKenzie Mt., 5.2 mi. (8.4 km). Ascent, 2240 ft. (680 m). Elevation, 3861 ft. (1177 m).

(99) Northville-Lake Placid Trail from Averyville Rd. to Duck Hole   Maps: C-6 & C-7

This is the most northerly section of the 130-mi. Northville-Lake Placid Trail, which starts near Northville close to the southern boundary of the Adirondack Park. The Adirondack Mt. Club has published a separate guidebook covering the entire trail for those interested in traversing this classic route. This partial description is included here for those interested in access to the remote areas at the headwaters of the Cold River. This guide also describes the Duck Hole to Shattuck Clearing section and Shattuck Clearing to Long Lake section (trail 133).

Trailhead: The start is on Averyville Rd. near Lake Placid. From the junction of Rtes. 73 and 86 in Lake Placid, proceed 0.2 mi. E on Rt. 73 and turn S on Averyville Rd. This crosses Old Military Rd. at 1.0 mi., where there is a large DEC sign marking the official terminus of the Northville-Placid Trail. Continuing straight ahead on Averyville Road, the trailhead is another 1.2 mi. on the L, just before a bridge over the Chubb River. There is a small turnout on the L, and additional parking at the top of the hill beyond the bridge on the R.

Leaving the road (0 mi.) and marked with blue DEC disks, the trail begins following an old road along the R bank of the Chubb River, but veers L away from the river at 0.1 mi. and soon arrives at the trail register. From the register the trail climbs at a steady, gradual grade until 0.5 mi., where it levels out and continues with short ups and downs. A dim fisherman's trail from Bear Cub Rd. to the Chubb River crosses the trail at 1.3 mi., and the trail begins crossing an extensive spruce swamp at 2.2 mi. At 2.4 mi., an unmarked trail diverges L, with the end of the spruce swamp coming at 2.5 mi. The trail crosses a large brook on a good bridge at 3.3 mi. and continues on to join an old tote road at 3.7 mi., where it swings L and begins a gradual climb to a beaver pond on the R at 4.1 mi. From here there is a view of a new slide on the W side of Nye Mt. which came down as a result of the earthquake of October 7, 1983.

The trail, now on the flat, passes to the E of the beaver pond, with another unmarked trail diverging R at 4.4 mi. Bearing L, the trail crosses a large brook at 4.8 mi., and crosses two more brooks before descending slightly to a bridge over the Chubb River at 6.1 mi. On the far side of the bridge the trail joins the original route from Averyville. Turning L and proceeding up the L bank of the Chubb River, the trail reaches a junction with a side trail leading L to Wanika Falls Lean-to at 6.7 mi. This trail climbs steeply and crosses the Chubb River on a bridge just above a small falls to reach the lean-to on the R bank 0.1 mi. from the main trail. The actual Wanika Falls are about 100 yds. above the lean-to.

From the junction with the side trail to Wanika Falls, the N-P Trail climbs steeply at first and then more easily to a height of land at 7.0 mi. and begins descending. Crossing several brooks as it descends, the trail levels out past a brook at 7.6 mi. and continues with easy ups and downs to Moose Pond Lean-to at 8.3 mi. This is a picturesque spot to camp, with wild and rugged views of the Sawtooth Range across the pond.

Past the lean-to, the trail descends to the L bank of Moose Creek at 8.5 mi., but soon leaves the brook and crosses a beaver dam at 8.8 mi. The trail now continues to parallel Moose Creek but remains some distance back from it. At 9.7 mi. the trail begins to climb away from Moose Creek and reaches a small height of land at 10.2 mi., after which it descends into the valley of Roaring Brook. At 10.5 mi. there is a short steep pitch up followed by a more moderate descent to the R bank of Roaring Brook at 10.6 mi. The trail now continues along the brook to a junction at 11.7 mi. with a trail L to Indian Pass and Upper Works (trail 127). Continuing straight ahead at this junction and now marked with both red and blue markers, the trail proceeds with several easy ups and downs to a large, open area leading down to the bridge and dam at Duck Hole at 12.2 mi.

Here there are two lean-tos and plenty of tent sites. One lean-to is just before the bridge and dam, and the other is in the woods on a point of land 100 yds. E of the dam. A ranger station at the W edge of the clearing was removed in December 1977 in order to bring the area into compliance with wilderness use guidelines. A blue trail crosses the dam and leads to Bradley Pond and the trailhead at Tahawus (trail 128). The N-P Trail heads W along an old truck trail which connects with a trail heading to Ward Brook and the trailhead at Coreys. See Southern Section for descriptions of all these trails.

Distances: Parking area on Averyville Rd. to Wanika Falls, 6.7 mi.; to Moose Pond Lean-to, 8.3 mi.; to junction with Preston Ponds Trail, 11.7 mi.; to Duck Hole, 12.2 mi. (19.6 km).

(100) Scarface Mt.   Map: C-5

Owing to the construction of a federal prison, the former access to Scarface has been closed, but in the fall of 1981 the DEC completed a new approach to this peak. This new route adds nearly a mile to the old route, but it is easy walking and the unique views from this seldom-visited summit still make this trip worthwhile.

Trailhead: The present trail starts 0.1 mi. down Ray Brook Rd. from Rt. 86, directly across from DEC Region 5 Headquarters. A large sign marks the start, and there is a small parking lot off the road.

From the parking lot (0 mi.), the trail goes through a pine forest, crosses the now-abandoned railroad tracks, and comes to an elaborate bridge over Ray Brook at 0.5 mi. Climbing the opposite bank on a series of steps, the trail continues on the flat to a clearing at 0.7 mi. and then gradually ascends to a higher plateau and clearing with a large rock in its center. Just beyond this point, at 1.5 mi., the trail joins a road which was the original route. Note this turn well for the return trip.

Turning L, the trail descends slightly along this road and then turns sharp L off the road at 1.7 mi. Continuing mostly on the level, the trail crosses a brook at 2.2 mi. After several alternating steep and easy pitches, the trail comes close to the top of a col on the ridge leading W from Scarface, and then at 3.0 mi. begins a steep climb to a ledge at 3.1 mi. from which there are fine views to the SW, W, and NW. (A vague side trail leads L 200 yds. to a view N from the top of the "scar," but slick moss on the rock at the view makes this a potentially very dangerous spot.) From the first ledge, the marked trail bears R and up. Fifty yds beyond the first ledge a 25-yd. bushwhack to the R leads to a ledge with excellent views to the SE, S, and W. At 3.2 mi. the trail comes to more open rock with the best views to the SE and S. The trail continues at easy grades, terminating at 3.4 mi. on a western summit of Scarface, which now offers only obscured views. The viewless, untrailed summit of Scarface is approx. 0.4 mi to the E.

Distances: Parking lot on Ray Brook Rd. to junction with old route, 1.5 mi.; to ledge near summit of Scarface, 3.4 mi. (5.4 km). Ascent from parking lot, 1480 ft. (451 mi). Elevation, 3088 ft. (941 m).

(101) Baker Mt.   Map: B-5

This little mountain offers some of the best views of lakes and mountains for the amount of effort involved. From its partially wooded summit, lookouts provide views of Moose and McKenzie mts. to the E, many of the high peaks to the SE and S, and many lakes to the SW and W.

Trailhead: Start at the N end of Moody Pond just N of the village of Saranac Lake. Coming into Saranac Lake on Rt. 86 from Lake Placid, turn R onto McKenzie Pond Rd. at the traffic islands with an NBT branch bank on the R. After crossing the railroad track 200 yards from the bank, immediately turn L on Pine St., which recrosses the track in one-half mile. In another one-quarter mile, at the top of a hill, East Pine St. goes R on a bridge over the railroad track and leads in one-half mile to the N end of Moody Pond. E Pine St. can also be reached by turning off Rt. 3 just N of the village onto Pine St. The start is marked with a standard DEC sign and the trail is marked with red DEC markers.

From the road (0 mi.) the trail ascends an old road, crosses under a power line, and turns sharp R 120 yds. from the start. In another 75 yds. the trail bears L, climbs past an old quarry for 50 yds., and then bears R—avoiding the trail that continues along the upper edge of the quarry. At 0.2 mi. a house is visible on the R, and now the trail climbs to a brief level area at 0.4 mi. Climbing again soon, the marked trail splits at 0.6 mi. The R branch offers more views, but is steeper and more exposed than the L branch. The two routes rejoin at a large ledge at 0.8 mi. just below the summit at 0.9 mi. (Markers are scarce, especially on the descent. Use care in following this trail as there are several unmarked side trails.)

Distance: Moody Pond to summit of Baker Mt., 0.9 mi. (1.4 km). Ascent, 900 ft. (274 m). Elevation, 2452 ft. (747 m).

(102) Ampersand Mt.   Map: A-7

The view from the totally bald summit of this former fire tower peak is one of the best in the Adirondacks. Sitting on the boundary between the mountains and the lake country, Ampersand offers the best of both views. The name for the peak apparently comes from Ampersand Creek, which was so named because it twisted and turned so much that it resembled the ampersand symbol, "&."

Trailhead: The start is on Rte. 3, 8.1 mi. W of Saranac Lake and 7.3 mi. E of the junction of Rtes. 3 and 30 E of Tupper Lake. There is a large turnout on the N side of the road which is also the parking area for the 0.5-mi. trail leading down to Middle Saranac Lake and Ampersand Beach—a nice spot to swim after the climb.

Leaving the S side of the highway (0 mi.) at a small DEC sign, the trail, marked with red DEC disks and yellow paint blazes, proceeds past a locked gate on the level on an old jeep road. This section of the trail has been well maintained and is very easy walking as it gently rises and falls through a beautiful, mature forest. At 0.8 mi. the trail crosses a long, wet section on an extensive series of bridges and at 1.2 mi. begins a steady climb to the site of the former observer's cabin, which is reached at 1.7 mi.

Turning sharp R, the trail follows up the L bank of a small brook at easy to moderate grades, but at 1.9 mi. it steepens and becomes quite eroded in spite of obvious recent efforts to stabilize it. This rather unpleasant section of trail ends at 2.4 mi., as the grade eases just before the crest of the ridge. The trail now swings L and climbs easily up to a large split boulder on the R at 2.5 mi. Just beyond, the trail reaches a height of land and descends slightly before turning sharp R and climbing onto the open rocks. From here, the trail is marked profusely with yellow paint blazes to the summit at 2.7 mi.

The site of the former fire tower is just beyond and slightly below the true summit. There is a tablet on a rock face near this spot dedicated to the memory of Walter Channing Rice, 1852-1924, the "Hermit of Ampersand, who kept Vigil from this peak, 1915-1923." The summit used to be wooded, but Verplanck Colvin in his survey had the trees removed from this essential survey station. Erosion set in and washed all the soil away, and now nothing remains but the bare rock.

Distances: Route 3 to site of observer's cabin, 1.6 mi.; to summit of Ampersand, 2.7 mi. (4.4 km). Ascent from highway, 1775 ft. (541 m). Elevation, 3352 ft. (1022 m).

(103) Taylor Pond Trail   Map: F-1

This trail was reopened by the DEC in 1984. Although designated as a snowmobile trail, it sees little of this use and is generally a pleasant walking trail where solitude is practically guaranteed. As a hiking trail the loop around the pond is not particularly scenic since it remains back from the shore and provides direct access only to the lean-to on the E shore; but it does offer a long, nearly flat walk through a variety of forested terrain. The trail also provides access to bushwhacks up Douglas or Cranberry Mt.

There is a relatively undeveloped state campground at the start of the trail, offering primitive tent sites with well water and privies. It thus does not attract many large trailers or campers, but makes an ideal base for hiking or canoeing. As of 1992 there was a $4 per-night charge for camping and a $3 charge for day use, with canoes available for rent. Camping on the lakeshore is restricted to the three lean-tos and one designated site on a peninsula on the NE shore.

Trailhead: Taylor Pond is located just off the Silver Lake Road approximately 10 mi. W of Ausable Forks and 2 mi. E of Silver Lake. The mile-long gravel access road is marked, in season, with a DEC sign for the Taylor Pond State Campground.

Starting at the caretaker's cabin (0 mi.), the trail goes straight for 50 yds. and then bears R to the end of the campground road in another 200 yds. Now on an old tote road with occasional snowmobile trail markers, the trail climbs over a low ridge and at 1.3 mi. reaches a junction with a trail L. (This junction, like many others on this trail, is not marked, and hikers must remain alert and look for the trail markers at each junction.) Continuing on, the trail swings farther R with a bit of the NW bay visible. At 1.7 mi., another unmarked trail diverges L to the designated campsite on the point.

Now following a series of old roads, the trail swings sharp L at 1.8 mi. and again at 2.0 mi., after which it crosses a beautiful, fern-filled swamp before swinging sharp R and up at 2.1 mi. Soon crossing a stream, the trail begins a steady, gradual climb to a junction at 2.8 mi. Turning L on a better road, the trail swings R at 3.0 mi. and climbs some more to a junction at 3.3 mi. Turning L, the trail continues to climb in gentle stages until it swings L and away from the good road at 3.6 mi. Now somewhat grown in, the trail descends to within 100 vertical feet of the pond at 5.0 mi., parallels the shore, and then pulls away again at 5.5 mi. and becomes rougher as it begins to circle the SW end of the pond.

At 6.0 mi. the trail crosses an inlet (no bridge) and then swings sharp L and up onto a flat shelf. The trail here is little used and quite vague, but the walking is easy with just enough markers to keep one on course. Reaching a second inlet at 6.5 mi., again with no bridge, the trail continues vague to a road at 7.0 mi., after which the walking is easier to a lean-to at 8.1 mi. Beyond the lean-to the trail follows a wider road that gradually pulls away from the pond. Several other roads diverge R and the trail climbs gradually to a junction at 9.5 mi. The snowmobile trail continues straight ahead on the most obvious road, coming out on the Silver Lake Road E of the campground. The shortest return to the campground is to turn L and down to another junction at.10.3 mi. Turning L, the trail goes up over a small knoll and down to the end of the dam at the NE corner of the pond. Crossing the dam, the trail reaches the caretaker's cabin at 10.5 mi.

Trail in winter: Because this trail sees little snowmobile traffic, it makes a good ski trip, with the only potential problem being the two inlets at the S end that lack bridges.

Distances: Caretaker's cabin to S end of pond, 6.0 mi.; to E shore lean-to, 8.1 mi.; complete loop around pond, 10.5 mi. (16.8 km).

Dorothy W. Caldwell

An Adirondack Brook

Eastern Section

This section is comprised mainly of the hikes included in both the Cascade-Keene-Hurricane and the Boquet Valley regions in previous editions of this guidebook. This region now stretches from Poke-o-Moonshine Mt. at the N end, to trails around North Hudson at the S end. The area is characterized by lower rocky peaks with young second growth forests and many views from numerous ledges. Included in this region are the entire Jay and Hurricane Primitive Areas as well as most of the Giant Wilderness Area.

The Cascade Mt., Pitchoff Mt. and Owls Head Trails are now included in the Northern Section, but information on trailless hiking in the Jay Range and other mountains N of Hurricane has been added to this section. Also added is a trail to Round Pond near North Hudson, as well as information on approaches to Northway access points to the Dix Wilderness Area.

With its proximity to the Champlain Valley, this area was the first to be visited by white men, and the natural route along the Boquet and Schroon Rivers, now followed by Rt. 9, was important as early as the Revolutionary War. This area was also the first part of the Adirondacks to be settled, and many of the now seemingly remote areas were once productive farms that existed for many generations. The higher hillsides have nearly all been lumbered or burned, which means there is little virgin timber to appreciate, but the multitude of views makes this an interesting area to explore.

Trails in winter: Unless noted otherwise, these trails are not suited for skiing. There are a few unplowed roads, most notably Glen Road between Upper Jay and Lewis, that make for nice skiing. There are also a number of old roads in the northern part of the Jay Primitive Area that are not marked routes, but do provide good skiing.

The following are some of the best hikes the area has to offer.

Short Hikes:

Poke-o-Moonshine Mt.—2.4-mi. round trip. This popular fire tower peak offers tremendous views of lakes and mountains for just over 1 mi. of climbing.

The Crows—3.5-mi. round trip. These two rocky peaks offer numerous views with a complete loop finishing with a pleasant walk down a dirt road. Many shorter variations are also possible.

See also—Table of Short Hikes in Appendix III.

Moderate Hikes:

Hurricane Mt. from Rt. 9 N—5.3-mi round trip. Excellent views with not too much strenuous climbing.

Bald Peak—7.7-mi. round trip. A spectacular hike, finishing with a long, open ridge leading to an unparalleled view of the Champlain Valley. See description for East Trail to Giant and Rocky Peak Ridge.

Harder Hikes:

Giant from the East via Rocky Peak Ridge with descent via Giant Ridge Trail—11.0-mi. point to point. The outstanding hike in the Adirondacks, with more than 5 mi. of open walking. Over 5300 vertical feet of climbing means this hike is for experienced hikers only, but the rewards are commensurate with the effort. See descriptions for East Trail to Giant via Rocky Peak Ridge and Giant from Chapel Pond via Ridge Trail (see St. Huberts section).

Trail Described	Total Miles	Page
Hurricane Mt. from Rt. 9N	2.6	205
Hurricane Mt. from the East		
(Route 9N near Elizabeth-town)	1.5	206
Hurricane Mt. from Keene (North Trail)	3.0	207
Lost Pond	2.1	208

Hurricane Mt.

There are three approaches to this popular rocky summit, with the trail from Rt. 9N being the most popular. Hurricane offers one of the most commanding views of any of the lesser peaks, and because of this it was an important survey station for Verplanck Colvin during his Adirondack survey. For many years there was an active fire tower on this peak, but the tower has been abandoned and may be removed altogether in the near future. The view encompasses much of the length of Lake Champlain and the Green Mountains in Vermont as well as many of the high peaks. There are also plenty of blueberries starting in early August.

(104) Hurricane from Rt. 9N   Map: G-7

Trailhead: This trail leaves the N side of Rt. 9N at the height of land 3.6 mi. E of the junction of Rtes. 9N and 73 between Keene and Keene Valley and 6.8 mi. W of the junction of Rtes. 9N and 9 at the S end of the village of Elizabethtown.

Marked with red DEC disks, the trail leaves the highway (0 mi.), following a tote road at first up steeply but soon leveling off and becoming a foot path at 0.3 mi. The trail now continues nearly on the level through mostly thick conifers as it crosses a series of four small brooks. Crossing the last one at 1.1 mi., the trail heads into hardwood forest and begins to climb steadily. The first of several steep pitches begins at 1.7 mi., and the trail alternates between steep and easy climbing to the crest of the ridge and the junction with the ADK trail from Keene (trail 106) at 2.5 mi. Turning R, the trail soon climbs up over the summit rocks and reaches the summit at 2.6 mi.

Distance: Route 9N to summit of Hurricane, 2.6 mi. (4.3 km). Ascent from highway, 2000 ft. (610 m). Elevation, 3694 ft. (1126 m).

(105) Hurricane Mt. from the East   Map: G-7

This approach was the one used by the DEC in manning the fire tower when it was active. The last 1.2 mi. of road on this approach have not been maintained regularly in recent years, but under most conditions ordinary passenger cars can be driven to the parking lot 0.5 mi. short of the end of the road. Beyond this parking lot the road steepens, and even 4WD vehicles cannot be assured of making it to the site of the observer's cabin at the end of the road. The trail is very steep from the observer's cabin, which coupled with the poor road, makes it less popular than its shorter distance might indicate.

Trailhead: The start is at the end of a road that branches R off Rt. 9N 2.2 mi. from the junction of Rtes. 9N and 9 at the S end of the Village of Elizabethtown. The dirt road goes R just before a bridge and climbs steadily to a gate at 2.7 mi., where it narrows. Continuing on and then swinging L at 3.1 mi., the road soon enters state land with a small parking area on the R at 3.4 mi. Parking here is advisable since the road steepens after this point with a greater chance of washouts, and spots to turn around are very few.

Leaving this parking lot (0 mi.), proceed up the road to the site of the former observer's camp at the end of the road at 0.5 mi. Past this point, the trail drops down a few yards to a stream, with a lean-to on the R just past the stream. From here the trail begins climbing moderately, but after crossing another stream at 0.7 mi., it climbs steeply with only a few breathers until it emerges on the rocks just before reaching the summit at 1.5 mi.

Distances: Parking area to end of road, 0.5 mi.; to summit of Hurricane, 1.5 mi. (2.4 km). Ascent from parking area, 1500 ft. (450 m). Elevation, 3694 ft. (1126 m).

(106) Hurricane from Keene   Maps: G-6 & G-7

Commonly known as the North Trail to Hurricane, this is the longest approach to Hurricane but the grades are moderate throughout. There also is an attractive and little-used lean-to just over a mile from the end of the road, which makes this approach a wonderful first camping trip for young families. The trail is marked with ADK markers and maintained by the Hurricane Chapter of ADK.

Trailhead: The start is at the end of O'Toole Rd. off East Hill Rd. above Keene. From just S of the center of the hamlet of Keene, proceed E 2.3 mi. up a long hill. Just past the Mountain House, bear L on O'Toole Rd. where East Hill Rd. makes a sharp R turn. This point can also be reached by following Hurricane Rd. approximately 4.0 mi. from Rt. 9N. Proceed up the dirt road 1.2 mi. to Crow Clearing, where cars may be parked.

Leaving the R side of the clearing (0 mi.), the Hurricane Trail crosses a bridge over a small brook, crosses another small stream at 0.4 mi., and continues mostly on the level to Gulf Brook Lean-to at 1.1 mi., where an ADK trail bears L to Lost Pond (trail 107).

Turning sharp R in front of the lean-to, the Hurricane Trail crosses Gulf Brook and begins a gradual to moderate ascent. At 1.2 mi. the trail crosses a small brook, which it recrosses several more times before finally ending up on the R bank at 1.2 mi. Veering L, the trail now climbs at a steady, moderate grade through a beautiful birch forest to the junction with the trail from Rt. 9N (trail 104) at 2.8 mi. Continuing straight ahead, the trail soon reaches the summit rocks and then the summit at 3.0 mi.

Distances: Crow Clearing to Gulf Brook Lean-to, 1.1 mi.; to summit of Hurricane, 3.0 mi. (4.8 km). Ascent from Crow Clearing, 1600 ft. (490 m). Elevation, 3694 ft. (1126 m).

(107) Lost Pond   Map: G-6

The trail to this hidden little body of water branches L from the North Trail to Hurricane at Gulf Brook Lean-to, 1.1 mi. from Crow Clearing (see trail 106). Bearing L at the lean-to (0 mi.), the trail, with ADK markers, follows near the R bank of Gulf Brook until it turns sharp L and up at 0.3 mi. The trail climbs steadily with a few switchbacks until it levels off about 300 yds. before reaching the end of Lost Pond at 0.7 mi. The trail continues around the W shore of the pond to the Walter Biesemeyer Memorial Lean-to at 1.1 mi.

An unmarked trail continues past the lean-to approximately 0.3 mi. to the summit of Weston Mt., also known as Rocky Spar Peak. The view from this rocky summit ranges from Hurricane to Marcy to Whiteface, with only the NE blocked by some low trees. The mostly unmarked trail now continues down the N side and along Nun-da-ga-o Ridge (trail 109).

Distances: Crow Clearing to Gulf Brook Lean-to, 1.1 mi.; to Biesemeyer Lean-to on Lost Pond, 2.1 mi. (3.4 km).

(108) The Crows   Map: G-6

These two rocky pinnacles which dominate the landscape at the top of East Hill have long been favorites of local hikers. They offer a variety of views from their many ledges, including 28 major peaks from Big Crow. Some care is needed in following this trail both going up and down, as it makes many sharp turns winding through the many ledges. Big Crow can also be ascended separately in 0.7 mi. if one drives to Crow Clearing (see trail 106 for description of Hurricane from Keene).

Trailhead: The start is 2.0 mi. above Keene on East Hill Rd. or 0.2 mi. W of the Mountain House. There are no signs at the start, but there is an ADK trail marker on a large maple next to the road. The first part of this trail is on private land and hikers must be very careful to stay on the trail until reaching state land, and of course not camp or build fires on this private land.

Leaving the road (0 mi.), the trail climbs first at an easy grade through an overgrown field. After several steeper pitches interspersed with easier climbing, the trail passes a rock face on the L at 0.4 mi., shortly after which an alternate route diverges L. (This route climbs the partially open W ridge of Little Crow and rejoins the older route at the W summit. This alternate route is not as well marked, so stay alert, especially if descending this route, so as not to miss the L turn to return to the old route.)

Bearing R at this intersection, the regular trail soon reaches the first view. After a short, easy stretch, the trail again climbs steeply to a ledge with better views at 0.6 mi. Now mostly on bare rock, the trail continues to climb to the W summit of Little Crow and soon on to the E and true summit at 0.9 mi. Elevation, 2450 ft. (747 m).

The trail now descends gradually to the col between the two Crows at 1.1 mi. Climbing at first on a traverse, the trail soon swings R and climbs to the summit of Big Crow at 1.4 mi., elevation, 2800 ft. (853 m). Continuing on the flat across the summit, the trail begins descending steadily at 1.4 mi. and reaches a junction at 1.6 mi. Trail L (trail 109) leads to Nun-da-ga-o Ridge. Continuing to descend after this junction, the trail levels off at 1.8 mi. and reaches Grow Clearing at 2.1 mi. From here it is 1.2 mi. down the road to the Mountain House and another 0.2 mi. to the starting point.

Distances: Road to Little Crow, 0.9 mi.; to Big Crow, 1.4 mi.; to Crow Clearing, 2.1 mi.; round trip 3.5 mi. (5.6 km).

(109) Nun-da-ga-o Ridge   Map: G-6

Also called the Soda Range on USGS maps, this series of ledges stretching in a shallow arc between the Crows and Weston Mt. offers a variety of unique views. Though recently improved from its nearly lost condition, this trail is only lightly used and sparsely marked, so care is needed to follow it. Carry a map and compass just in case; distances are estimated.

The trail starts on the Crows trail (trail 108) 0.4 mi. from Crow Clearing. (See trail 106 for driving directions.) Turning R from the Crows trail, the Nun-da-ga-o Ridge Trail slabs across a side hill to the notch between Big Crow and the ridge at 0.2 mi. The trail then climbs over one bump and on to the first good ledge at 0.5 mi. From here, several more short ups and downs lead to a steep switchbacking ascent to the summit of Nun-da-ga-o Ridge at 1.4 mi. This is the best view on the ridge, but more views follow as the trail works its way down over several other bumps to the notch at the base of Weston Mt. at 2.5 mi. From here it is a steady climb through a beautiful birch forest to the summit of Weston at just under 3.0 mi. (To descend via Lost Pond, follow description for Lost Pond, trail 107).

Distances: Crow Clearing to junction with Nun-da-ga-o Ridge Trail, 0.4 mi.; to summit of ridge, 1.8 mi.; to Weston Mt., 3.4 mi.; to Lost Pond, 3.7 mi.; complete circuit back to Crow Clearing, 5.8 mi. (9.3 km).

Trailless Peaks North of Hurricane

Stretching for nearly 15 mi. N of Hurricane through the Hurricane and Jay Mt. Primitive Areas is an interesting series of peaks, none of which have trails—except for Poke-o-Moonshine Mt., whose trail is described separately below. Although none of these peaks have trails, many have outstanding views. There are numerous old roads into the area, and the forests are generally open second growth, making for generally easy traveling. What follows are some brief descriptions of what is available in this area, and some hints on how to approach these peaks. Beyond this, hikers must rely on map and compass to find their way. Hikers must also be aware that many of the approaches to these peaks are on private land. There appears to be little land on the described ways to these peaks that is actually "posted," but land can change hands or current owners can become more protective. Please respect any posted property and while traveling on unposted private land, do not do anything that might cause the owner to want to post his property.

Peak 3373—Also labeled as "Ausable No. 4," this peak has some interesting wide ledges giving excellent views to the S and E. The best approach is from the Lost Pond Trail (trail 107) where that trail turns sharp L 0.3 mi. above Gulf Brook Lean-to. Continue straight ahead through an old lumber clearing and slowly slab upwards to the top of this broad ridge, which is then followed to its N end. There are several other ledges to be found along the way as well.

The Jay Range

Reaching a height of 3600 feet with many bald summits, these peaks, though officially trailless, are popular enough to have a fairly well-defined path to the top of their bare ridge. The easiest and formerly the most popular approach from the Glen Road unfortunately has been posted by the landowner as of 1988. The landowner cited overuse by hikers (apparently busloads on occasion) and other abuses by nonhikers as the reason for this closure. All other land fronting on Glen Road near this approach is also private, with private land extending nearly to Merriam Swamp. One cannot, therefore, simply bypass this one piece of posted land.

Jay Range Access

An acquisition made in 1991 by the DEC now offers a relatively direct public access to the summits of the Jay Range from close to the former access point on Glen Rd. As of this writing (1992), there is no established trail on the upper section of this approach and hikers will have to use care in descending to find one's way back down through this narrow corridor to the road. Although somewhat more difficult than the old approach, this new approach is by far the easiest to Jay Mt. and should become popular in the future.

The new approach is on Glen Rd. at its junction with Luke Glen Rd., 1.2 mi. north of the former access at the farm at the intersection of Styles Brook and Glen Rds. The DEC hopes to eventually create a small parking area at this access point, but parking is not a problem on this lightly traveled road. The new acquisition's S boundary line offers the best route for the first mile. It is located just S of Luke Glen Rd. and is marked with fresh yellow paint blazes and a "Forest Preserve" sign. The boundary line is clearly marked and cut out for approximately 0.5 mi. to a corner marking the end of the new access corridor. This is the beginning of the larger piece of state land comprising the Jay Mt. Wilderness Area.

Continuing E from this corner, an older property line blazed with faded red paint goes up over a steep knoll (with red pines and a view to the R) and then over a few small bumps for another 0.5 mi. to a blazed property corner. From this point, the understory thickens and makes the going somewhat more difficult with better going found by detouring slightly to the L (N) before heading up the steep ridge to more open going. The rocks at the top of the ridge, which offer a 360-degree view, are reached at approximately 1.5 mi. from the road. From here, one can follow the mostly open ridge for approximately another 1.5 mi. to the summit of Jay. (Other possible approaches to the Jay Range are across Ward Lumber Company property from the official end of Nugent Rd. or from the NE at the end of Seventy Rd. near Lewis. There are no trails or marked routes from any of these other approaches.)

Saddleback Mt.—At 3615 ft., this mountain offers a variety of views from its summit. One can approach it from the height of land to the S on the road between Upper Jay and Lewis, along the ridge from Jay, or from the same approach as for Slip Mt. (see below).

Slip Mt.—This also offers a rocky top, with the best approach being from the E on West Hill Rd. leading out of Lewis. Just before the road crosses Spruce Mill Brook, turn R and hike up a private driveway bearing L until the driveway reaches Derby Brook, which is followed to a flat area beneath the summit of Slip. Slip Mt. can also be climbed via its long NE ridge from the end of Seventy Rd. Both *Seventy Mt.* and *Bald Peak* on this ridge offer views, and there are several other views along the ridge, including a spectacular view of Slip's steep E face.

Death Mt.—Farther to the N, this mountain has an open summit and can be approached from the end of Seventy Rd. One can also continue on the summit of Jay along the obvious ridge.

Mt. Fay—This prominent, rocky little bump to the E is a rewarding short climb with views of the Boquet River Valley. Approach Mt. Fay from the end of Seventy Rd.

Bluff Mt.—This 2930-ft. mountain leading up from Jay is found to the N of the old road connecting Seventy Rd. in Lewis with the Lincoln Hill Rd. It has a prominent cliff on its S side. One can scramble up the steep S face from the height of land on the Jay-Lewis Road, or take the easier SW shoulder from just W of the height of land.

Baldface Mt.—The peaks to the N of Bluff Mt. are generally lower and seem to have greater access problems, but several are worth exploring, including Baldface Mt. just N of Poke-o-Moonshine Mt. Baldface is approached from Rt. 9 near Butternut Pond. Be aware that there is another jeep road about 0.3 mi. to the E of the one shown on the current maps.

Flagstaff Mt.—Topped by USGS station Fordway, at the far NE end of the area, this is a good 30-minute jaunt up from the gravel road along the R bank of the Ausable River. The views of Lake Champlain and some of the surrounding farmland are well worth the effort.

Clearly, the only limit to hiking in the Jay Range is one's own imagination.

(110) Poke-O-Moonshine Mt.   (Page map)

This fire tower peak is extremely popular because of its tremendous view of Lake Champlain and of the high peaks seen in the distance to the SW. Its unusual name appears to be a combination of two Algonquin Indian words, "Pohqui" and "Moosie," which mean, respectively, "broken" and "smooth." The name then, later corrupted by the settlers, seems to refer to the smooth rocks of the summit or the prominent slab on the SE side and the broken rocks of the impressive cliff on the E side.

Trailhead: The trail starts at the state campground on Rt. 9, 9.3 mi. N of the junction of the road from Lewis to Exit 32 on the Adirondack Northway and 3.0 mi. S of Exit 33. In season, a day-use fee is charged for parking in the campground. The campground caretakers strongly discourage parking on the highway, although it is not posted against parking. Thus, be prepared either to pay the fee or add a quarter-mile or so to your hike and walk in from S of the campground. When the campground is closed, park on the highway opposite the trailhead at the S end of the campground.

Starting from the S end of the campground (0 mi.), the red-marked trail enters the woods and immediately begins climbing, steeply at times, to the base of a cliff at 0.3 mi. Skirting the cliff on the L, the trail switchbacks R to a good lookout on the R at 0.3 mi. The grade now eases somewhat but remains steady to a saddle S of the summit at 0.8 mi. Here are the remains of the fire observer's cabin with a lean-to approximately 65 yds. to the L.

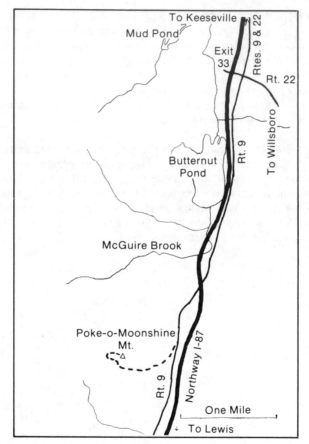

Poke-o-Moonshine Mt.

Base maps are Ausable Forks and Willsboro Bay, both 7.5 by 15 minute metric series maps.

From this saddle there are two trails leading up to the R. The L trail is now marked as the official route; it leads up past a lookout on the L and along a shelf before turning R and up to the summit plateau. Turning R again, the trail goes through open woods to the summit and tower at 1.2 mi. (The R trail leading up from the observer's cabin is the old route, now badly eroded, which leads past an old spring house and then up steeply through a slot in the summit cliffs. It joins the current trail 0.1 mi. below the summit.)

Distance: Campground to summit of Poke-o-Moonshine, 1.2 mi. (1.9 km). Ascent, 1280 ft. (390 m). Elevation, 2180 ft. (664 m).

(111) Giant from Route 9N   Map: G-7

This is one of the longer approaches to Giant, but it has its attractions for those who don't like company while approaching a popular peak like Giant. (See St. Huberts section for history and naming of Giant.) This trail from Rt. 9N, also referred to as the North Trail, offers generally easy grades, an interesting lookout, a unique geological formation, and a secluded and seldom-used lean-to. The Owl Head Lookout (not the plural form, to distinguish it from the peak above the Cascade Pass Road) is also popular as a short day trip, with its magnificent view of the E face of Giant as well as Rocky Peak, Lake Champlain, and the Green Mountains.

Trailhead: Start on Rt. 9N at a large DEC sign, 4.5 mi. W of the junction with Rt. 9 at the S end of the village of Elizabethtown or 5.5 mi. E of the junction of Rtes. 9N and 73 between Keene and Keene Valley. Off the highway, there is a small parking lot and trail register on the L of a private gravel road. Park here (0 mi.).

Continue down the road on foot and cross a small bridge in 150 yds. Immediately after the bridge, the trail (now marked with red markers) turns sharp L off this road and begins a gradual climb as it joins and then leaves a relatively new lumber road. Entering state land at 0.4 mi., the trail continues its gradual climb before leveling out and then reaching Slide Brook at 1.1 mi. There are several possible campsites in this area.

Crossing Slide Brook on a good bridge, the trail climbs steeply up the bank of the brook, swings L and crosses a small tributary brook before beginning a steady easy to moderate climb above the R bank of the small brook. Returning to the brook, the trail crosses it several times as it works up through a small ravine. At the top of the ravine at 1.8 mi., the trail swings sharply R, crosses a few boggy areas, and continues to swing slowly to the R as it climbs at a moderate grade to the top of the ridge at 2.5 mi. Here there is a junction with a side trail leading L and up 0.1 mi. to the summit of Owl Head Lookout. (Climbers ending their trip here should go 0.1 mi. L when returning to the main trail for a spectacular view of the cliffs on the Lookout.)

The trail soon begins to descend through a small open area to a small valley at 2.7 mi., after which it climbs briefly and then descends again before starting up through a very open grove of maples at 3.4 mi. Just beyond this point, there is a good view from rocks just off to the L of the trail. There is one more short descent before continuing the climbing to the top of High Bank, a remarkable bank of glacial gravel with only a few birches growing on it, which is reached at 4.1 mi. Continuing on, the trail crosses a dry stream bed at 4.4 mi. At 4.6 mi. there is a view of the slides on Giant 50 ft. on the L.

The grade continues steady and moderate, but begins to slacken at 5.7 mi., just before a junction with a side trail leading 50 yds. L to a lean-to. Past the lean-to the grade eases off as the trail approaches the junction with the ATIS trail from Hopkins (trail 52) at 6.1 mi. Turning L, the trail begins climbing steeply out of the col. At 6.2 mi. there is a sharp switchback to the L to negotiate a small cliff band. From here the grade continues steep for a few yards, but slowly eases until it levels off at 6.8 mi. Descending slightly, the trail resumes its climb and arrives at a ledge on the R at 7.2 mi., soon after which the trail levels out and crosses other ledges to the summit at 7.4 mi. (ATIS trails 47 and 48 continue over the summit to St. Huberts.)

Distances: Rt. 9N to Owl Head Lookout, 2.6 mi.; to lean-to, 5.7 mi.; to junction with trail from Hopkins, 6.1 mi.; to summit of Giant, 7.4 mi. (11.9 km). Ascent from Rt. 9N, 3327 ft. (1014 m). Elevation, 4427 ft. (1349 m). Order of height, 12.

Trailless Route to Knob Lock

(See Peaks Without Maintained Trail in Introduction)

Located S of Rt. 9N between Keene and Elizabethtown, the expansive rocks on the summit of this 3209-ft. peak offer 360-degree views of Hurricane, Whiteface, and the Champlain Valley. Since the summit is less than a mile from the road, one would expect this to be a popular climb; but the N slopes are guarded by numerous cliffs and thick scrub while the other slopes have fewer cliffs but even thicker scrub. Thus, reaching this summit is more of a challenge than its size or distance from a road would indicate. There is as yet no general agreement on the "best" route, and no established herd paths.

Possible approaches include starting at the Hurricane trailhead (see trail 104) and proceeding SE about 0.2 mi., avoiding the brook leading SW to the slopes of Tripod, and then following a brook that flows from the notch between Knob Lock and Tripod. About 0.5 mi. from the road, follow a smaller brook that heads toward the summit. Another possibility is to follow the North Trail to Giant (trail 111) for about 1.0 mi. and then ascend the prominent E ridge of Knob Lock, which has a good deal of open rock but also some very thick going between the end of the ridge and the summit. A third possibility is to ascend an indistinct NE ridge starting from Rt. 9N opposite a small sand pit located 0.6 mi.W of the trailhead for the North Trail to Giant. Be aware that just to the east is private land. After a thrash through alders next to a brook, head S to the crest of the first ridge and then SW (with some additional thrashing) to the summit. Be careful on the descent because it is easy to be led too far to the E and onto posted land or to head N too soon and end up on top of some of the many cliffs on this side of the mountain

(112) East Trail to Rocky Peak Ridge and Giant   Map: H-9

This route up the long E ridge of Rocky Peak Ridge and on to Giant is a very challenging but also very rewarding climb. Nearly half of the trail is in the open, and there are exceptional views at nearly every turn. Bring plenty of water along on any day, and think twice before attempting this route on a particularly hot day, but on a cool day with fall colors at their height this trail is probably the best hike in all of the Adirondacks. For those with less ambition, two intermediate points, Blueberry Cobbles at 2.0 mi. and Bald Peak at 3.9 mi., are also worthy objectives.

Except for a small stand of first-growth hemlock near the start of the trail, this entire route is through smaller second growth. This is the result of the great fire of 1913, which burned all of Rocky Peak and much of Giant. Nearly all of the views along this route are a direct result of this last great fire in the Adirondacks.

Trailhead: The trail begins at a parking lot on Rt. 9, 4.9 mi. N of the junction with Rt. 73 and 1.3 mi. S of the New Russia Post Office.

From the parking lot the trail crosses a nearly grown-up field, begins to climb an old tote road, and comes to the L bank of a small stream at 0.7 mi. Following up the L bank, the trail enters a flat notch at the far end of which it swings L and climbs to the first view on the L at 1.6 mi. A second view is just off the trail to the R at 1.8 mi.

Continuing up, the trail comes to the first lookout on Blueberry Cobbles on the L at 1.9 mi. and then comes to a junction at 2.0 mi., with a red trail which bypasses the top of Blueberry Cobbles leading R. (In season there should be no doubt that Blueberry Cobbles is most appropriately named.) The yellow trail L leads past many other views of the Boquet Valley and the Dix Range before turning sharp R and down at 2.3 mi. to Mason Notch, where the red bypass trail rejoins it. The trail climbs over the lightly wooded summit of Mason Mt. (2330 ft.) at 2.8 mi. before descending to Hedgehog Notch at the base of Bald Peak. There is an interesting cleft in the rock just to the L of the trail. Now the trail begins to climb steeply over mostly bare rock to the summit of Bald Peak (3060 ft.) at 3.9 mi., where there are good views in all directions.

Turning L and following the ridge W, the trail passes a huge balanced glacial erratic at 4.0 mi. and then begins to descend the R side of the ridge to Dickerson Notch at 4.2 mi. From the notch, the trail begins a long climb to the prominence at the E end of the summit ridge. Unlike most of the trail so far, there are only a few views to serve as excuses to rest, but there is one good ledge on the R as the grade begins to ease off just before reaching the bald summit of Rocky Peak (4060 ft.) at 5.4 mi.

The trail now crosses several minor rocky bumps before descending to the outlet to Mary Louise Pond (also referred to as Lake Marie Louise) at 6.1 mi. Skirting the N side of the pond, the trail now climbs the beautiful open meadows to the summit of Rocky Peak Ridge at 6.7 mi. From here are views in all directions, with the slides on Giant's E face dominating. Total ascent from the parking lot, 4700 ft. (1277 m). Elevation, 4420 ft. (1347 m). Order of height, 20.

Bearing NW, the trail descends steadily into the col between Giant and Rocky Peak Ridge at 7.4 mi. and immediately begins to climb steeply, first through an open meadow and then into the woods. Angling R, the trail comes to a junction with a side trail at 7.7 mi. (Trail R leads 60 yds. to a spectacular view of some of the slides on the E face of Giant.) Swinging back to the L after this junction, the trail soon gains the crest of a ridge and follows this up to its junction with the ATIS trail from St. Huberts at 7.9 mi. Turning R, it is an easy hike to the summit of Giant at 8.0 mi.

Distances: Parking lot to Blueberry Cobbles, 1.9 mi.; to Bald Peak, 3.9 mi.; to summit of Rocky Peak Ridge, 6.7 mi.; to summit of Giant Mt., 8.0 mi. (12.9 km). Total ascent from parking lot, 5300 ft. (1466 m). Elevation, 4627 ft. (1410 m). Order of height, 12.

(113) Sunrise Trail to Mt. Gilligan   Map: H-9

Formerly known as Sunrise Mt., this little peak rises directly above the Boquet River and offers views of Pleasant Valley, Rocky Peak Ridge, and the Dixes from the summit and the several lookouts along the way.

Trailhead: The trail starts from Rt. 9, 3.6 mi. N of its junction with Rt. 73 and 2.6 mi. S of the New Russia Post Office. A dirt road leads to a bridge over the river, with a fisherman's parking lot just before the bridge. Park here (0 mi.), cross the bridge, and turn L off the road after 150 yds. just before reaching a house on the L.

Marked with ADK markers, the trail proceeds on the flat for a few hundred yards before climbing to a higher shelf up to the R and then, after some more flat going, climbs steeply up to the first lookout at 0.3 mi., with a good view of Dix.

Continuing on, the trail dips briefly and then climbs steadily to another lookout at 0.6 mi. Now the grade is easier along the top of the ridge before it dips down and crosses an old lumber road in a small col at 0.8 mi. Climbing past an interesting overhung rock, the trail reaches a broad, open area at 0.9 mi., with good views of Rocky

Peak Ridge and the Dix Range. Just after this ledge, the trail joins and briefly follows an old lumber road before branching L and up to the final lookout at 1.1 mi. at the end of the trail. The wooded summit of Mt. Gilligan is about 100 yds. beyond.

Distance: Parking area near Rt. 9 to lookout below summit of Mt. Gilligan, 1.1 mi. (1.8 km). Ascent, 670 ft. (204 m). Elevation, 1420 ft. (433 m).

(114) Trail from Sharp Bridge Campsite to Round Pond and East Mill Flow   Map: H-12

This trail is a relatively flat and pleasant walk through some fine woods, giving access to picturesque Round Pond as well as the beautiful and unique open area known as East Mill Flow. This trail was cut about 1975, but has not been consistently maintained recently. It is still quite passable and one only needs to be careful not to lose it in the alders at a few of the stream crossings.

Trailhead: The start is at Sharp Bridge Campground on Rt. 9, 7.1 mi. N of the village of North Hudson and 2.9 mi. S of Exit 30 on the Adirondack Northway. Parking is at the gravel turnout just outside the gate.

From the parking area (0 mi.), the trail goes to the far end of the large, flat field near the Schroon River and then goes along the L bank of the river on an old road. Crossing several small brooks, the trail comes to an old bridge abutment at 0.8 mi. This was apparently the original crossing point used as early as the 1830s both by the predecessor of Rt. 9 and by a road leading W from Port Henry to Tahawus and beyond. Turning sharp L at this point, the trail follows this old road for several miles.

The trail climbs briefly, drops to cross a small brook, and then begins a steady climb to a height of land at 1.5 mi. Dropping down the other side in two short pitches, the trail continues mostly on the level through several magnificent stands of white pine to the R bank of East Mill Brook at 2.7 mi., at the S end of East Mill Flow. Swinging R, the trail drops down and makes a somewhat difficult crossing of the brook before scrambling up the far bank and continuing along the E side of this extensive open swamp. At 3.4 mi. the trail crosses the outlet to Round Pond in a thick clump of alders, turns sharp R, and heads up a gentle grade. At 3.6 mi., just before coming within sight of Round Pond, the trail turns sharp R off the old road and proceeds to the outlet of Round Pond at 3.9 mi. (The old road leads straight ahead to the NW shore of Round Pond with a good campsite located across the pond on some low rocks.)

From the outlet, the trail climbs S away from the pond and skirts numerous small swampy areas as it crosses a low divide and proceeds down to a junction with an unmarked trail leading L at 4.5 mi. (Trail L leads along E shore of Trout Pond to rough access road.) Continuing R, the trail makes its way along the W shore of Trout Pond and comes to the North Hudson-Moriah Rd. at 5.2 mi. This trailhead is approximately 5.3 mi. from Rt. 9, N of North Hudson, and is not marked by any sign.

Trail in winter: This is an excellent ski trip from Sharp Bridge to Round Pond.

Distances: Sharp Bridge Campground to East Mill Flow, 2.7 mi.; to outlet to Round Pond, 3.9 mi.; to North Hudson-Moriah Rd., 5.2 mi. (8.4 km).

Dix Range via North Fork of the Boquet River

The trailless peaks of the Dix Range may be approached via this unmarked hunter's trail. There are several interesting ponds in this area, as well as some nice camping spots. Although the trail is fairly plain, there are no signs or markers, and one should carry a map and compass in the event one loses the trail.

Trailhead: *The trail begins on Rte. 73 on the S side of the N Fork of the Boquet River, at a stone bridge approximately 1.5 mi. N of the junction of Rtes. 73 and 9.*

Leaving the highway (0 mi.), the trail goes up along the R bank of the stream to a crossing point at 0.4 mi. Now heading away from the Boquet, the trail crosses a small stream and returns to a bank high above the river 150 yds. later at 0.7 mi. There is a good swimming hole and picnic spot at the small flume in the river, which can be seen through the trees.

From this swimming hole, the trail climbs high above the river before turning L and down to cross it at 1.2 mi. Heading SW, the trail crosses another large tributary at 1.4 mi., with Lillypad Pond just out of sight to the L of the trail. The trail now climbs easily and then descends to the L bank of the S Fork of the Boquet at 2.3 mi. The trail continues up the L bank, much of the time high above it, passing the "Rock of Gibraltar" on the L at 3.1 mi. and coming to the L bank of a tributary coming down from Dix at 3.3 mi. From here there are easy approaches to most all of the Dix Range, as well as several outstanding camping spots in this remote and seldom-visited area.

From the crossing of this tributary a herd path continues close to the South Fork, eventually reaching the base of the slide on East Dix. For the first half mile the herd path crosses and recrosses the South Fork, but then settles on the R (S) bank at the first major tributary coming in from the S. Although slightly widened, this is not the brook from the base of the slide. The latter is found another half mile along the herd path that leads directly to the base of the slide and even provides an alternative to some of the lower sections of the slide that have become too overgrown with moss to be easy going. At the top of the slide, bear R for the easiest access to the crest of the ridge, but watch the loose rock.

Northway Access Points to the Dix Wilderness Area

With the construction of the Adirondack Northway through this area in the mid 1960s, there came a need to provide access across this controlled-access highway, since parking was of course prohibited on the highway itself. There are now three points where one can easily cross the Northway along the ten-mile stretch from North Hudson to Exit 30 near Underwood. These access routes connect with the valleys of Lindsay Brook, West Mill Brook, and Walker Brook, and are described briefly below.

(115) Lindsay Brook Access   Map: H-12

This route, marked with red markers, starts S of the Schroon River opposite Sharp Bridge Campground (see trail 114). Going up a road for 0.1 mi., the trail turns sharp R and crosses a stream, negotiates a flooded area, and continues on through a pine forest to a culvert under the Northway at 0.9 mi. No trail continues beyond this culvert.

(116) West Mill Brook Access   Map: H-12

This route begins 1.6 mi. S of Sharp Bridge Campground or 5.5 mi. N of the village of North Hudson. There is a large wooden signpost at the start of a narrow dirt road which leads down to West Mill Brook at 0.2 mi., where there is a good ford. (Park just before on R at times of high water.) From the ford, the road crosses an extensive, open sandy, area and reaches a concrete culvert under the Northway at 0.8 mi. At 1.1 mi. there is a parking area just before a gate controls further access along the old road leading along the R bank of West Mill Brook. This road leads approximately 2 mi. farther W before turning S and becoming obscure.

(117) Walker Brook Access   (No map)

This access is 3.7 mi. S of Sharp Bridge Campground or 3.4 mi. N of North Hudson. Just south of two houses, there is an old green metal signpost at the end of a dirt road. Go down this road for 0.3 mi. and park where a poorer road bears R. Bear in mind that this is private land and that the driveway beyond 0.3 mi. is not a public road.

Go R and down this poorer road to the L bank of the Schroon River. Just upstream is a good wooden foot bridge leading to a good road on the far side, which is followed uphill to a flat area 0.5 mi. from Rt. 9. Bear R just beyond and cross under the Northway through a concrete culvert at 0.7 mi. Walker Brook is approximately 0.2 mi. beyond, with an old road leading up its R (S) bank giving access to Camels Hump, Niagara, and Nipple Top mts.

Cold River from Ouluska Lean-to

Tom Dunn

Southern Section

This region stretches across the southern edge of the High Peaks Wilderness Area and a small portion of the Dix Wilderness Area. With the exception of the well-traveled trails leading to Marcy and Dix, much of this area is remote and seldom visited. There are outstanding opportunities for solitude, and one must be willing to backpack to reach much of the terrain within the section's boundaries.

The following descriptions are the ones formerly found in the Elk Lake and Sanford Lake Regions of previous editions of this guidebook; sections of the Northville-Placid Trail from Long Lake to Duck Hole have also been incorporated into this section.

Trails in winter: More of the trails in this section are skiable, but unless specific details are given, one should assume that the trail is steep enough to require snowshoes and possibly crampons.

Except for Goodnow Mt., there are no short hikes in this area, and very few moderate hikes; but there are great possibilities for extended backpacking trips beyond the obvious traverse of the Northville-Placid Trail. For the serious and experienced hiker, this area is the place to go to find new challenges.

Short Hikes:

Goodnow Mt.—3.0-mi. round trip. An easy ascent on a good trail leads to a fire tower with expansive views of the high peaks and of the equally wild country to the S.

See also—Table of Short Hikes in Appendix III.

Moderate Hikes:

Summit Rock in Indian Pass—8.7-mi. round trip. Except for the final half mile, this is an easy hike to a close-up view of the largest (nearly 1000 ft. high) cliff in the Adirondacks. See description for Indian Pass from Upper Works.

Camp Santanoni on Newcomb Lake—9.0-mi. round trip. The road to Newcomb Lake has easy grades and leads to an authentic "great camp" on the shore of a beautiful lake.

Harder Hikes:

Dix Mt. via Hunters Pass with return via Beckhorn—13.9-mi. round trip. An interesting loop trip on this impressively rugged peak with outstanding views from the summit.

Newcomb Lake, Shattuck Clearing, Duck Hole, Henderson Lake backpacking trip—35.2-mi. point to point. This 4- to 5-day trip leads along little-used trails past three attractive lakes with good campsites and also parallels the ruggedly beautiful Cold River for several miles. It requires only a short shuttle between start and finish points. See descriptions for: Road to Newcomb Lake, Foot Trail to Shaw Pond, Moose Pond Horse Trail, Cold River Horse Trail, Shattuck Clearing to Duck Hole via Northville-Placid Trail, and Duck Hole via Henderson Lake.

Elk Lake Area

Trailhead: To reach the trails starting from Elk Lake, leave the Adirondack Northway (Interstate 87) at Exit 29 in North Hudson. Then go W 4 mi. on Blue Ridge Rd., following signs for Newcomb. Turn R off Blue Ridge Rd. onto a *gravel road marked with a sign for Elk Lake Lodge. At 5.2 mi. on this gravel road there is a parking lot on the R just before the road drops down to Elk Lake. The road beyond here is private and open only to guests at Elk Lake Lodge. In winter, this road is usually plowed only as far as Clear Pond, 3.3 mi. from Blue Ridge Rd.*

All of the trails starting from this parking lot cross private land, and hikers should observe the normal courtesies when on private land, which means that there is no camping permitted for 5 mi. along the Elk Lake-Marcy Trail or for 1.9 mi. along the Dix Trail. Furthermore, both of these trails are closed to the public during the big-game hunting season (next to last Saturday in October to first Sunday in December). All privately maintained trails branching from the public trails are closed at all times. Refer to the map accompanying this guidebook for the exact location of private lands in this area.

(118) Elk Lake-Marcy Trail   Map: F-12

This is one of the longer approaches to Marcy and involves an additional climb and descent of about 700 ft. over the Boreas-Colvin Range before actually beginning the ascent of Marcy. The condition of the trail has improved considerably in recent years. The ATIS has assumed responsibility for maintaining this trail from the crest of the Colvin Range to Four Corners. The trail has been cut out regularly, most of the wet areas bridged, and the ADK trail crew has added a now-legendary 60+ step rock staircase above Panther Gorge. There is also a new lean-to at Panther Gorge. The only problem is the E portion of Marcy Swamp where beavers have been intermittently active, potentially causing a few hundred yards of wet trail. Because much of this trail is on private land, hikers should be aware that no camping is permitted until approximately 6.5 mi., with the exception of a small piece of state land at 5.0 mi. that offers no attractive campsites unless one detours 0.2 mi. N on the Colvin Range connection (trail 60).

Leaving the DEC signpost across the road from the parking lot (0 mi.), the blue-marked trail climbs through thick woods for a few yards and then descends and crosses a private trail at 0.1 mi. Continuing to descend, the trail crosses The Branch (outlet to Elk Lake) on a suspension bridge at 0.3 mi. and then climbs gently to a lumber road at 0.4 mi. Turning L on the road, the trail crosses Nellie Brook and then takes an immediate R up a steep bank. Quickly leveling off, the trail zig-zags along a series of old overgrown lumber roads and emerges on a wide gravel lumber road at 0.7 mi. Turning R on this road, the trail takes the R fork at 1.1 mi., crosses Nellie Brook a few yards later, and climbs over a ridge.

The trail descends to cross Guideboard Brook at 1.7 mi., and at 2.0 mi. a private trail comes in from the R. Continuing along the lumber road, the trail takes a R fork at 2.2 mi. and then turns L off the road at 2.4 mi. The trail now climbs over a hill and descends to Guideboard Brook at a point just below a beaver dam. Passing the beaver pond on its E side, the trail crosses Guideboard Brook at the head of the pond at 2.8 mi. and follows up a tributary to an old road at 2.8 mi. From here, the trail climbs with a few steep pitches to the top of the pass through the Boreas-Colvin Range at 3.3 mi. Elevation, 2650 ft. (808 m). Ascent from Elk Lake, 600 ft. (180 m).

From this pass, the trail descends moderately, crosses a small brook at 3.5 mi. and continues along a side hill with short ups and downs, followed by a moderate climb to another height of land at 4.3 mi. Elevation, 2590 ft. (789 m). From here, the trail descends moderately and crosses an old lumber road at 4.6 mi. Continuing down, at 4.8 mi. the trail passes a collapsed building on the R, which is all that is left of a lumber camp. Turning L at this old building, the trail descends to another lumber road at 4.9 mi., which the trail follows for a few yards before turning sharp R and down and entering state land shortly before reaching a junction at 5.0 mi. Trail R leads along Pinnacle Ridge over Mt. Colvin and Blake Peak to St. Huberts (trail 60).

The Elk Lake-Marcy Trail continues to descend to a junction at 5.2 mi., where it again enters private land. (Trail R and L at this junction is private and closed to the public.) Continuing straight ahead a few yards, the trail crosses the Upper Ausable Lake inlet on a two-log bridge. (Heading toward Elk Lake, be sure to make a sharp L at the E end of this bridge.) The trail is now on the flat in Marcy Swamp with evidence of recent beaver activity until just before it reaches a series of log bridges and at 5.5 mi. enters an open area affording a view of Marcy. The trail then re-enters the woods and begins to climb at 5.7 mi.

At 6.1 mi. the grade steepens and remains steady to a junction at 6.5 mi. (Trail R is private and closed to the public.) Now on the level, the trail again enters state land at 6.6 mi. and begins climbing the first of several pitches. At about 7.0 mi. the trail levels off in a wet area, crosses a fair-sized brook at 7.7 mi., and then traverses a small bog, with Marcy Brook coming into view on the L. Shortly after, the trail turns sharp R away from an old tote road the trail had briefly followed. Soon swinging back L, the trail parallels Marcy Brook to a brook crossing at the confluence of two streams (PBM 3012 ft. on large rock between two brooks) at 8.3 mi.

Continuing on, the trail enters thick woods at 8.7 mi. and passes the new Panther Gorge Lean-to on the R just before a short descent to the junction at 9.0 mi. with the ATIS trail leading R to Haystack (trail 58). Turning L, the Elk Lake-Marcy Trail crosses Marcy Brook and bears R and up a steep climb. (Watch carefully for the markers leading to the R, as there are several plain but false trails leading straight up the far bank of the brook.) At 9.1 mi. the trail crosses a small brook and resumes the steep climb. After a few more steep pitches, the grade begins to ease off, but the trail remains very rough all the way to Four Corners and the junction with the yellow trail from Lake Colden and Upper Works at 10.2 mi. (trail 121). Red trail L leads 0.5 mi. to the summit of Skylight (trail 122). This junction is the former site of Four Corners Lean-to, but because it is above 4000 ft. no camping is permitted here now.

Turning R with yellow markers, the trail climbs steadily up a rocky, eroded section of trail. At 10.4 mi. there is a boulder on the L which has split away from the mountain, forming a crevice. A few yards through this crevice there is a lookout at Gray Peak and Lake Tear. Swinging R, the trail continues the ascent to a good lookout on the R at 10.6 mi. Reaching timberline soon after, the trail climbs over bare rock to the top of Schofield Cobble at 10.7 mi. This little prominence is named for Peter Schofield, an early climber in the High Peaks whose favorite campsite was "Junction Camp" as Four Corners was then called. Schofield was also a member of the New York Board of Trade and Transportation and in his official capacity he played an important part in securing the adoption of the "forever wild" clause in the 1894 state Constitution. The name was suggested by Russell M.L. Carson in *Peaks and People*.

After dipping slightly beyond Schofield Cobble, the trail, marked with cairns and yellow paint blazes, begins its final steep ascent to the summit of Marcy at 11.0 mi. See "Mt. Marcy" in Introduction for history and description of the view. At the summit the trail joins the trail from Heart Lake, which also connects with the trails to Johns Brook Lodge and Keene Valley (trails 1 and 61).

Distances: Elk Lake parking lot to pass over Boreas Colvin Range, 3.3 mi.; to Upper Ausable Lake Inlet, 5.2 mi.; to Panther Gorge Lean-to, 9.0 mi.; to junction at Four Corners, 10.2 mi.; to summit of Marcy, 11.0 mi. (17.6 km). Total ascent from Elk Lake, 4200 ft. (1280 m). Elevation, 5344 ft. (1629 m). Order of height, 1.

(119) Dix via Hunters Pass   Map: F-12

Dix Mt. was named by Ebenezer Emmons in 1837 for John A. Dix, then Secretary of State for Governor Marcy and later governor himself. He also served as U.S. Senator, Secretary of the Treasury, and Major General in the Civil War. The first ascent was in 1807 by a surveyor named Rykert, who had the task of running a line that now forms the southern boundary of the town of Keene and passes directly over the summit.

There are two trails from Elk Lake (see "Elk Lake Area" heading above for trailhead info), coinciding for the first 4.3 mi. The Hunters Pass Trail is 0.7 mi. longer but has a little less steep climbing and some interesting views from above Hunters Pass.

Leaving the parking lot (0 mi.) with red DEC markers, the trail proceeds mostly on the level, crosses a private trail, and reaches a wide gravel lumber road at 0.5 mi., where the trail turns L. (Hikers returning on this section of trail should watch very carefully for the sharp R turn off the lumber road.) Gentle rises and falls lead to Big Sally Brook at 1.6 mi., and the wide road ends shortly afterwards at another brook crossing. From here the trail is quite wet to the yellow-blazed state land boundary at 1.9 mi. Continuing on the flat and crossing two small brooks, the trail crosses the first of several small brooks that are discolored by iron as a result of the great Macomb slide of 1947. At 2.3 mi. the trail crosses a larger brook, which is the favored approach to the Macomb slide. (See below.)

Just past this brook are some possible campsites on both sides of the trail, after which the trail crosses another brook and comes to Slide Brook Lean-to on the L at the edge of a large clearing at 2.3 mi. There has been some question as to which of these two brooks is actually Slide Brook, but in reality both are, as the slide caused Slide Brook to split about 0.2 mi. above the trail.

Swinging L and slightly down through the clearing, the trail crosses a brook at the far edge of the clearing and continues on at easy grades through an open hardwood forest. At 3.1 mi., a small cairn on the R marks the beginning of a route to Hough and South Dix. The Dix Trail continues ascending for a few more yards before swinging L and beginning a steady descent to Lillian Brook Lean-to on the L bank of Lillian Brook at 3.6 mi. Swinging R and crossing the brook, the trail climbs to 3.8 mi. and then descends moderately to steeply to some rough going along a side hill above Dix Pond. Descending to the level of Dix Pond at 4.1 mi., the trail passes through two lumber clearings to a junction at 4.3 mi. with a yellow trail R to the Beckhorn (trail 120).

Continuing straight ahead, the trail crosses the East Inlet and begins a steady climb along the R bank of the brook. Eventually pulling away from the brook, the trail crosses a large tributary at 5.5 mi. and continues at a moderate grade, finishing with a steep pitch to Hunters Pass at 6.1 mi. Crossing to the far side of the boulder-strewn pass, the trail begins a steep to very steep climb up past some overhanging rocks to a short breather at 6.3 mi. The climbing soon resumes to another level stretch and view toward Nipple Top at 6.5 mi. Just beyond, the trail reaches "Balanced Rock" lookout, followed by slightly easier but still steady climbing to a junction at 6.9 mi. with the trail from Round Pond (trail 146).

Turning R, the climbing continues steady but not quite as steep along the ridge to the summit crest at 7.1 mi. From this point, hikers should use care to remain on the marked trail so as not to damage the fragile alpine vegetation. The going is now nearly level past one rock on the L with a U.S. Coast and Geodetic Survey marker and on to the summit with an old survey bolt at 7.3 mi. This bolt was placed by Verplanck Colvin in 1873 as part of his Adirondack Survey. The view is unobstructed in all directions, with Elk Lake seen to the SW, Lake Champlain and the Green Mts. to the E, and the Great Range to the NW. The trail with yellow DEC disks from the lumber clearing via the Beckhorn continues straight over the summit.

Distances: Elk Lake parking lot to Slide Brook Lean-to, 2.3 mi.; to Lillian Brook Lean-to, 3.7 mi.; to junction with Beckhorn Trail, 4.3 mi.; to Hunters Pass, 6.1 mi.; to Round Pond Trail from Rt. 73, 6.9 mi.; to summit of Dix, 7.3 mi. (11.8 km). Ascent from Elk Lake, 2800 ft. (853 m). Elevation, 4875 ft. (1486 m). Order of height, 6.

(120) Dix via Beckhorn   Map: F-11

This trail leads up the steep SW ridge of Dix to a small subsidiary peak known as the Beckhorn, a name conferred by Old Mountain Phelps because of its resemblance to the beckiron on a blacksmith's anvil. Take the red-marked Dix Trail (trail 119) to the lumber clearing at 4.3 mi. Leaving the junction (0 mi.) with the yellow markers, the trail soon begins climbing steeply, with one short, easier stretch, before reaching a small brook at 0.5 mi. Climbing out of the brook, the trail gains the crest of a ridge with some more easy going until the climbing starts again at 0.9 mi. From here the trail climbs at a steady, steep grade, with a few views possible back to Elk Lake, to a slight sag at 1.5 mi., followed by more steep climbing to the open rocks just below the Beckhorn. Now following cairns and paint blazes, the trail passes over the Beckhorn at 2.1 mi., down steeply, and on to the summit at 2.3 mi.

Distances: Elk Lake parking lot to junction at lumber clearing. 4.3 mi.; to summit of Dix, 6.6 mi. (10.6 km). Ascent from lumber clearing, 2600 ft. (792 m). Elevation, 4875 ft. (1486 m). Order of height, 6.

Unmaintained Trails in the Dix Range

(See Peaks Without Maintained Trails in Introduction)

Macomb, South Dix, East Dix, Hough

Macomb honors the memory of Alexander Macomb, who defeated the British in the Battle of Plattsburgh on September 11, 1814. Hough bears the name of one of the early Adirondack conservationists, Franklin B. Hough (pronounced "Huff").

The most popular current route up Macomb follows Slide Brook to the base of a new slide that leads to a point just N of the summit. The great slide of 1947, formerly the most popular route, is now less so owing both to the difficulty of findings its base in a tangle of alders and to the amount of moss and lichen growing back on the rock.

To find either slide, take the Elk Lake-Dix Trail (trail 119) to Slide Brook, 2.3 mi. from Elk Lake. Follow the N bank of this brook E for about 0.6 mi. to the end of the recently widened brook bed. (The tributary that comes in from the SE just below this point is the route to the older slide.) The widened brook is now followed for just over 0.5 mi. to the base of the new slide coming down from the R. The first part is quite loose, but angling to the L puts one on firmer ground. From the top of the slide it is about 0.3 mi. to the top of the ridge and then about 200 yds. to the R (S) to the summit of Macomb. A return via the old slide makes a nice round trip and affords an excellent view from the S summit at the head of the old slide.

Another possible route follows the valley of West Mill Brook up from Rt. 9 near North Hudson, beginning at the end of the West Mill Brook Northway Access (trail 116).

From Macomb to South Dix, the going is easy, following the ridge down to the col between the two peaks and then up spectacular open rocks below South Dix's summit. From South Dix to East Dix is likewise an easy walk of about an hour on a good herd path running along the crest of the ridge.

Going from South Dix to Hough, skirt the blowdown just N of the South Dix summit on its W side and then climb the hogback between South Dix and Hough. There is a bivouac site in the col between the hogback and Hough (with wet-weather water available). From Hough to Dix, continue along the ridge to the Beckhorn of Dix.

Alternate routes to the crest of the Dix Range leave the height of land on the Elk Lake-Dix Trail (trail 119) between the Slide and Lillian Brook valleys (0.7 mi. N of Slide Brook Lean-to). These routes follow an old lumber road to the S bank of Lillian Brook and then up to a flat area at about 3100 ft. Here one herd path bears R to the

McComb-South Dix col while another continues straight ahead to the Hough-South Dix col.

The Dixes may also be climbed from the NE via the North and South Forks of the Bouquet River (see Eastern Region). Another interesting approach to East Dix is from the E via Lindsay Brook, starting at the end of the Lindsay Brook Northway Access (trail 115).

Boreas Mt.

With the removal of the firetower, the access to this peak has been lost. For hikers this is no great loss because without the tower this summit does not offer any views commensurate with the effort required to reach the it.

Sanford Lake Area

The trails to Marcy, Lake Colden, Indian Pass, and Duck Hole all begin at or near the end of a road that leads from Rt. 28N near Newcomb past the presently inactive mining operations at Tahawus to the abandoned village of Adirondack, commonly referred to as Upper Works. This area has a long and interesting history, beginning in 1826 when an Indian guide led a party through Indian Pass to show them a vein of iron ore. For the next thirty years or so this was, in spite of transportation difficulties, a thriving operation which employed up to 400 men. The last expansion of the operation during this early phase was in 1854 and included the building of the great stone furnace, the remains of which can still be seen next to the road. This operation was built up the river from the original development located near the present center of mining operations, hence the name "Upper Works."

By 1858, operations had ceased, only to start again during World War II, when this deposit became a major source for the important metal titanium. Mining by the National Lead Company (now called NL Industries) continued after the war on an expanding basis, with the titanium used as a pigment for paint. In 1965, the entire village of Tahawus was moved to Newcomb to accommodate a new and larger excavation, and the tailings "desert" that the road crosses reached its present size. For various reasons, operations now have virtually ceased, but the property around these trailheads remains in the hands of the National Lead Company. This means that camping is not permitted at Upper Works, and that on some trails one must hike a considerable distance to reach state land where camping is permitted. See the map that accompanies this guidebook for the exact location of private land.

Trailhead: This access road is reached from Rt. 28N, 7.3 mi. N of Aiden Lair or about 5 mi. E of the Town Hall in Newcomb. An alternate approach is from Exit 29 on the Adirondack Northway (Interstate 87) via Blue Ridge Rd. Approximately 20 mi. from Exit 29, Blue Ridge Rd. joins the access road, 1.6 mi. from Rt. 28N.

About 6 mi. from Rt. 28N, the road forks with the main road continuing straight across a bridge over the Hudson to the mine. Turn L here on a narrower road marked with a sign for "Marcy and the High Peaks." At 2.0 mi. from this turn, there is a parking lot on the L for the Bradley Pond Trail to Duck Hole (trail 128). At 2.8 mi., one passes the large stone furnace on the R; and at 3.0 mi. there is a parking lot on the R for the Hanging Spear Falls approach to Flowed Lands (trail 123) as well as the route to Allen Mt. Shortly beyond are some abandoned buildings, and the parking lot at Upper Works is reached at 3.5 mi.

(121) Mt. Marcy and Lake Colden via Calamity Brook Trail   Map: C-10

This is the shortest approach to Marcy from the S and it is an attractive route highlighted by the camping areas on Flowed Lands and Lake Colden and the pretty falls and flumes on the Opalescent River. For years, many hikers believed, for understandable reasons, that the name "calamity" was applied to this trail because of its condition, but recently ADK and DEC trail crews have done extensive work on this trail and it is now relatively dry and much more pleasant to hike.

Starting at the Upper Works parking lot (0 mi.) with red and yellow markers, the trail follows a wide road, bearing L at a junction at 0.1 mi. (Road R at this junction is the old route of the Calamity Brook Trail.) The trail then crosses the outlet of Henderson Lake at 0.2 mi. and bears R to avoid a private road leading to the shore of the lake. After a short climb and descent, the trail comes to a junction at 0.4 mi. with a yellow trail straight ahead for Indian Pass and Duck Hole (trails 125 and 127). Turning sharp R on a good trail with red markers, the trail rejoins the old route at 0.7 mi. Now climbing at an easy grade near the R bank of Calamity Brook, the trail crosses the brook on a suspension bridge at 1.3 mi. and continues mostly on the flat around the E side of an extensive wet area. At 1.8 mi. the trail recrosses Calamity Brook and comes to a junction with a blue-marked trail from the Indian Pass Trail (trail 126). (End of red markers.)

Turning R, the trail follows the R bank of the brook at a gentle grade, but then pulls away from the brook at 2.1 mi. and begins a steady, moderate climb. Shortly above a switchback to the R at 2.3 mi., the grade begins to ease, and the trail enters state land at 2.4 mi. as the trail continues a gradual climb. At 2.9 mi. the trail swings sharp L away from the old tote road and soon descends a ladder to a bridge over the brook. (At low water one can save a few steps by crossing the brook on the stones.) Crossing the bridge, the trail quickly rejoins the tote road and climbs at a moderate grade until 3.3 mi., where it eases. The trail is now gently rolling, crossing numerous small streams and reaching an open area with many log bridges at 4.1 mi. After a short climb and descent, the trail reaches another open marsh which it skirts on the R side and reaches the N end of Calamity Pond at 4.3 mi.

A side trail leads 20 yds. straight ahead to the Henderson Monument, erected in memory of David Henderson who was accidentally shot and killed (the "calamity") on this spot while scouting for additional water sources to power the blast furnaces at the iron works. His scouting efforts eventually led to the construction of Flowed Lands dam, which could at one time divert the entire flow of the Opalescent down Calamity Brook and past the blast furnaces.

Turning sharp R, the Calamity Brook Trail climbs gradually along a very rocky section of trail to a junction at Flowed Lands at 4.7 mi., with the two Calamity Lean-tos up to the R. The red trail R is the Hanging Spear Falls Trail (trail 123) which leads to several lean-tos on Flowed Lands and eventually back to the road below Upper Works. As of 1984, the dam at Flowed Lands had been partially breached because it was deemed unsafe. This accounts for the current low water level in the lake. The DEC may rebuild the dam at a lower level to bring the water about half way back up to its former height.

Turning sharp L and now with red markers again, the trail crosses the now dry channel by which the Opalescent River was once diverted to Calamity Brook. The trail follows around the NW shore of the lake and at 5.0 mi. begins a climb up behind a rocky promontory before descending again to lake level and crossing Herbert Brook at 5.4 mi. (One approach to Mt. Marshall goes L here; see below.) Continuing on with a few short climbs and descents, the trail reaches a junction at the top of the ladder leading to the bridge over Lake Colden Dam at 5.7

mi. Blue trail straight ahead (trail 69) leads in 300 yds. to two of the six lean-tos in the vicinity, and in 0.5 mi. to Lake Colden Interior Outpost on the NW shore of the lake and then on to Heart Lake.

Turning R and down across the dam (still with red markers), the trail passes a former lean-to site on the L and several designated camping areas and comes to a trail register and junction at 5.8 mi. Yellow trail L (trail 68) leads along the E shore of Lake Colden to Avalanche Pass and Heart Lake. A lean-to is located about 100 yds. beyond on the R bank of the Opalescent River, although this lean-to is slated for eventual replacement by a structure on a new site E and uphill from the trail register. Another lean-to is located across the river and 0.2 mi. down the L bank. (At most water levels, one can cross the Opalescent just below the Lake Colden Dam, but at high water levels use the suspension bridge described below.)

Bearing R from the trail register, the trail soon reaches a suspension bridge over the Opalescent and turns sharp L on the far side. Continuing up the L bank at easy grades, the trail passes a waterfall at 6.1 mi. and ascends a ladder at 6.4 mi. to some ledges above a beautiful flume in the Opalescent. The grade eases above the flume and, after crossing a small tributary, the trail joins an old tote road and climbs away from the river at easy to moderate grades. At 7.3 mi. the trail reaches a height of land and descends a moderate grade to the junction with the abandoned Twin Brook Trail at 7.4 mi. (Unmarked routes to Cliff and Redfield diverge R and up the abandoned trail.) This is the end of the red markers, and the trail is now marked with yellow DEC disks, the color of the former Twin Brook Trail.

From here, the trail bears L and gently down 200 yds. to Uphill Lean-to located on the L bank of Uphill Brook. (This lean-to is slated for replacement in 1994 on a new site to the L of the trail.) Past the lean-to, the trail continues down and crosses Uphill Brook on stones near its confluence with the Opalescent River. The trail now follows close to the L bank of the Opalescent at an easy grade to a junction at 8.0 mi. with the blue-marked Lake Arnold trail (trail 73). The rebuilt Feldspar Lean-to is found 100 yds. up this trail. Turning R, the Marcy Trail soon begins climbing at a moderate grade, crosses a tributary at 8.1 mi., and begins a steady, steep climb up a section of trail high above the L bank of Feldspar Brook. This section of trail has received extensive stabilization work in the past few years and now bears little resemblance to the eroded mess that used to pass for a trail.

At about 8.8 mi. the grade begins to moderate and finally becomes level just before reaching the outlet to Lake Tear of the Clouds, the highest pond source of the Hudson River (elevation, 4346 ft.) at 9.2 mi. Across this little body of water, fringed with spruce and balsam, the rocky dome of Mt. Marcy rises in full view.

Bearing R, the trail ascends a few yards to the former site of Lake Tear Lean-to. (Camping is prohibited in this area as it is over 4000 ft. in elevation.) Continuing on, the trail drops back to the lake level and continues mostly on the level through some very wet terrain to Four Corners, where it joins the blue trail from Elk Lake (trail 118) at 9.5 mi. The red trail R (trail 122) leads 0.5 mi. to the summit of Skylight. As at Lake Tear, no camping is permitted at this former lean-to site because it is above 4000 ft. in elevation.

Turning L and still with yellow markers, the trail climbs steadily up a rocky, eroded section of trail. At 9.7 mi. there is a boulder on the L that has split away from the mountain, forming a crevice. A few yards through this crevice there is a lookout at Gray Peak and Lake Tear. Swinging R, the trail continues the ascent to a good lookout on the R at 10.0 mi. Reaching timberline soon after, the trail climbs over bare rock to the top of Schofield Cobble at 10.1 mi. This little prominence is named for Peter Schofield, an early climber in the High Peaks whose favorite campsite was "Junction Camp" as Four Corners was then called. Schofield was also a member of the New York Board of Trade and Transportation and in his official capacity he played an important part in securing the adoption of the "forever wild" clause in the 1894 state Constitution. The name was suggested by Russell M.L. Carson in *Peaks and People.*

After dipping slightly beyond Schofield Cobble, the trail, marked with cairns and yellow paint blazes, begins its final steep ascent to the summit of Marcy at 10.3 mi. (See "Mt. Marcy" in Introduction for history and description of the view.) At the summit the trail joins the trail from Heart Lake, which also connects with the trails to Johns Brook Lodge and Keene Valley (trails 1 and 61).

Trail in winter: This has long been a popular ski trip for advanced intermediate skiers. At least one foot of snow is needed to cover the rocks. With luck, the stream crossings will be frozen as the suspension bridges are tricky. From Calamity Lean-tos, ski across Flowed Lands and find the trail to Lake Colden on the L bank of the Opalescent River.

Distances: Upper Works parking lot to Calamity Lean-tos at Flowed Lands, 4.7 mi.; to junction at Lake Colden dam, 5.7 mi.; to Uphill Lean-to, 7.5 mi.; to junction with Lake Arnold Trail near Feldspar Lean-to, 8.0 mi.; to Four Corners and junction with Elk Lake-Marcy Trail, 9.5 mi.; to summit of Marcy, 10.3 mi. (16.6 km). Ascent from Upper Works, 3800 ft. (1158 m). Elevation, 5344 ft. (1629 m). Order of height, 1.

(122) Skylight from Four Corners   Map: D-10

From Four Corners, the junction of the Elk Lake and Calamity Brook trails to Marcy, a red-marked trail leads S and up to the open, rounded dome of Mt. Skylight. Leaving the junction (0 mi.), the trail makes a steady climb up a wet, rocky trail to timberline at 0.4 mi. From here the grade is easier through an open alpine meadow with cairns to mark the way to the summit at 0.5 mi. There are outstanding views of the surrounding peaks, with 30 major peaks discernible. Legend states that if a climber fails to carry a rock from timberline to place on one of the two huge cairns on the summit, it will surely rain.

Distance: Four Corners to summit of Skylight, 0.5 mi. (0.8 km). Ascent from Four Corners, 578 ft. (176 m). Elevation, 4926 ft. (1501 m). Order of height, 4.

Unmaintained Trail to Gray Peak

(See Peaks Without Maintained Trails in Introduction)

This mountain, the highest of the trailless peaks, was named by Colvin for Professor Asa Gray, one of the most noted botanists of his day. Start at the outlet of Lake Tear of the Clouds (see trail 121) and climb over a ridge and across into a valley. (When descending, do not be misled down this valley, as it is very rough going and joins Feldspar Brook well below Lake Tear.) The route then heads N to the summit ridge, striking it about 200 yds. W of the summit. Another route leads from the lowest extension of timberline on the W side of Marcy, dipping to the S of the ridgeline at times to avoid cliffs, but this route involves traversing some of the thickest scrub imaginable with no continuous herd path yet developed. Should one attempt this route, remember to walk on the bare rock when above timberline to avoid trampling any alpine vegetation. (See Introduction.)

Unmaintained Trails to Cliff and Redfield

(See Peaks Without Maintained Trails in Introduction)

Redfield

This peak was named by Colvin for Professor William C. Redfield, meteorologist and organizer of the first expedition to Marcy. It was Redfield who first described Marcy as the "High Peak of Essex" after a reconnaissance up the Opalescent River above Lake Colden before the first ascent in 1837.

The best route to Redfield's summit follows Uphill Brook from Uphill Lean-to (see trail 121) to a point about 0.3 mi. above a high waterfall on the main stream where a tributary comes in from the R (S). Follow this tributary and then head straight for the summit to avoid bad blowdown on the NE section of the summit ridge.

Another route to Redfield leads from Lake Tear of the Clouds SW to the summit. Stay below the summit ridge until directly under the top of the mountain. There is no continuous herd path on this route.

Cliff

This self-explanatory name was bestowed by Colvin. Start from the height of land between Cliff and Redfield on the abandoned Twin Brook Trail, which can be reached from the Mt. Marcy via Lake Colden trail (trail 121). Head W, in general keeping to the R of the higher cliffs. Reaching the NE summit, follow the broad ridge SW about 0.5 mi. to the true summit, which rises steeply beyond the col.

(123) Flowed Lands via Hanging Spear Falls   Map: C-11

This much longer approach to Flowed Lands leads past the beautiful Hanging Spear Falls, one of the highest in the Adirondacks. This trail also is the start of the most popular approach for Allen Mt. However, now that Twin Brook Lean-to has been removed and camping is prohibited at the former lean-to site, the first legal area to camp is nearly 6 mi. from the road and is almost a 1-mi. detour from the approach to Allen. Hikers also should be aware that there is no bridge across the Opalescent River at Flowed Lands, and this crossing can be difficult in high water.

Trailhead: The trail starts at a parking lot on the R side of the road to Upper Works, 3.0 mi. from the junction with the road leading to the mining operations. (See above, under Sanford Lake Area, for complete driving directions.)

From the trail register (0 mi.), with yellow markers, the trail follows a road 0.1 mi. to the R bank of the Hudson River where it turns R a few yds. to a suspension bridge. Crossing the bridge, the trail soon rejoins the road and continues on the level to a long bridge over the N end of Lake Jimmy at 0.6 mi. At 0.7 mi. the trail reaches a junction with trail to Mt. Adams (trail 124) and swings sharp R.

The trail now crosses a small stream and several small wet areas and comes to a gravel road at 1.2 mi. Turning sharp R onto the road, the trail turns sharp L and down on another road at 1.4 mi. and swings R again in another 100 yds. Now a footpath again, the trail soon comes to the shore of Lake Sally with occasional views across the lake at the N edge of the tailings "desert." After a last view of the lake at 1.9 mi. the trail heads SE over a low divide and comes to the Opalescent River at 2.6 mi. Swinging L, the trail follows near the R bank of the river to an open area and a private gravel road leading R across the river at 3.7 mi.

The yellow trail continues to follow a gravel road along the R bank of the river until the trail bears R off the road and down to a bridge across the Opalescent River at 3.8 mi. At the far side the trail turns L and climbs at an easy grade along an old tote road, sometimes leaving the old road to avoid washouts or blowdown areas. Hiking this trail in either direction, one must remain alert in this section for sharp changes of direction; but it is otherwise very easy walking as the trail crosses a brook at 4.2 mi. and later the Lower Twin Brook at 5.1 mi. on the broken remains of an old lumber bridge. At 5.3 mi. the trail reaches the former site of Twin Brook Lean-to which was removed in 1992. It will not be replaced, and because this is private land, camping at this site is now prohibited.

Continuing to the L and now with red markers, the trail soon crosses Upper Twin Brook, bears L along the edge of a large lumber clearing, and ascends gradually to a gravel lumber road coming in from the R at 5.5 mi. continuing to ascend gradually on this road to a crest at 5.7 mi., the trail descends and soon branches R from the lumber road, coming to a yellow post marking the boundary of state land at 5.9 mi. At 6.4 mi. the trail reaches the L bank of the Opalescent River but soon climbs away from the river on an old tote road.

At 7.5 mi. the trail crosses a brook and begins to climb more steeply along a side hill near the gorge. Shortly after this stream crossing there is a side trail L (which rejoins the old road 70 yds. further on) leading to several views of Hanging Spear Falls. At a certain volume of water, the falls are divided by a rock which gives the appearance of a "hanging spearhead." The trail continues its steep climb, passing another lookout on the L at 7.6 mi. and reaching easier going soon after. The trail now follows the L bank of the river at easy grades to the breached dam at Flowed Lands at 8.1 mi. See Calamity Brook Trail (trail 121) for history and current status of this dam. (From the dam, a yellow-marked side trail leads R 0.6 mi. to Livingston Point Lean-to. With the current low water levels it is also relatively easy to continue along the open shore of Flowed Lands to the lean-tos at Lake Colden, but this route is not marked and will likely become more of a bushwhack in the years to come as the alders grow on the formerly flooded areas.)

Turning L at the dam, the trail crosses the river on stones below the dam and comes to a side trail at the far side which leads L and up 50 yds. to Griffin Lean-to. The main trail climbs up away from the shore and after several ups and downs comes to a side trail R at 8.3 mi. leading to Flowed Lands Lean-to, which has one of the prettiest locations of any lean-to in the Adirondacks. Continuing past this junction, the trail climbs over one more knoll and descends to a junction at the shore of the lake near the Calamity Lean-tos at 8.5 mi. Trail L and straight ahead is Calamity Brook Trail (trail 121) leading to Upper Works or Lake Colden and Marcy.

Trail in winter: Although rarely skied, the trail is skiable all the way to the base of the climb to Hanging Spear Falls at 7.5 mi. If one is willing to struggle for 0.5 mi., this is a feasible, if long, route to Flowed Lands.

Distances: Parking lot to Twin Brook Lean-to site, 5.3 mi.; to Hanging Spear Falls, 7.6 mi.; to Flowed Lands Dam, 8.1 mi.; to junction with Calamity Brook Trail, 8.5 mi. (13.7 km).

Unmaintained Trail to Allen

(See Peaks Without Maintained Trails in Introduction)

This mountain was named by Rev. Joseph Twichell for his close friend, Rev. Frederick B. Allen, who became superintendent of the Episcopal City Mission in Boston. The naming took place on a camping trip to Upper Ausable Lake with Charles Dudley Warner and Dr. Horace Bushnell when they were caught in the great cloudburst of August 20, 1869, that caused the great slide (or "avalanche," as in the lake) on Mt. Colden.

The formerly popular approach to Allen using the gravel lumber roads along the S Branch of the Opalescent River has been closed for several years at the request of the landowner. Currently, the most used route follows a herd path from the site of the former Twin Brook Lean-to on the trail to Flowed Lands via Hanging Spear Falls (trail 123). The route to Allen begins by heading SW to Lower Twin Brook, which it follows along its NW side. About 0.3 mi. from the marked trail the herd path strikes a gravel lumber road, turns L for 100 yds., and then turns R and proceeds to the far end of a sand pit where the herd path resumes. In about a mile, the herd path crosses the brook and heads generally SE, contouring to a low pass. Descending the valley SE of the pass past beaver ponds, the route crosses a sizable brook shortly before crossing Skylight Brook to join the old route. Continuing NE up the Skylight Brook valley for some 0.7 mi., the herd path turns SE again following a tributary, the beautiful Allen Brook, past its source to the ridgetop a short distance S of the summit. Allow at least 4 hours from the trail at Twin Brook lean-to site.

Climbing Allen from either Skylight or the Elk Lake-Marcy Trail involves travel through blowdown and thick second growth without the aid of herd paths.

(124) Mt. Adams   Map: C-11

The fire tower on this peak has been abandoned for many years and is currently unsafe to climb. There are practically no views from this summit without the tower, making this a less than attractive climb. The DEC has discontinued to marking the trail to this summit but it is still relatively easy to follow although it has not received recent maintenance. The Mt. Adams Trail diverges L from the Hanging Spear Falls Trail to Flowed Lands (trail 123) 0.8 mi. from the parking lot and is marked with red markers. It ascends at first by easy grades past the old observer's cabin and then at moderate to finally very steep grades to the summit, 2.4 mi. from the parking lot, having ascended 1800 ft.

(125) Indian Pass from
Upper Works   Map: C-10

This trail leads to Summit Rock in Indian Pass, where it connects with the trail from Heart Lake. The view of Wallface's huge cliff from Summit Rock is one of the most impressive views in the Adirondacks, and is a good objective for a day hike or as a point to be included in a backpacking trip.

Trailhead: The trail starts at the Upper Works parking lot (see above, under Sanford Lake Area, for driving directions) with yellow markers and coincides with the red-marked Calamity Brook Trail (trail 121) initially.

From the trail register (0 mi.) the trail follows a wide gravel road, bearing L at a side road at 0.1 mi. and continuing on to a bridge over the outlet to Henderson Lake at 0.2 mi. Bearing R at the end of this bridge, the trail climbs slightly and continues to a junction at 0.4 mi. (Red trail R is the Calamity Brook Trail, trail 121). Continuing straight ahead, the gravel road ends at 0.5 mi. and the trail bears R and begins a gradual climb to a crest at 0.8 mi., after which it descends. After some more ups and downs on this old jeep road, the trail bears R while the road goes straight ahead to a ford, and soon comes to a junction at 1.5 mi. with the red-marked trail L leading to Duck Hole (trail 127). Yellow markers end here.

Continuing straight ahead with red markers, the Indian Pass Trail enters state land at 1.7 mi., with Henderson Lean-to on the L near Indian Pass Brook just beyond. Passing behind the lean-to, the trail comes to an old lumber clearing and junction at 2.0 mi. The blue-marked trail going straight at this junction is the crossover to Calamity Brook (trail 126). Turning L, the Indian Pass Trail crosses the brook and proceeds at easy grades to Wallface Lean-to at 2.7 mi. near the R bank of Indian Pass Brook.

Still pretty much on the level, the trail veers away from the brook; just before reaching a large rock on the R at 2.9 mi., there is a view of Wallface ahead. After crossing three smaller brooks, the trail crosses the outlet to Wallface Ponds at 3.2 mi. and recrosses Indian Pass Brook at 3.9 mi. The grade soon becomes steep as it winds among large boulders and ledges. After a short downgrade at 4.1 mi. the trail again climbs steeply, with a ladder necessary at one point, until it reaches a side trail leading L a few yds. to Summit Rock at 4.4 mi. This is not the actual summit of the pass, but has by far the best view and is the usual destination coming from either direction. The actual height of land is another 0.5 mi. beyond, and the trail continues 6.0 mi. more to Heart Lake (trail 75).

Trail in winter: Skiable for the first three miles or close enough to get some spectacular views of Wallface, but definitely not skiable to Summit Rock.

Distances: Upper Works to junction with Duck Hole Trail, 1.5 mi.; to Henderson Lean-to, 1.7 mi.; to junction with crossover to Calamity Brook Trail, 2.0 mi.; to Wallface Lean-to, 2.7 mi.; to Summit Rock, 4.4 mi. (7.0 km). Ascent from Upper Works, 870 ft. (265 m). Elevation, 2660 ft. (810 m).

(126) Indian Pass-Calamity Brook Crossover   Map: C-10

This trail leads through a pass at the end of the MacIntyre Range to connect the Indian Pass and Calamity Brook Trails. Its construction dates back to a time when the Tahawus Club controlled the area near Upper Works and would not permit hikers to pass through. An alternate route was thus needed to allow hikers to travel between Duck Hole and Lake Colden. With the current trail layout, however, this crossover trail saves no distance between these two points and involves some rough, wet trail—complicated by recent beaver activity—plus 500 ft. of additional climbing. Hikers approaching from Indian Pass do save almost a mile, but the trail is now infrequently used.

From the junction, 2.0 mi. from Upper Works on the Indian Pass Trail (0 mi.), the grade is easy at first, but soon becomes steeper as the trail follows a brook, crossing and recrossing it several times before climbing more steeply to the top of the pass at 0.9 mi., having gained 500 ft. from the Indian Pass Trail. Descending, the trail skirts a meadow at 1.0 mi. and follows a brook, crossing it several times and reaching a beaver swamp at 1.7 mi. After some tough going around the R side of the swamp, the trail crosses the swamp at 1.8 mi. and follows a soggy tote road to the L of the brook and finally reaches dry ground at 2.0 mi. The trail reaches the junction with Calamity Brook (trail 121) at 2.1 mi.

Distance: Indian Pass Trail to Calamity Brook Trail, 2.1 mi. (3.4 km).

(127) Duck Hole via
Henderson Lake   Map: C-10

This is the easiest route to Duck Hole and involves relatively little climbing compared to the route via Bradley Pond. The trail begins at Upper Works (see above, under Sanford Lake Area, for driving directions) and follows the Indian Pass Trail (trail 125) to the junction at 1.5 mi. Leaving the junction (0 mi.), the trail immediately crosses Indian Pass Brook on a good log bridge and turns L, but soon swings R and away from the brook and at 0.3 mi. crosses a beaver flow.

Past the beaver flow, the trail is mostly level to a junction at 0.6 mi. with a trail leading L and down to a private dock on Henderson Lake. Swinging R, the trail crosses a long series of bridges over a wet area and reaches a brook, which it crosses at 0.7 mi. Recrossing the brook at 0.8 mi., the trail veers away and approaches the R bank of another brook, which it follows up past some interesting cascades at 0.9 mi. Just beyond, the trail skirts a beaver pond on its L side and continues on to a brook crossing at 1.3 mi. Recrossing this brook twice more, the trail begins a moderate climb that levels off at 1.8 mi. Descending slightly, the trail is now mostly level through an almost imperceptible divide between the St. Lawrence and Hudson watersheds, having gained only 370 ft. (113 m) from Henderson Lake.

Dropping slightly after the pass, the trail comes to a junction in the middle of a series of bridges over some wet areas. (Trail straight ahead leads to a private dock on the Preston Ponds.) Turning sharp R, the trail soon begins climbing along the outlet to Hunter Pond, crossing it at 2.4 mi. The trail continues up the L bank, reaches Hunter Pond at 2.7 mi., crosses the outlet, and skirts the pond to the N before climbing a short steep pitch to the top of a pass at 2.8 mi. Starting down, the trail skirts a beaver pond on its R side at 3.0 mi. and joins an old lumber road just past the pond. The trail now descends a wet and eroded section of lumber road to the remains of Piche's lumber camp at 3.2 mi.

After the camp, the trail crosses to the R side of the brook and continues descending at easy grades before veering away from the brook and descending more steeply over old corduroys with Lower Preston Pond visible through trees to the L. Crossing a small swamp at 4.0 mi., the trail climbs easily to a boundary line, enters state land at 4.2 mi. and, after another descent and climb to a height of land, descends to the NE shore of Duck Hole at 4.4 mi. Turning N and after several more short, steep ups and downs, the trail reaches the L bank of Roaring Brook, which it crosses on stones to a junction with the Northville-Placid Trail (trail 99) on the far bank at 4.9 mi. There is no bridge, and this crossing could be difficult in times of high water.

Turning L and now with red and blue markers, the trail proceeds with several easy ups and downs to a large,open area leading down to the bridge and dam at Duck Hole at 5.3 mi. There are two lean-tos at Duck Hole, and plenty of tent sites. One lean-to is just before the bridge and dam, and the other is in the woods on a point of land 100 yds. E of the dam. A ranger station at the W edge of the clearing was removed in December 1977 in order to bring the area into compliance with wilderness use guidelines. A blue trail crosses the dam and leads to Bradley Pond (trail 128) and the trailhead at Tahawus. The N-P Trail heads W along an old truck trail which connects with a trail heading to Ward Brook and the trailhead at Coreys (trails 129 and 133).

Trail in winter: Very skiable as far as the Preston Ponds. Access to the ice on the ponds is trespassing and the climb to Hunter Pond is very difficult on skis. Otherwise, this is a very skiable route to Duck Hole.

Distances: Trail junction S of Henderson Lean-to near bridge over Indian Pass Trail to E end of Preston Ponds, 2.3 mi.; to junction with N-P Trail at Roaring Brook, 4.9 mi.; to Duck Hole, 5.3 mi. (8.6 km). (Distance from Upper Works, 6.9 mi. or 11.1 km).

Trailless Route to MacNaughton

(See Peaks Without Maintained Trails in Introduction)

MacNaughton is named after James MacNaughton, grandson of Archibald McIntyre, who headed the original Adirondack Iron Works. Though not officially one of the 46 peaks, it is the one mountain to be raised to the 4000-ft. status on the 1953 USGS map. (With the publication of the new series of metric maps with 10-meter contour intervals, the highest contour elevation when converted to feet is less than 4000 feet, although the actual top elevation is probably above 4000 feet.) The upper reaches of the mountain are almost completely covered with blowdown.

Leave Duck Hole via Henderson Lake Trail (trail 127) at the brook crossing beyond the beaver pond about 0.6 mi. NW of Hunter Pond. Follow the SE side of the brook valley nearly to the summit ridge. Climb N over two summits to the register on the third and NW summit. All three summits are about the same height, the middle one having a good view.

Two other routes to MacNaughton are possible. One is from the Wallface Ponds on a compass line generally SW; the other is from Indian Pass following the outlet to the Wallface Ponds, bearing generally NW from the flat swampy area above the steeper descent of the outlet. There are no plain herd paths on MacNaughton. Cripple brush is thick and blowdowns are numerous.

(128) Duck Hole via Bradley Pond   Map: C-11

This trail leads to Duck Hole through the pass between the Santanoni Range and Henderson Mt. and gives access to the routes up to trailless Santanoni, Panther and Couchsachraga peaks (see below).

The first 4.3 mi. of this trail is on private land, where no camping is permitted, and the previously used routes to the trailless Santanonis that left this trail before it reached state land are now closed.

Trailhead: *The trail begins at a parking lot on the L side of the road to Upper Works, 2.0 mi. N of the bridge to the mining operations. (See above, under Sanford Lake Area, for complete driving directions.) There is a large parking lot 100 yds. back from the road.*

From the trail register (0 mi.), the trail follows a good gravel road with blue markers at gentle grades. At 1.1 mi. it crosses the outlet to Harkness Lake, where there is a great view of Wallface Mt. The trail now climbs over a small rise, drops down, and begins a longer climb that eases just before the trail makes a sharp R turn off the road at 1.8 mi.

The trail now descends along the R bank of a brook, crosses the brook on a good bridge, and continues on the flat through a grassy clearing with plenty of raspberries. At the far end of the clearing, the trail swings L and crosses Santanoni Brook at 2.1 mi. on an elaborate bridge with a series of log steps up the far bank. At the top of the bank, the trail swings L onto an old tote road and begins ascending at easy to moderate grades up the valley.

At 2.4 mi. the trail encounters some recent lumber roads which cross and recross the trail for about 300 yds., after which the trail continues a steady, moderate climb to a series of beautiful cascades on the L at 3.4 mi. At 3.5 mi. the trail passes the abandoned Santanoni Trail on the L (now closed to the public) and continues to a crest at 3.6 mi. After a short descent, the trail crosses a wet area on a series of good bridges, but beyond here the trail is almost unremittingly wet until well past Santanoni Lean-to. At 4.3 mi. the trail enters state land and the current legal route to the Santanonis diverges L across a beaver dam at Bradley Pond. Continuing on, the trail reaches a brook and former lean-to site at 4.4 mi. The new Santanoni Lean-to is located on a knoll above and to the R of the former site, but established, legal campsites are so far quite limited. This is the top of the pass, 2950 ft. (900 m), 1110 ft. (338 m) above the trailhead.

Past the lean-to the trail begins to descend. It is often difficult to distinguish the trail and the brook for the first part of the descent until at 4.8 mi. the trail crosses a larger stream, swings to the R and then back L to recross the stream, and then continues down to a crossing of the L fork of the main stream at 5.1 mi. Turning R on relatively flat ground, the trail crosses the main brook but returns to the L bank at 5.6 mi. Still mostly on the flat, the trail detours to the L to avoid some recent beaver and blowdown activity and crosses a beaver dam at 6.0 mi.

The trail wanders through more blowdown areas and climbs above the swamp where there are views of Panther to the SW. At 6.6 mi. the trail returns to the L bank of the stream. From here it is mostly very enjoyable walking along the picturesque stream. At 7.1 mi. the trail crosses again to the R bank and continues on the level to a corner of private land at 7.8 mi., where it turns L and crosses the brook for the final time and climbs over a small ridge to the SW shore of Duck Hole at 7.9 mi. Skirting the pond, the trail crosses a rock crib dike at 8.0 mi. and soon comes to the dam with the lean-to and trail junction just beyond at 8.2 mi. Here the trail meets the Northville-Placid Trail (trails 99 and 133), marked here with blue and red markers. It leads R to Averyville Rd. near Lake Placid with a connection to the trail from Upper Works (trail 127). To the L, the N-P Trail leads to Shattuck Clearing and Long Lake with a connection to the trail to Ward Brook and Coreys (trail 129).

Trail in winter: Both the climb to Bradley Pond and the descent off the N side of the pass are for advanced skiers, but overall this is a skiable route. It is rarely done, but makes a beautiful though very rugged 14-mile loop when combined with trail 127, Duck Hole via Henderson Lake.

Distances: Parking lot to Santanoni Lean-to, 4.4 mi.; to Duck Hole, 8.2 mi. (13.2 km).

Unmaintained Trails in the Santanoni Range

(See Peaks Without Maintained Trails in Introduction)

Santanoni

The name of the highest peak W of the Hudson River and the dominating one in the range is derived from the name Saint Anthony; it filtered down through the French Canadians to the Abenaki Indians who adopted their own pronunciation of the word. The traditional approach was a herd path starting 3.4 mi. from the old Tahawus Club road on the trail to Duck Hole via Bradley Pond (trail 128), but being on private land, this route is now closed to the public. A legal, and currently the most used route, leaves the above trail 4.3 mi. from the old Tahawus Club road and about 0.3 mi. S of the Santanoni Lean-to at a beaver dam. Crossing the beaver dam and then following a survey line past the northern end of Bradley Pond, it climbs steeply over rough terrain to state land about a third of the way up Panther Mountain, beyond which a herd path contours westerly some 0.3 mi. to the brook descending from the Panther-Santanoni ridge. A half mile of rock-hopping up the brook leads to a herd path that reaches the ridge about 0.5 mi. S of the summit of Panther at the point where a herd path leads W down a ridge to Couchsachraga. The route to Santanoni leads S along the ridge, a distance of more than a mile.

Ermine Brook Slide: A new and challenging route to Santanoni follows a slide that came down Santanoni's W face in September, 1985. The route leaves the Moose Pond Horse Trail (trail 138) where it crosses Ermine Brook, 1.4 mi. past Moose Pond. Take the R fork (looking up) just over 0.5 mi. from the trail to stay in the main branch of Ermine Brook. The base of this long, narrow slide is reached about 2 mi. from the trail. From the top of the slide it is a few yards to the crest of the ridge and then nearly 0.5 mi. to the summit of Santanoni.

Panther

The most used route to Panther's attractive summit employs the approach described above for Santanoni. It turns N at the top of the ridge, the distance from this point to Panther's summit being about 0.5 mi.

Couchsachraga

Pronounced "Kook-sa-kra-ga," this term is an ancient Algonquin name for the Adirondacks that means "dismal wilderness." Most people today reach Couchsachraga by way of herd paths leading W down the long ridge from the point 0.5 mi. S of Panther's summit where the route from the trail to Duck Hole via Bradley Pond strikes the ridge (see above). Travel from the Panther-Santanoni ridge to Couchsachraga can take two hours or more. The easiest way back from Couchsachraga to the above-mentioned trail is to return by the same route.

Another approach is from the Cold River area up a stream crossed by the horse trail (trail 134) about 6.0 mi. E of Shattuck Clearing and 4.0 mi. W of the Northville-Placid Trail NW of Duck Hole. An effectively abandoned trail from the Santanoni Preserve joins the horse trail at this point.

(129) Duck Hole from Coreys
via Ward Brook Truck Trail   Map: A-8

This is the western access to Duck Hole and the High Peaks Region and also offers the easiest access to the routes up the Seward Range (see below).

Trailhead: The start is on a road that leaves Rt. 3 12.7 mi. W of the traffic light in Saranac Lake and 2.7 mi. E of the junction of Rtes. 3 and 30 E of Tupper Lake. This road is marked with a large DEC sign for "High Peaks via Duck Hole." It is paved through the little settlement of Coreys, but turns to gravel at about 1.5 mi., crosses Stony Creek at 2.5 mi., and continues to a parking area on the R, 5.8 mi. from Rt. 3. As the signs indicate, the road enters a private preserve shortly beyond the parking lot, and this is as far as the public may travel. From this parking lot, both a foot trail and a horse trail depart for the Ward Brook Truck Trail and Duck Hole. The horse trail is not described here because it exactly parallels the hiking trail, is considerably wetter, and is generally unsuited for hiking.

Leaving the trail register (0 mi.) with red markers, the foot trail bears L and crosses a swamp on some good bridges and climbs a bank to higher ground at 0.6 mi., where an old trail comes in from the R. Now mostly on the level and soon joining the posted property line of the Ampersand Club, the trail comes to the Calkins Brook Trail at 1.2 mi. (Road L is blocked by a gate at the boundary of private land. Road R leads to Calkins Brook and Shattuck Clearing trail 130).

Continuing past the road and still mostly level, the trail crosses several brooks and passes within sight of Blueberry Pond on the L at 2.3 mi., crosses a large brook at 3.5 mi., and at 4.5 mi. comes to Blueberry Lean-to on the R. Just beyond the lean-to, the trail joins the Ward Brook Truck Trail coming in from the L from the private Ampersand Club. (Hikers heading toward Coreys must be sure to make this sharp L turn off the truck trail.)

Turning R on the road, the trail passes the junction with the horse trail at 4.7 mi. and then crosses three fair-sized brooks before reaching Ward Brook Lean-to at 5.4 mi. The first of these brooks is the favored approach to Seward (see below). The first brook beyond Ward Brook Lean-to is the favored approach to Seymour; after this brook the trail climbs easily to a crest before dipping down a bit to two lean-tos and a horse barn at 6.1 mi.

Climbing again at easy to moderate grades, the trail reaches its highest point at 7.0 mi. and descends in several stages to an open swamp at 8.4 mi. before climbing over another hill and dropping down to a junction with the Northville-Placid Trail (trail 133) at 8.7 mi. Continuing on with red and blue markers, the trail comes to the two Cold River Lean-tos (Nos. 1 and 2) at 9.1 mi. Just past the lean-tos, the trail crosses Moose Creek just above its confluence with the Cold River, climbs the far bank, and then follows along the R bank of the Cold River to a junction at 9.4 mi. with Cold River Horse Trail R (trail 134) which fords the Cold River and continues down the E side of the river to Shattuck Clearing with a connection to the Santanoni Preserve and Newcomb (see below).

Past this junction, the trail climbs over a low ridge and arrives at the trail junction and former site of the ranger station at 10.3 mi. Blue trail R crosses the dam and leads to Bradley Pond and the road below Upper Works (trail 128). Trail bearing L with blue and red markers is the continuation of the N-P Trail leading to Lake Placid (trail 99) and with a connection to a trail leading to Henderson Lake and Upper Works (trail 127). There are two lean-tos and several good campsites at Duck Hole. One lean-to is located by the dam and the other is 100 yds. E of the dam on a beautiful wooded point.

Trail in winter: Because the road is not plowed beyond the bridge over Stony Creek, add 3.3 mi. to all distances for winter travel. This route is very skiable for as far as time permits.

Distances: Parking area to Blueberry Lean-to, 4.5 mi.; to Ward Brook Lean-to, 5.4 mi.; to Northville-Placid Trail, 8.7 mi.; to Cold River Lean-tos, 9.1 mi.; to Duck Hole, 10.3 mi. (16.6 km).

(130) Shattuck Clearing from Coreys via Calkins Brook Truck Trail (No map)

This is the shortest access to Shattuck Clearing and the Cold River from the W. It follows valleys to the W of the Seward Range at generally easy grades. For much of its distance it parallels Calkins Brook, which is, however, frequently referred to as Calkins "Creek." Since all maps show this stream as "Brook," this designation is used throughout for consistency. Except for the first 1.2 mi., this entire route is on gravel roads that are also part of the Cold River Horse Trail system.

Trailhead: The trail begins at the same parking lot, on the road from Coreys, where the Ward Brook approach to Duck Hole begins. (See above for driving directions.)

From the trail register at the parking lot (0 mi.), this trail coincides with the trail to Duck Hole for 1.2 mi. to the junction with the Calkins Brook Truck Trail (trail 130). Turning R, the road climbs at an easy grade to a junction with the horse trail at 1.4 mi. (Trail R leads back to the parking lot. Trail L leads to Ward Brook Truck Trail, trail 129.) Continuing straight ahead, the Calkins Brook Truck Trail continues climbing at easy grades to a height of land at 2.1 mi., after which the road dips, climbs again, and then begins a gradual, rolling descent. At 3.4 mi. the road comes to the R bank of Calkins Brook, soon crosses and then recrosses the brook at 3.7 mi., and continues the descent. At 4.2 mi. the road climbs sharply and begins a series of slight ups and downs leading to a junction at 4.9 mi. with the Raquette River Horse Trail (trail 131), which leads 5.5 mi. to the road to Raquette Falls and the parking lot near the bridge over Stony Creek.

Continuing straight ahead, the road makes a rolling descent to a clearing with the two Calkins Brook Lean-tos and a horse barn at 6.1 mi. Swinging L, the road crosses Calkins Brook and begins to climb past a large sand pit. The grades are easy at first, but increase to moderate before reaching a height of land at 7.0 mi. The road now begins a long, gradual descent through occasional small clearings to a larger clearing at 8.1 mi, with a brief view back toward the Seward Range. At 8.8 mi. the road skirts the R side of a large alder swamp with even better views before crossing Boulder Brook at 8.9 mi. and climbing over a small knoll and down to a junction at 9.6 mi. (Trail L leads 200 yds. to Latham Pond, where there are a view of the Sewards and some good campsites, but no longer any lean-to.)

Turning R, the road gently descends through a beautiful grove of pines to a junction on the R bank of the Cold River at 10.4 mi. (Road L leads up along the R bank of the Cold River to two lean-tos. Cold River #3 is 0.4 mi. from this junction and Cold River #4 is 0.6 mi., at the point where the Northville-Placid Trail crosses the Cold River on a suspension bridge.) Turning R at this junction for 200 yds., the road comes to the site of a former lumber bridge over the Cold River. There is a reasonably easy ford just above, and the road climbs the far bank to the site of the former Shattuck Clearing ranger station at 10.6 mi. Like the station at Duck Hole, this structure was removed in 1977 to bring this area into compliance with wilderness area guidelines.

At Shattuck Clearing is a junction with the blue-marked Northville-Placid Trail (trail 133). Trail R leads 12.5 mi. to Rt. 28N near Long Lake. Trail L leads 0.7 mi. to the suspension bridge over the Cold River and then on to Duck Hole at 11.9 mi. Trail L also leads to the Cold River Horse Trail (trail 134), which follows the E bank of the Cold River to Duck Hole and connects with another horse trail leading to Newcomb. The Wolf Pond Truck Trail which also leads L from Shattuck Clearing (and is followed for short distances by both the N-P Trail and the Cold River Horse Trail) leads to Rt. 28N, W of Newcomb; but since it crosses the private lands of the Huntington Forest it is closed to the public for hiking and is not an access route to Shattuck Clearing.

Also to the R from Shattuck Clearing is the Pine Point Trail, which branches R from the N-P Trail 0.1 mi. from the clearing. It is somewhat overgrown and difficult to follow as it leads 0.3 mi. down the L bank of the Cold River to a point about 1.0 mi. above the mouth of Calkins Brook. The end of this trail is at the upper limit of canoe navigation on the Cold River.

Trail in winter: Same as for trail 129. The shorter winter approach to Calkins Brook is via Raquette Falls Horse Trail.

Distances: Parking lot on Coreys Rd. to junction with Calkins Brook Truck Trail, 1.2 mi.; to junction with Raquette River Horse Trail, 4.9 mi.; to Calkins Brook Lean-tos, 6.1 mi.; to Latham Pond junction, 9. mi.; to Shattuck Clearing, 10.6 mi. (17.0 km).

(131) Shattuck Clearing and Calkins Brook via Raquette River Horse Trail (No map)

This approach to the Calkins Brook Horse Trail is 0.6 mi. longer than the one described above, but for those walking from Coreys or for winter travelers when the road is not plowed beyond Stony Creek, this road saves 2.8 mi.

Trailhead: The trail begins at a parking area on the R side of Coreys Rd., which leaves Rt. 3 12.7 mi. W of the traffic light in Saranac Lake and 2.7 mi. E of the junction of Rtes. 3 and 30 E of Tupper Lake. This road is paved for about 1.5 mi. through the little settlement of Coreys and then turns to gravel, crosses Stony Creek at 2.5 mi., and comes to the parking lot 2.8 mi. from Rt. 3.

From the trail register (0 mi.), the trail follows a gravel road, avoiding a road R 100 yds. from the register, and continues with easy ups and downs, crossing several brooks. At 1.5 mi., where an obscure lumber road goes R toward the river, the trail goes L and climbs away from the river along a small brook. Crossing the brook at 1.7 mi., the trail levels off and at 2.1 mi. comes to a trail leading R to Hemlock Hill Lean-to. Beyond this, the trail dips down to a junction at 2.2 mi. with a trail R to Raquette Falls (trail 132).

The horse trail bears L, follows Palmer Brook, and then bears away from it over a hill. Descending to a swamp, the trail crosses Palmer Brook at 2.7 mi. and climbs over another hill and descends to cross a brook at 3.4 mi. This marks the end of the gravel-based road and the beginning of a very muddy section.

Crossing another brook at 3.5 mi., the trail begins a long climb. At 4.6 mi. the trail crosses a small brook and climbs steeply for about 50 yds., after which the grade eases and the trail reaches the top of a pass at 5.1 mi. After a short, level stretch, the trail descends steeply to the junction with the Calkins Brook Truck Trail (trail 130) at 5.5 mi. From here it is 1.2 mi. to the Calkins Brook Lean-tos and 5.7 mi. to Shattuck Clearing.

Trail in winter: Day skiers often push a fair distance along this trail, but don't count on broken track beyond the height of land before Calkins Brook. This trail is very skiable to Shattuck Clearing and beyond.

Distances: Parking lot to junction with Raquette Falls Trail, 2.2 mi.; to junction with Calkins Brook Truck Trail, 5.5 mi.; to Calkins Brook Lean-tos, 6.7 mi.; to Shattuck Clearing, 11.2 mi. (18.0 km).

(132) Raquette Falls   (No map)

This spot on the Raquette River is more often visited by canoeists on the route from Long Lake down the Raquette River, but it is also a worthwhile and relatively easy hike. Besides the series of falls on the Raquette River, there are a DEC Interior Outpost, two lean-tos, and many good campsites at Raquette Falls.

The trail starts at the same parking lot as the Raquette River Horse Trail (trail 131) and follows the horse trail for the first 2.2 mi. Turning R at the junction next to Palmer Brook, the trail crosses the brook, climbs over a knoll, and drops down to the edge of a slough of the Raquette River at 2.8 mi. After several more ups and downs, the trail begins a longer climb at 3.5 mi. and reaches the top of the hill at 3.8 mi. The trail now descends some steep switchbacks to the edge of an old clearing and then continues on the flat to a signpost at 4.2 mi. at the junction with the Raquette Falls canoe carry. Trail R leads a few yds. to the river at the lower end of the carry. Trail L leads just over 1 mi. to the upper end of the carry. The best view of the falls is found by going about 100 yds. up the canoe carry and looking for a vague trail leading R to the bank of the river and up along the top of a small gorge. Just up and to the L of the signpost are the DEC Interior Outpost and a large field with the lean-tos located on the edge of the field.

Trail in winter: This is one of the classic Adirondack ski tours. Count on broken track to the falls as well as good snow being likely here even if it is not plentiful elsewhere.

Distances: Parking lot to junction at Palmer Brook, 2.2 mi.; to Raquette Falls, 4.2 mi. (6.8 km).

Unmaintained Trails in the Seward Range

(See Peaks Without Maintained Trails in Introduction)

Seymour

This peak was named for Horatio Seymour, several times governor of New York. The popular route ascends the first brook 0.1 mi. SE of Ward Brook Lean-to. The most westerly branch leads to an easily ascended old slide track, above which the going is easy to the top of the ridge. Follow the ridge SW to the summit. Ascent from the SW by way of Ouluska Pass Brook is more difficult because of blowdown. Descent into Ouluska Pass, the col between Seymour and Seward, is complicated because of blowdown and cliffs.

Seward, Donaldson and Emmons

Seward was named for William Henry Seward, who succeeded William L. Marcy as governor. He was one of the founders of the Republican Party and Secretary of State in Lincoln's cabinet. Donaldson, the first Adirondack peak to be named during the 20th century, stands as a monument to Alfred Lee Donaldson, who wrote the first and most complete history of the Adirondacks. The southernmost peak in the Seward Range honors the memory of Ebenezer Emmons, state geologist and leader of the 1837 expedition that made the first ascent of Mt. Marcy, and the man who gave the name "Adirondacks" to this mountain region.

The usual route to Seward begins at the bridge 0.2 mi. SE of the clearing where the red foot trail from Coreys (trail 129) joins the fire truck trail. This is also the third bridge NW of Ward Brook Lean-to. After starting on the E side of the brook, follow traces of old tote roads on the W side to the end of the second growth, where blowdown begins. Avoid the ridge to the W. For easier going, climb part way up the ridge to the E, eventually striking the NE ridge of Seward, which leads to the summit. Herd paths descend to the S flanks of the western Seward ridge, reaching Donaldson more or less on a compass line from Seward's summit. The route to Emmons from Donaldson follows the ridge.

Today, most people reaching Emmons over Seward and Donaldson from the Ward Brook Lean-to area find it easier to return by retracing their steps over the latter two peaks, but there are other alternatives. The return via the Northville-Placid Trail and the Duck Hole truck road, formerly the usual route, now takes longer than returning over Donaldson and Seward. Additionally, this route is now more difficult to find because once-open lumber roads are more overgrown, but it does make a challenging wilderness loop or the best alternative should bad weather dictate against hiking on a high ridge.

To descend to the Northville-Placid Trail, find a herd path leaving the ridge about 0.3 mi. N of the Emmons summit. This route descends through blowdown into the valley leading SE to a brook from Ouluska Pass (which is located between Seward and Seymour). The large lumber clearing next to Ouluska Brook that was once such a prominent landmark has now grown in so that it is more difficult to find, and a key to an easy return to Ward Brook is an old tote road leading E from this clearing. The best current landmark is the junction with Ouluska Brook of a large brook coming from Emmons. The lumber clearing is 0.3 mi. above this junction, and the tote road can be found by generally heading NE from the junction. Once found, the tote road leads in about a mile to the Northville-Placid Trail (trail 133) at a point 0.9 mi. NE of the former Noah John Rondeau hermitage.

A more difficult route to the Seward Range is from the W by way of Calkins Brook. This stream is reached from Coreys by way of the Ward Brook Trail (trail 129) and the Calkins Brook truck trail (trail 130). Avoid striking directly for Emmons from the head of Calkins Brook. It is easier to cross over the summit of Donaldson.

(133) Shattuck Clearing from Long Lake via Northville-Placid Trail   Map: A-10

This approach to Shattuck Clearing is a section of the 132-mi. Northville-Placid Trail running from Northville, near the southern boundary of the Adirondack Park, to Lake Placid. This trail is described in full in a separate guidebook, *Guide to Adirondack Trails: Northville-Placid Trail*, published by the Adirondack Mt. Club. The description below and the description of the section from Shattuck Clearing to Duck Hole are adapted from the 1988 edition, written by Bruce Wadsworth. The trail generally follows the E shore of Long Lake for the first 7.5 mi. but is sometimes forced to detour away from the lake to avoid private property. There are several attractive lean-tos and many campsites on the lake in this section, but hikers should be aware that some of the land is private, in particular a large inholding from 5.6 mi. to 7.5 mi.

Trailhead: The trail begins at a parking lot on Tarbell Rd. leading N from Rt. 28N, 1.5 mi. E of the junction of Rtes. 28N and 30 in Long Lake Village. There is a large DEC sign on the highway. At 0.7 mi. up Tarbell Road there is a parking area on the R at the top of a hill, and the trail starts just beyond on the R.

Leaving the road (0 mi.) the trail descends to a trail register and continues to descend to the outlet to Polliwog Pond at 0.6 mi. Crossing the brook on a wide board bridge, avoid a trail L at 0.9 mi. and cross another brook at 1.1 mi. Just past this brook, an unmarked trail leads L to the two Catlin Bay Lean-tos. The first is visible from the N-P Trail and the second is reached by continuing to the shore of Long Lake and circling L and over a small rise to the lean-to sitting in a beautiful location above the lake.

Continuing straight through the junction, the N-P Trail proceeds over easy ups and downs and soon enters the High Peaks Wilderness Area. At 2.0 mi. the trail bears L and then back R, coming near Long Lake and following the shore to a sandy beach and stream at 2.4 mi. Swinging away from the lake, the trail climbs, descends, and climbs again to a height of land 200 ft. above the lake at 3.2 mi. Now descending, the trail crosses a brook at 4.0 mi. and comes within view of a large clearing on the L at 4.1 mi., where there are two privies and several side trails. This is Kelley's Point, and two lean-tos are visible on the lakeshore from the clearing. These are perhaps the most attractive lean-tos on this section of trail, but they are heavily used by both hikers and canoeists.

Passing behind the clearing, the N-P Trail reaches a junction at 4.5 mi. with the now unmaintained trail leading R to Kempshall Mt. Without the tower, which the DEC removed several years ago, there is virtually no view from the summit and this is no longer a worthwhile side trip. The trail L leads a short distance to the lake. Continuing on, the N-P Trail soon joins a wide tote road, crosses a brook at 5.2 mi. and reaches a junction at 5.4 mi., with a side trail leading to the first of two lean-tos at Rodney Point. There is a spring on the L about halfway to the lean-to, and a nice sandy beach on the shore makes this a pleasant place to camp. After a short ascent, a less noticeable trail leads L at 5.5 mi. to the second Rodney Point lean-to.

Just beyond this junction, the N-P Trail leaves state land and crosses several brooks as well as some private water pipes before coming to a muddy bog which it skirts at 6.7 mi. After crossing a small brook at 7.4 mi., the trail comes to a junction at 7.6 mi., with a side trail leading 0.1 mi. L to the two lean-tos at Plumleys. The first lean-to sits on a grassy knoll with a commanding view of the lake, and the second one is 50 yds. further N along the shore. Both lean-tos are attractive camping spots and are worth the side trip even for a lunch break.

Leading out of Plumleys, there is a maze of side trails, and hikers must be careful to look for the blue markers. The N-P Trail joins a good tote road, swinging away from the lake, crossing a small brook at 8.0 mi., and then climbing to a height of land at 8.5 mi. Gradually descending from this crest at 9.3 mi., the trail enters a fine stand of white pine developed after a forest fire and differing from the surrounding forest. Just past this stand of pines, the trail crosses a brook flowing out of an open marsh (or vlei) at 9.9 mi.

At 10.2 mi. the N-P Trail reaches a barely discernible junction with a vague trail R leading 0.9 mi. to Round Pond. A side trip to this pond, though worthwhile for its solitude, is now more of a bushwhack than a trail walk. Continuing past this junction, the trail reaches a wide vlei with a stream crossing made somewhat difficult by the haphazard collection of boards and logs that serves as a bridge. The trail then passes a large clearing on the R and at 10.5 mi. comes to Pine Brook, which is easily crossed on stones. The trail is now pleasant walking to some beaver activity at 11.3 mi., where it abruptly turns L off the tote road to circumvent the beaver pond. Once past this obstacle, the N-P Trail joins a gravel road at 11.7 mi. and turns R and down.

Just after joining the gravel road, the vague Pine Point Trail, also with blue markers, diverges L (see trail 130, end of description), but the N-P Trail continues R and down to a junction at Shattuck Clearing at 11.8 mi. The ranger station formerly on this site was removed by the DEC in 1977 to bring this area into compliance with wilderness area guidelines. The gravel road L from the junction is the Calkins Brook Truck Trail which leads to a ford of the Cold River and on to Coreys in 10.6 mi. (See trail 130.) The gravel road R is the continuation of the N-P Trail to Duck Hole as well as the Cold River Horse Trail (trail 134). The Wolf Pond Truck Trail, which also leads R from Shattuck Clearing (and is followed for short distances by both the N-P Trail and the Cold River Horse Trail), leads to Rt. 28N, W of Newcomb; but since it crosses the private lands of the Huntington Forest it is closed to the public for hiking and is not an access route to Shattuck Clearing.

Trail in winter: The entire N-P Trail is skiable and has been skied in one continuous trip on several occasions. This section is very pleasant skiing even with an overnight pack, but a tour this long is not for novices. Depending on surface and wind conditions, it may be easier to ski on Long Lake as far as Plumleys.

Distances: Parking lot to Catlin Bay Lean-tos, 1.1 mi.; to Kelley's Point lean-tos, 4.1 mi.; to first Rodney Point Lean-to, 5.4 mi.; to trail to Plumleys (two lean-tos), 7.6 mi.; to Round Pond trail junction, 10.2 mi.; to Shattuck Clearing, 11.8 mi. (19.0 km).

(133) Duck Hole from Shattuck Clearing via Northville-Placid Trail   Map: A-10

This section of the N-P Trail generally follows the NE bank of the Cold River to Duck Hole. This is the wildest section of the entire trail, with the trailless Seward and Santanoni ranges flanking the valley of the Cold River. Leaving the junction at Shattuck Clearing (0 mi.), the N-P Trail bears slightly R on a gravel road to a somewhat obscure L turn off the road at 0.2 mi. There is a small clearing and campsite at this turn. The trail soon crosses a suspension bridge over Moose Creek, with a good view of the Santanoni Range from the bridge. Beyond this bridge, a pleasant trail leads to another suspension bridge over the Cold River at 0.7 mi., from which there is also a good view of the Santanonis. At the far side, the trail comes to a junction with a trail leading L a few yards to Cold River Lean-to #4. Just beyond this junction, the N-P Trail joins a gravel lumber road. (Cold River lean-to #3 is .02 mi. to the left on this road, which continues on to connect with the Calkins Brook Truck Trail and is also an alternative route from Shattuck Clearing.) The N-P Trail turns R on this gravel lumber road, which was constructed in the early 1950s to allow lumbermen to clean up some of the terrific damage left by the 1950 hurricane. This area is now quite open and there are many views of the surrounding peaks for the next several miles.

After one short descent and climb, the trail descends to the Cold River at a large pool, known as Big Eddy, at 2.0 mi. An interesting falls drops into this pool and the water turns gracefully in its eddy. Beyond Big Eddy, the road climbs away from the river, crosses a brook on a bridge at 3.1 mi., and after a short, steep climb the trail turns sharp R and leaves the gravel road at 3.6 mi. The trail descends steeply and crosses two steep gullies before reaching Seward Lean-to at 4.0 mi.

Just above the lean-to, a large outcrop of rock forms a natural dam called Miller's Falls, where one can swim. Just below the falls, a dark gray dike cuts through the lighter-colored anorthosite granite, and several potholes have been carved in the bedrock. Past the lean-to, the trail again climbs a steep bank to an open area above the river at 4.2 mi. and then descends to the river at 4.4 mi. Now following the river closely, the trail crosses a grassy, muddy stretch at 5.3 mi. and at 5.7 mi. a painted tree indicates a nearby benchmark (PBM 1876) located on a boulder 25 ft. E of the trail. Crossing first a smaller brook, the trail crosses Ouluska Brook at 6.1 mi. and reaches Ouluska Lean-to just beyond at 6.2 mi.

Beyond the lean-to, the trail follows the Cold River to a sharp bend in the river where the trial climbs away from the river and an old lumber road enters from the L at 6.6 mi. Almost immediately, however, the trail swings sharp R away from the road and climbs gradually to the top of a knoll which was the site of Noah John Rondeau's "Hermitage." It was on this high, open bluff that Rondeau lived off and on (mostly on) from 1915 to 1950. He built two diminutive cabins and developed a unique life style that has been the subject of a book and numerous articles. He left the woods briefly in 1947 to appear at the New York Sportsman's Show, where he became the feature attraction. Leaving the woods for good during the 1950 hurricane, he continued to appear at other sportsman's shows, dying in Lake Placid in 1967 at the age of 84.

From Rondeau's, the trail turns sharp L and down across a small valley and then descends gradually to the old lumber road. At 7.0 mi. a newer but badly overgrown lumber road goes R; it was once a connection to a lumber bridge over the Cold River to the Cold River Horse Trail on the SE bank. Continuing straight ahead, the N-P Trail begins climbing, passing a yellow boundary post marking one's passage from Essex to Franklin County, and coming to a large brook which is crossed on stones at 7.5 mi. The trail continues to climb, and an old tote road enters from the L at 7.8 mi.

Just past this old road, the trail swings R, levels off, and begins to descend at 8.0 mi., with a pond visible to the L. With one short interruption, the descent continues to a large brook at 8.7 mi. Crossing this brook, the trail climbs briefly and then continues to descend to another large brook at 9.3 mi., with a small clearing on the far side. Heading across the clearing, the trail soon reaches the R bank of the outlet to Mountain Pond, climbs along the bank, and crosses the brook on a bridge at 9.6 mi. Just beyond, the pond is visible to the L and a series of small ups and downs leads to the junction with the Ward Brook Truck Trail (trail 129) at 10.3 mi.

Turning R and now with red and blue markers, the trail comes to the two Cold River Lean-tos (Nos. 1 and 2) at 10.7 mi. Just past the lean-tos, the trail crosses Moose Creek just above its confluence with the Cold River, climbs the far bank, and then follows along the R bank of the Cold River to a junction with Cold River Horse Trail at 11.0 mi. (trail 134). This trail fords the Cold River and continues down the E side of the river to Shattuck Clearing with a connection to the Santanoni Preserve and Newcomb.

Past this junction, the trail climbs over a low ridge and arrives at the trail junction and former site of the ranger station at 11.9 mi. Blue trail (trail 128) crosses the dam and leads to Bradley Pond and the road below Upper Works (see above). Trail bearing L with blue and red markers is the continuation of the N-P Trail leading to Lake Placid (trail 99) and with a connection to a trail leading to Henderson Lake and Upper Works (trail 127). There are two lean-tos and several good campsites at Duck Hole. One lean-to is located by the dam and the other is 100 yds. E of the dam on a beautiful wooded point.

Trail in winter: Except for some rough going approximately 0.5 mi. either side of Seward Lean-to, this section of trail is easily skiable even with a backpack—a definite requirement on this remote section.

Distances: Shattuck Clearing to turn-off for Cold River lean-tos nos. 3 & 4, 0.7 mi.; Seward Lean-to, 4.0 mi.; Ouluska Lean-to, 6.2 mi.; Rondeau's Hermitage, 6.7 mi.; junction with Ward Brook Truck Trail, 10.3 mi.; Cold River lean-tos nos. 1 & 2, 10.7 mi.; Duck Hole, 11.9 mi. (19.1km)

(134) Cold River Horse Trail from Shattuck Clearing to Ward Brook Truck Trail   Map: A-11

This seldom-used section of the Cold River Horse Trail System travels through low, rolling terrain SE of the Cold River. For much of its length, it follows an old gravel lumber road and is delightfully easy walking through spectacularly remote country where solitude is practically guaranteed. The final mile leading to the Ward Brook Truck Trail, however, is unfortunately quite wet and rather unpleasant to walk, with the additional problem that there is no bridge over the Cold River at the N end of the trail, and crossing could be difficult in high water.

From the junction at the former site of the ranger station at Shattuck Clearing (0 mi.), the horse trail follows the gravel road SE for 0.8 mi., where it turns L onto another gravel road. (Road straight ahead is the Wolf Pond Truck Trail, which is closed to the public where it enters private land just over 1 mi. beyond.) From this junction, the trail descends at a gentle grade to Moose Pond Stream at 1.8 mi., with two lean-tos on the far side.

Past the lean-tos, the trail climbs at easy to moderate grades to a junction at 2.6 mi. with a blue-marked horse trail to Moose Pond and Newcomb (trail 138). Turning sharp L, the Cold River Horse Trail descends in gradual rolls to an open area at an old gravel pit at 3.5 mi. and passes a pond on the L at 4.7 mi. Continuing along with short ups and downs, there is a good view of the Seward Range at 5.3 mi.; at 6.9 mi., just before crossing a large stream, the trail comes to a junction. (Red trail R is unmaintained foot trail to Newcomb Lake; trail 136). Continuing straight ahead, the trail reaches another junction at 7.8 mi. (Abandoned trail L follows an old lumber road to a ford of the Cold River and on to the N-P Trail.)

Swinging R, the trail comes to Northern Lean-tos at 8.2 mi. Shortly beyond these lean-tos, the gravel-based road swings R while the horse trail continues straight ahead and becomes quite wet, remaining so nearly all the way to the crossing of the Cold River at 10.1 mi. and the junction with the Ward Brook Truck Trail (trail 129) just beyond. To the R it is 0.9 mi. to Duck Hole and to the L 0.3 mi. to the Cold River lean-tos.

Trail in winter: *Although the 1.5-mi. section at the N end is more difficult to ski, the rest of this route is quite easy.*

Distances: *Shattuck Clearing to turn-off from Wolf Pond Truck Trail, 0.8 mi.; to Moose Pond Stream Lean-tos, 1.8 mi.; to junction with Moose Pond Horse Trail, 2.6 mi.; to Northern Lean-tos, 8.2 mi.; to Ward Brook Truck Trail, 10.2 mi. (16.4 km).*

The Santanoni Preserve

This tract of land was transferred from private ownership to the State of New York in 1972 through the efforts of the Adirondack

Conservancy. Most of this land is now part of the High Peaks Wilderness Area and provides a SE approach to the Cold River area. Except for skiers and mountain bikers going to Newcomb Lake, this area has so far received very little use even though it offers some outstanding opportunities for hiking, fishing, horseback riding, and skiing. The centerpiece of the area is two-mile-long Newcomb Lake, which has two lean-tos and many campsites along its pristine shores.

Remaining from the days of private ownership are two roads leading to Newcomb Lake and Moose Pond, as well as a huge log structure known as Camp Santanoni on the NE shore of Newcomb Lake. The road to Newcomb Lake is still hard-packed and suitable for bicycles, and some people have used various wheeled carriers to transport boats to Newcomb Lake via the road. At one time boats were available for rent on Newcomb Lake, but this is no longer the case. No special camping permits are now required, although of course the normal restrictions that apply to camping on any state land still pertain.

Trailhead: The trails described below all start from the gatehouse of the Santanoni Preserve, on a road that leaves Rt. 28N 0.3 mi. W of the Town Hall in the Village of Newcomb. A small sign for the Santanoni Preserve marks this road which crosses a narrow iron bridge, passes the stone gatehouse on the R, and comes to a small parking area on the R at the top of the hill, 0.3 mi. from Rt. 28N

(135) Road to Newcomb Lake and Camp Santanoni Map: B-12

This wide gravel road leads at easy grades from the gatehouse near Newcomb to Camp Santanoni, a now abandoned "great camp" at the E end of Newcomb Lake. From the trail register (0 mi.), the road is practically level to some old farm buildings at 0.9 m. Past the farm, the road swings L and up to an open field at 1.1 mi., where one can see the Santanonis. Descending slightly, the road comes to a beautiful moss-covered stone bridge and begins a steady, gradual climb to a junction at 2.2 mi. with a road L to Moose Pond and the Cold River Horse Trail (trail 138).

Turning R, the grade soon eases and the road begins a gentle descent across a side hill with more beautiful stonework and some glimpses of the Santanonis through the trees. At 3.6 mi. the red-marked trail along the S side of Newcomb Lake (trail 136) branches L, after which the road drops down to a picnic area on the S shore of the lake at 3.9 mi. Swinging R, the road crosses a bridge and then swings back L along the NE side of a narrow channel and on to Camp Santanoni at the E end of Newcomb Lake at 4.5 mi. This immense, rambling log structure plus numerous out-buildings were built by the Pruyn family of Albany, using material cut on the site. Since this structure has been placed on the National Register of Historic Places, the land surrounding the camp can be classified as an "historic district," meaning that this four-walled structure may remain even though this is Forest Preserve. Yet to be determined is what exact use would be made of this structure if it were to be preserved. Since the structure itself has deteriorated over the years it remains to be seen first whether it can be feasibly preserved and second what its use will be. In the meantime, don't wait to go and see it.

Trail in winter: Since 1972, when this area was opened to the public, this road has probably seen more skiers each year than hikers; for not only is it easy skiing all the way to Newcomb Lake, but the smooth gravel road coupled with Newcomb's propensity to accumulate snow has meant that many times this has been about the only good cross country skiing in the entire Northeast. The Visitor's Interpretive Center in Newcomb (telephone: 518-582-2000) is a good source of information on current ski conditions.

Distances: Trail register near gatehouse to junction with Moose Pond Road, 2.2 mi.; to foot trail along S shore, 3.6 mi.; to picnic area on S shore, 3.9 mi.; to Camp Santanoni, 4.5 mi. (7.2 km).

(136) Foot Trail from Newcomb Lake to Shaw Pond and Cold River Horse Trail

Map: B-12

This trail leads from the road along the S shore of Newcomb Lake, giving access to a lean-to on the lake shore. It then continues NW toward the Cold River. Since its construction in 1976, it has received very little use and even less maintenance beyond the W end of Newcomb Lake. It is now quite obscure in spots, and following it requires great care. The section from Shaw Pond (near Moose Pond) to the Cold River Horse Trail is particularly obscure and, being somewhat redundant due to the nearly parallel Moose Pond Horse Trail, will probably be officially abandoned in the near future. The section from Newcomb Lake to Shaw Pond as described below will probably remain open because it provides a useful connection from the beautiful camping areas on Newcomb Lake to Moose Pond and the Cold River area.

The trail with red markers starts 3.6 mi. up the road to Newcomb Lake (trail 135). From the road (0 mi.), the trail drops down and soon joins an old road which follows a broad shelf above a swamp. After a steep descent at 0.7 mi. the trail crosses one brook and begins a rolling descent to a second brook crossing at 1.0 mi., with a beaver dam to the L and a large open area to the R. At 1.2 mi. a side trail with blue markers branches R and leads 300 yds. to a lean-to on a beautiful rocky point on the S shore of Newcomb Lake. This is one of the nicest campsites anywhere.

Continuing on the flat, the trail comes to a small ladder leading down to a bridge over the main inlet to the lake at 1.8 mi. Some care is needed to follow the trail through the thick alders beyond the bridge. Climbing the far bank, the trail comes to a junction at 1.9 mi. with a yellow trail R leading along the N shore of the lake to a lean-to and the end of the road at Camp Santanoni (trail 137). Beyond this junction, the trail is flat through a thicket of fir trees next to an extensive open swamp until it swings R and up at 2.6 mi. The trail now follows a series of old roads with several sharp turns which, though marked with a few disks, requires close attention. At 2.8 mi. the trail crosses a large beaver dam and meadow and joins an old grassy road which slowly swings L around a large swamp.

Taking a sharp R off this road at 3.5 mi., the trail joins another old road, which it follows up and down along a side hill to the L bank of a large stream at 4.1 mi. The trail now swings sharp R without crossing the stream and follows another vague road. At 4.2 mi. the trail joins a slightly better road and goes R and up some steep to moderate grades; the trail leaves the road, becomes a foot path and comes to a crest at 4.5 mi. Continuing to a higher crest at 4.6 mi., the trail now descends, crosses a brook, and comes within sight of Shaw Pond at 5.1 mi. Proceeding along the W shore of the pond, the trail reaches a large beaver dam at the outlet at 5.4 mi.

The marked trail continues across this dam and along the SW slopes of Little Santanoni and Couchsachraga to the Cold River Horse Trail at about 12.5 mi. As stated above, this final section of trail is practically nonexistent and will probably soon be officially abandoned. However, an easy bushwhack of less than 0.1 mi. to the L from the end of the Moose Pond Horse Trail (trail 138), 0.2 mi. beyond Moose Pond. It is only about 2.5 mi. longer to Northern Lean-tos or the Ward Brook Truck Trail via the Moose Pond and Cold River Horse Trails than by the foot trail, and the walking is far easier.

Distances: Santanoni Preserve gatehouse to turnoff from road to Newcomb Lake, 3.6 mi.; to turnoff to lean-to, 4.8 mi.; to junction with trail on N shore of Newcomb Lake, 5.5 mi.; to Shaw Pond, 9.0 mi. (14.5 km).

(137) Trail Along N Shore of Newcomb Lake
Map: B-12

This trail leads from Camp Santanoni past several campsites and on to the Ward Pond Brook Lean-to and a junction with the S shore trail leading to Shaw Pond. Starting from Camp Santanoni (0 mi.)at the end of the road to Newcomb Lake (trail 135), the trail goes past some out-buildings to the E shore of the lake. There are no signs or markers at the start, but the route is obvious next to the shore past a campsite, at an old bath house at a small beach, and on to some campsites near the mouth of Sucker Brook at 0.3 mi. From these campsites, the trail swings R and up to an old lumber road where it turns L, crosses Sucker Brook, and now with a few yellow markers climbs to a crest at 0.7 mi. Continuing to follow the lumber road, the trail descends, climbs over another hill and descends to Santanoni Brook at 1.5 mi. The road ends past this brook, but the trail continues on the flat to Ward Pond Brook Lean-to on the N shore of the lake at 1.6 mi. This little-used lean-to is in excellent condition and is nearly as nice a site as its companion lean-to on the S shore. Passing behind the lean-to, the trail continues on the flat to the junction with the S shore trail at 2.3 mi.

Distances: Camp Santanoni to campsites on Sucker Brook, 0.3 mi.; to Ward Pond Brook Lean-to, 1.6 mi.; to junction with S shore trail, 2.3 mi.(3.7 km.).

(138) Moose Pond Horse Trail
Map: B-12

Following good road for most of its distance, this trail provides access to some nice campsites on Moose Pond and then connects with the Cold River Horse Trail System. From the Santanoni Preserve gatehouse (0 mi.), follow the road to Newcomb Lake (trail 135) to the junction at 2.2 mi. Turning L, the road is gently rolling until it begins a steady descent at 3.6 mi. Crossing a brook at the bottom of the descent, the road swings R and climbs gently to a large clearing at 4.7 mi. There are some good views as the road climbs up through this large open area. After some more gently rolling terrain, the road enters another clearing at 6.0 mi. Turning L, the road climbs a steady, moderate grade to a height of land and then descends to a junction near Moose Pond at 6.7 mi. (Road L leads 0.2 mi. to two campsites on Moose Pond.) Bearing R, the road (now marked with blue horse trail disks) passes several large open swamps, crosses Ermine Brook at 8.1 mi., and swings L. The road now goes up and down along a side hill above the outlet to Moose Pond before dropping steeply down to Calahan Brook at 10.4 mi. This is the end of the gravel road.

The trail now climbs moderately to an old lumber road at 10.7 mi., turns sharp R and continues climbing to a better road at 10.9 mi. Again turning sharp R, the trail follows this sometimes muddy road along a gently rolling profile to the junction with the Cold River Horse Trail (trail 134) at 11.8 mi. (Trail straight ahead leads to Moose Pond Stream Lean-tos and Shattuck Clearing. Trail R leads to Northern Lean-tos and Duck Hole.)

Trail in winter: An old road, this is ideal for skiing with just a bit more terrain to make the actual skiing somewhat more interesting than the Newcomb Lake Road. A few years ago one cross country ski manufacturer had as its slogan, "As far as you want to go"—a slogan that perfectly sums up the possibilities not only for this trail but for the whole truck trail/horse trail system near the Cold River.

Distances: Santanoni Preserve gatehouse to turn-off from road to Newcomb Lake, 2.2 mi.; to Moose Pond, 6.7 mi.; to junction with Cold River Horse Trail, 11.8 mi. (19.0 km.).

(139) Goodnow Mt. (Page map)

Although not technically in the High Peaks region, this wonderful, easy hike to a summit with an intact fire tower is too good to ignore. Not only does this peak offer a marvelous view of the high peaks, but the trail to the summit is now a self-guided nature walk with interpretive pamphlets (available at the trailhead) that are keyed to marked posts along the trail. Although not directly related, this hike is now a perfect complement to the displays at the Visitor Interpretive Center at Newcomb. A new parking area and 0.9 mi. of new trail were completed in the summer of 1993. The new route adds 0.4 mi. to the overall distance to the summit.

This trail is entirely on the private land of the Archer and Anna Huntington Forest owned by the College of Environmental Science and Forestry (ESF) in Syracuse. It is ESF students and faculty who produced the interpretive pamphlets and coordinated a grant that enabled the Town of Newcomb to hire a work crew. The latter built the new parking area and trail—a trail complete with frequent benches for resting. ESF staff continue to maintain the fire tower. Because this is private land, no camping or fires are permitted, and the area is closed from sunset to sunrise. No hunting is permitted on this private preserve, so this is a good choice for hikers who are concerned about possible danger during the hunting season.

Trailhead: The trail starts on Rt. 28N, 1.5mi. W of the entrance to the Visitor Interpretive Center W of the hamlet of Newcomb. This point is also 11.4 mi. E of Long Lake. A large white sign marks the turn to a new parking area and kiosk which contains a register and interpretive pamphlets.

The trail is marked by red markers with small black arrows. From the parking area (0 mi.), the trail climbs moderately for 200 yds. before swinging R and continuing with small rises and falls along a shelf parallel to the highway. Reaching a bridge across a small brook at 0.5 mi., the trail swings L and at 0.7 mi. begins to climb moderately. After a steady climb, the trail reaches the crest of a ridge and joins the old trail at 0.9 mi.

Swinging sharply L, the trail descends slightly before climbing to a flat notch with a well and old horse barn at 1.5 mi. Climbing gradually to the crest of the ridge, the trail dips and then climbs easily to the tower on the summit at 1.9 mi. There are some views to the E and S without climbing the tower, but from the tower one can see 23 of the major peaks, with the Santanoni Range, Algonquin, and Marcy particularly prominent.

Trail in winter: *The new start for this trail is narrower and steeper than the original route. It is no longer feasible as a ski trip, but its short distance and the absence of any really steep terrain make it an ideal introductory snowshoe trip.*

Distance: Rt. 28N to summit of Goodnow Mt., 1.9 mi. (3.1 km). Ascent from road, 1040 ft. (317 m.) Elevation, 2690 ft. (820 m).

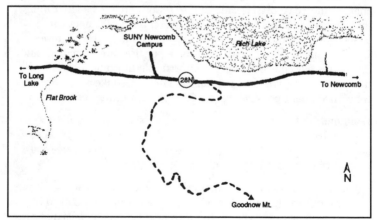

Goodnow Mt.
Base map is Newcomb quadrangle, 15 min. series, 1954.

Wallface from Scott Clearing

Tom Dunn

Appendix I

Glossary of Terms

Bivouac Camping in the open with improvised shelter or none at all.

Bushwhacking To make one's way through bushes or undergrowth without the aid of a formal trail.

Cairn A pile of stones to mark a summit or route.

Chimney A steep, narrow cleft or gully in the face of a mountain, usually by which it may be ascended.

Cobble A small stony peak on the side of a mountain.

Col A pass between two adjacent peaks.

Corduroy A road, trail or bridge formed by logs laid side by side transversely to facilitate crossing swampy areas.

Couloir A deep gorge or gully on a hillside.

Cripplebrush Thick, stunted growth at higher elevations.

Dike A band of different colored rock, usually with straight, well-defined sides. Formed when igneous rock is intruded into the existing rock. Dikes can manifest themselves either as gullies, if the dike rock is softer (as in the Colden Trap Dike), or as ridges.

Duff   Partly decayed vegetable matter on the forest floor. It can burn easily. Burning duff has started many forest fires.

Lean-to   A three-sided shelter with an over- hanging roof on the open side.

Lumber road   A crude road constructed for the purpose of hauling logs.

Tote road   A better road constructed in connection with logging operations and used for hauling supplies to a lumber camp, etc. Often built with corduroy, many of these roads are still evident after 80 years, and are often used as the route for present-day trails.

Vlei   A marsh or swampy meadow (pronounced "vly").

Appendix II

Highest One Hundred Adirondack Mountain Peaks

In order to stimulate greater interest in the very substantial outlying mountainous area, a list of the highest 100 mountains in the Adirondacks has been prepared. It is presented with the idea of making hikers aware of the many possibilities for interesting and worthwhile climbs and explorations in all parts of the Adirondack Park. It is not presented with the idea that one should climb them all, or form a club. Forty of the new listings are presently trailless, and some are privately owned, with permission needed to climb.

Heading the list are the original 46 high peaks. These were all originally thought to be at least 4000 ft. high by early surveys, but more recent surveys have lowered several of these peaks. These original 46 peaks are, however, still the peaks recognized by the Adirondack Forty-Sixers as the requirement for membership, and they are the group referred to as the "high" or "major" peaks. The criteria for these original 46 peaks were that each peak be at least .75 mi. distant from the nearest higher summit, or that it rise at least 300 vertical feet on all sides. In selecting the additional 54 peaks, the criteria used are a .75-mi. distance and a 300-ft. rise on all sides.

An asterisk (*) in the roster indicates that there is a footnote; the number of the footnote will correspond to the number on the roster. Under "Remarks," a "c" following elevation indicates that the elevation shown is that of the highest contour line. The symbol "Tr" indicates that there is presently a standard, maintained trail to the summit. An extra "T" means that there is a fire tower on the summit. A "P" indicates private ownership.

No.	Name	Elev.	Remark	Topographical Map & Sector
1	Mt. Marcy	5344	Tr	Mt. Marcy (W)
2	Algonquin Peak	5114	Tr	Mt. Marcy (W)
3	Mt. Haystack	4960	Tr	Mt. Marcy (C)
4	Mt. Skylight	4926	Tr	Mt. Marcy (W)
5	Whiteface Mt.	4867	Tr	Lake Placid (C)
6	Dix Mt.	4857	Tr	Mt. Marcy (SE)
7	Gray Peak	4840c		Mt. Marcy (W)
8	Iroquois Peak	4840c		Mt. Marcy (W)
9	Basin Mt.	4827	Tr	Mt. Marcy (C)
10	Gothics	4736	Tr	Mt. Marcy (C)
11	Mt. Colden	4714	Tr	Mt. Marcy (W)
12	Giant Mt.	4627	Tr	Elizabethtown (W)
13	Nipple Top	4620c	Tr	Mt. Marcy (E)
14	Santanoni Peak	4607		Santanoni (C)
15	Mt. Redfield	4606		Mt. Marcy (W)
16	Wright Peak	4580	Tr	Mt. Marcy (W)
17	Saddleback Mt.	4515	Tr	Mt.Marcy (C)
18	Panther Peak	4442		Santanoni (C)
19	Table Top Mt.	4427		Mt. Marcy (C)
20	Rocky Peak Ridge	4420c	Tr	Elizabethtown (W)
21	Macomb Mt.	4405		Mt. Marcy (SE)
22	Armstrong Mt.	4400c	Tr	Mt. Marcy (C)
23	Hough Peak	4400c		Mt. Marcy (SE)
24	Seward Mt.	4361		Santanoni (W)
25*	Mt. Marshall	4360		Santanoni (E)
26	Allen Mt.	4340c		Mt. Marcy (SE)
27	Big Slide Mt.	4240c	Tr	Mt. Marcy (N)
28	Esther Mt.	4240		Lake Placid (C)
29*	Upper Wolf Jaw Mt.	4185	Tr	Mt. Marcy (C)
30*	Lower Wolf Jaw Mt.	4175	Tr	Mt. Marcy (C)
31	Street Mt.	4166		Santanoni (NE)
32	Phelps Mt.	4161	Tr	Mt. Marcy (W)
33	Mt. Donaldson	4140		Santanoni (W)

No.	Name	Elev.	Remark	Topographical Map & Sector
34	Seymour Mt.	4120		Santanoni (W)
35*	Sawteeth	4100c	Tr	Mt. Marcy (C)
36	Cascade Mt.	4098	Tr	Mt. Marcy (N)
37	South Dix	4060	Tr	Mt. Marcy (SE)
38	Porter Mt.	4059	Tr	Mt. Marcy (N)
39	Mt. Colvin	4057	Tr	Mt. Marcy (C)
40	Mt. Emmons	4040		Santanoni (W)
41	Dial Mt.	4020	Tr	Mt. Marcy (E)
42	East Dix	4012		Mt. Marcy (SE)
43*	Blake Peak	3960c	Tr	Mt. Marcy (S)
44	Cliff Mt.	3960c		Mt. Marcy (W)
45	Nye Mt.	3895		Santanoni (NE)
46	Couchsachraga Peak	3820		Santanoni (C)
47	MacNaughton Mt.	4000		Santanoni (E)
48	Green Mt.	3980c		Elizabethtown (NW)
49*	Peak, Unnamed (Lost Pond)	3900c		Santanoni (E)
50*	Moose Mt.	3899		Saranac Lake (E)
51	Snowy Mt.	3899	TrT	Indian Lake (N)
52	Kilburn Mt.	3892		Lake Placid (S)
53*	Sawtooth Mts. (No. 1)	3877		Santanoni (W)
54.	Panther Mt.	3865		Indian Lake (N)
55	McKenzie Mt.	3861	Tr	Saranac Lake (E)
56	Blue Ridge	3860c		Indian Lake (W)
57	North River Mt.	3860c		Mt. Marcy (SW)
58	Sentinel Mt.	3838		Lake Placid (S)
59	Lyon Mt.	3830	TrT	Lyon Mt. (N)
60*	Sawtooth Mts. (No. 2)	3820c		Santanoni (N)
61*	Peak, Unnamed (Indian Falls)	3820c		Mt. Marcy (W)
62	Averill Peak	3810		Lyon Mt.

No.	Name	Elev.	Remark	Topographical Map & Sector
63	Avalanche Mt.	3800c		Mt. Marcy (W)
64	Buell Mt.	3786		Indian Lake (N)
65*	Boreas Mt.	3776	TrP	Mt. Marcy (S)
66	Blue Mt.	3760c	TrT	Blue Mt. (C)
67	Wakely Mt.	3760c	TrT	W. Canada Lakes (NE)
68	Henderson Mt.	3752		Santanoni (C)
69	Lewey Mt.	3742		Indian Lake (W)
70*	Sawtooth Mts. (No. 3)	3700c		Santanoni (N)
71	Wallface Mt.	3700c		Santanoni (E)
72*	Hurricane Mt.	3694	TrT	Elizabethtown (NW)
73	Hoffman Mt.	3693		Schroon Lake (E)
74	Cheney Cobble	3683		Mt. Marcy (SW)
75	Calamity Mt.	3620c		Santanoni (E)
76	Little Moose Mt.	3620c		W. Canada Lakes (NE)
77*	Sunrise Mt.	3614	TrP	Mt. Marcy (SE)
78	Stewart Mt.	3602		Lake Placid (S)
79*	Jay Mts.	3600		Ausable Forks (SW)
80.	Pitchoff Mt.	3600c	Tr	Mt. Marcy (N)
81	Saddleback Mt.	3600c		Ausable Forks (SW)
82	Pillsbury Mt.	3597	TrT	W. Canada Lakes (SE)
83	Slide Mt.	3584		Lake Placid (S)
84	Gore Mt.	3583	TrT	Thirteenth Lake (NE)
85	Dun Brook Mt.	3580c		Blue Mt. (E)
86	Noonmark Mt.	3556	Tr	Mt. Marcy (E)
87*	Mt. Adams	3540c	T	Santanoni (E)
88	Fishing Brook Mt.	3540c		Blue Mt. (NE)
89	Little Santanoni Mt.	3500c		Santanoni (SW)
90	Blue Ridge	3497		Blue Mt. (SW)
91*	Peak (Fishing Brook Range)	3480c		Blue Mt. (NE)
92	Puffer Mt.	3472		Thirteenth Lake (W)
93*	Sawtooth Mts. (No. 4)	3460c		Santanoni (N)

No.	Name	Elev.	Remark	Topographical Map & Sector
94*	Sawtooth Mts. (No. 5)	3460c		Santanoni (N)
95	Wolf Pond Mt.	3460c		Schroon Lake (N)
96	Cellar Mt.	3447		W. Canada Lakes (NE)
97*	Blue Ridge Mt.	3440c		Schroon Lake (NE)
98*	Morgan Mt.	3440c		Lake Placid (N)
99	Blue Ridge	3436		Raquette Lake (SE)
100*	Peak, Unnamed (Brown Pond)	3425		Indian Lake (N)

*25. **Mt. Marshall.** This is shown at Mt. Clinton on the 1953 map. See MacIntyre Range for history and naming of this peak.

29. and 30. **The Wolf Jaws.** The map reads Wolfjaw. Since "frog leg" is two words, it is assumed that "wolf jaw" is too. Early mountaineers used a single hyphenated word.

35. **Sawteeth.** This mountain was named for the profile of its several summit nubbles, which were said to resemble the teeth of a great saw. Sawtooth as shown on the 1953 map is incorrect but has been corrected on the 1978 "Mt. Marcy" 7.5-by-15 minute metric map.

43. **Blake Peak.** Blake Peak rather than Blake Mt. is the name in common use.

49. **Peak, Unnamed (Lost Pond).** This mountain is easily located because Lost Pond lies practically on its summit. The coordinates are 44 degrees 10'N x 70 degrees 02'W.

50. **Moose Mt.** (St. Armand Mt. on sign boards.) In spite of signs pointing to trails up this mountain, and several recent maps showing trails, there is no trail. See Northern Section for information on routes up this peak.

53. **Sawtooth Mts.** The Sawtooths comprise a large, completely wild area southeast of Ampersand Mountain. It is a region of many knobs, five of which qualify for the list. These have been numbered from one to five in order of descending altitude. Numbers 4 and 5 are the same height, but No. 4 is much more massive. The highest peak, elevation 3877 ft., is central to the region. The coordinates are 44 degrees 11'N x 74 degrees 07'W.

60. **Sawtooth Mts. (No. 2).** The 3820-ft. twin knobs of this summit mark the N end of a three-step ridge which lies W of the main 3877-ft. peak. The coordinates are 44 degrees 11'N x 74 degrees 08'W.

61. **Peak, Unnamed (Indian Falls).** Lying to the NW of Indian Falls on the trail from Marcy Dam to Mt. Marcy, the coordinates arc 44 degrees 08'N x 73 degrees 56'W.

65. **Boreas Mt.** With the removal of the fire tower, the trail is now closed and permission is needed to climb this peak.

70. **Sawtooth Mts. (No. 3).** Lying 0.5 mi. W of the Essex County line, this 3700-ft. peak marks the SE threshold of the Sawtooths. The coordinates are 44 degrees 10'N x 74 degrees 07'W.

72. **Hurricane Mt.** The fire tower is abandoned.

77. **Sunrise Mt.** The trail to this summit is mostly on private land and is closed to the public. Onc can approach without a trail from the E on public land, or one might try asking permission at Elk lake Lodge to ascend the trail.

79. **Jay Mts.** The 1953 map shows a 3340-ft. peak W of Grassy Notch for Jay Mt. This is believed to be an error.

87. **Mt. Adams.** The fire tower on this peak has been abandoned for many years, is officially closed, and is of questionable safety. The trail has not been maintained for several years, but is still followable.

91. **Peak (Fishing Brook Range).** This 3480-ft. unnamed peak marks the end of a long ridge leading SW from Fishing Brook Mt., 43 degrees 55'N x 74 degrees 19'W.

93. **Sawtooth Mts. (No. 4).** This 3460-ft. peak at the NW end of the Sawtooths lies about a mile SSE of Beaver Pond. Coordinates, 44 degrees 12'N x 74 degrees 10'W.

94. **Sawtooth Mts. (No. 5).** Also 3460-ft., this summit is found about 1 mi. NE of the pass between Ward Brook and Cold River country. Coordinates, 44 degrees 11'N x 74 degrees 08'W.

97. **Blue Ridge Mt. (Schroon Lake Map).** The 2825-ft. elevation shown for this mountain on the 1953 map is incorrect.

98. **Morgan Mt.** The DEC has reopened the trail to Cooper Kiln Pond which passes just to the N of the summit.

100. **Peak, Unnamed (Brown Pond).** This 3425-ft. peak is found about 3.5 mi. ENE of Wakely Dam. Brown Pond lies in a slight depression on its westerly slope. The coordinates are 43 degrees 44'N x 74 degrees 25'W.

Appendix III

Table of Short Hikes

For the benefit of those looking for easy introductions to the High Peaks Region, the following table lists destinations of less than 2.5 mi. (one way) from shortest to longer for each section in this guide. This table should help hikers unfamiliar with the region to identify worthwhile intermediate destinations within longer hikes. Each significant destination is listed separately with, in some cases, three destinations on one trail. The name and number of the complete trail description are included, along with a brief note as to the hiking terrain to assist in quickly choosing an appropriate hike. Bear in mind that even within this selected group of short hikes there is a big difference between the hike to the base of Roaring Brook Falls and the hikes to the summits of Blueberry, Noonmark or Cascade.

Many of these hikes are ideal for children. See the section on "Hiking with Children" in the Introduction of this guide.

Dist.	Objective	Trail Name & Number	Notes on Terrain
		KEENE VALLEY SECTION	
0.8	First ledge on Brothers	Big Slide via The Brothers (15)	Steep for 0.3 mi.
1.1	Summit of Baxter	Baxter from Rte. 9N (20)	Steep for 0.1 mi.
1.5	Summit of First Brother	Big Slide via The Brothers (15)	Steep for 1.0 mi.

Dist.	Objective	Trail Name & Number	Notes on Terrain
1.6	Summit of Baxter	Baxter from Beede Farm (21)	Steep for 0.1 mi.
1.7	First ledge on Blueberry	Porter Mt. from Keene Valley Airport (17)	Steep for 1.1 mi.
1.8	Summit of Roostercomb	Roostercomb from Keene Valley (18)	Steep for 1.3 mi.
1.9	Summit of Roostercomb	Roostercomb from Rte. 73 (19)	Steep for 1.1 mi.
2.0	Little Porter	Porter Mt. from Johns Brook (16)	Steep for 0.5 mi.
2.2	Tenderfoot Pools (swimming & fishing)	JBL via Southside Trail (3)	Mostly easy grades, one brook crossing, some rough footing.
2.4	Summit of Blueberry Mt.	Porter Mt. from Keene Valley Airport (17)	Steep for 1.3 mi.

ST. HUBERTS SECTION

0.3	Base of Roaring Brook Falls	Giant Mt. via Roaring Brook Trail (47)	Easy grades, some rough footing
0.6	Top of Roaring Brook Falls	(same as above)	Moderate grades
0.6	Round Pond	Dix Mt. from Rte. 73 (46)	Moderate grades
0.7	Washbowl & ledge w/view	Giant Mt. via Ridge Trail (48)	Steep for 0.5 mi.

Dist.	Objective	Trail Name & Number	Notes on Terrain
0.8	Mossy Cascade	Mossy Cascade Trail to Hopkins (51)	Easy grades, some rough footing
0.9	Waterfall	Deer Brook Trail to Snow Mt. (53)	Moderate grades, some rough footing
1.5	Summit of Nubble	Giant's Nubble (49)	Steep for 1.0 mi.
1.5 *	First ledge on Noonmark	Noonmark via Stimson Trail (43)	Steep for 1.1 mi.
1.7	Summit of Snow Mt.	Deer Brook Trail to Snow Mt. (53)	Steady, moderate grade, steep for 0.1 mi.
2.0 *	Gill Brook Flume	Road to Lower Ausable Lake (25)	Easy grades on road, 0.1 mi. on rough trail
2.4 *	Summit of Noonmark	Noonmark via Stimson Trail (43)	Steep for 2.0 mi.
2.5 *	Summit of Round Mt.	Round Mt. (45)	Steep for 0.8 mi.
2.5 *	Bear Run & Pyramid Brook waterfall	Cathedral Rocks & Bear Run (29)	Steep for 0.6 mi.

HEART LAKE SECTION

Dist.	Objective	Trail Name & Number	Notes on Terrain
1.1	Summit of Mt. Jo	Mt. Jo (77)	Steep for 0.5 mi.
2.2	Summit of Mt. Van Hoevenberg	Mt. Van Hoevenberg from S. Meadow Rd. (79)	Moderate for 0.8 mi., steep for 0.3 mi.

---

*Distance includes walk from parking area.

Dist.	Objective	Trail Name & Number	Notes on Terrain
2.3	Marcy Dam (small pond with views)	Mt. Marcy via Van Hoevenberg Trail (61)	Easy to moderate grades
2.4	Rocky Falls	Indian Pass from Heart Lake (75)	Easy to moderate grades

NORTHERN SECTION

Dist.	Objective	Trail Name & Number	Notes on Terrain
0.4	Summit of Cobble Hill	Cobble Hill (95)	Very steep for 0.2 mi., some scrambling
0.6	Summit of Owls Head	Owls Head (93)	Steep for 0.2 mi., some rough footing
0.6	Owen Pond	Owen, Copperas & Winch Ponds (87)	Easy to moderate grades
0.7	Beaver pond & rock with view of cliffs	Old Mountain Rd. (from Lake Placid end) (94)	Easy grades
0.9	Summit of Baker Mt.	Baker Mt. (101)	Steep for 0.5 mi.
0.9	Summit of Silver Lake Mt.	Silver Lake Mt. (86)	Steep for 0.2 mi.
1.3	Copperas Pond (view of Whiteface)	Owen, Copperas & Winch ponds (87)	Easy to moderate grades
1.6	Ledge w/balanced rocks	Pitchoff Mt. (92)	Steep for 0.6 mi.
1.8	Summit of Catamount Mt.	Catamount Mt. (85)	Steep for 1.1 mi., very steep scrambling for 0.1 mi.

Dist.	Objective	Trail Name & Number	Notes on Terrain
2.4	Summit of Cascade Mt.	Cascade Mt. (90)	Steep for 1.5 mi.
2.5	Whiteface Landing (dock w/view and swimming)	Whiteface Mt. from Connery Pond (81)	Easy grades

EASTERN SECTION

Dist.	Objective	Trail Name & Number	Notes on Terrain
0.8	Summit of Big Crow (from Crow Clearing)	The Crows (108)	Steep for 0.5 mi.
1.0	Summit of Little Crow	The Crows (108)	Steep for 0.7 mi.
1.1	Mt. Gilligan	Sunrise Trail to Mt. Gilligan (113)	Steep for 0.4 mi.
1.2	Summit of Poke-O-Moonshine (fire tower still in use)	Poke-O-Moonshine (110)	Moderate to steep for 1.0 mi.
1.5	Summit of Hurricane (abandoned fire tower)	Hurricane Mt. from the East (105)	Steep for 1.1 mi.
1.6	First ledge on Blueberry Cobble	East Trail to Rocky Peak Ridge & Giant (112)	Steep for 0.4 mi.
2.1	Lost Pond (lean-to)	Lost Pond (107)	Mostly easy grades, moderate for 0.5 mi.
2.3	Summit of Blueberry Cobble	East trail to Rocky Peak Ridge & Giant (112)	Steep for 0.5 mi.
2.6	Owl Head Lookout	Giant from Rt. 9N (111)	Easy to moderate grades, steep for 0.1 mi.

Dist.	Objective	Trail Name & Number	Notes on Terrain
SOUTHERN SECTION			
1.1	Old farm & field w/view	Newcomb Lake & Camp Santanoni (135)	Easy grades on graded, gravel road
1.5	Summit of Goodnow Mt. (fire tower still in use)	Goodnow Mt. (139)	Moderate for 1.2 mi.

Appendix IV

Opportunities in the Region for Some People with Disabilities

The following is a list of access opportunities in the High Peaks region for people who use wheelchairs or have other physical limitations. **These trails and access points do not conform to formal accessibility standards and are subject to changes in weather conditions.**

The trails in this particularly rugged region of the Adirondacks are challenging for all visitors. Before undertaking trail or boat trips, users of this appendix may find it helpful to have a friend knowledgeable about their capabilities scout the trip beforehand.

Scenic Vistas

Almost every road on the High Peaks map offers scenic vistas at one point or another, but listed below are the "classic" views from the roadside.

Keene Valley Airport. Rt. 73, 2.5 mi. N of hamlet of Keene Valley.

Town of Newcomb scenic overlook. Rt. 28N.

Quinn Elementary School. In Tupper Lake, 200 yds. S of Rtes. 3 & 30 on Stetson Rd., 1 mi. E of stoplight at jct. of Rtes. 3 & 30.

Adirondak Loj Rd. Rt. 73, 4 mi. SE of village of Lake Placid.

Summit of Whiteface. 8-mi. toll road from Wilmington on Rt. 86. Parking, excellent views 300 vertical ft. below summit. Access to summit via 100-yd. tunnel to elevator that reaches summit house.

Whiteface Mt. Ski Center chairlift to summit of Little Whiteface.*
Located on Rt. 86 between Lake Placid and Wilmington. Ascent is via
two successive chairlifts. No wheelchairs can go on chairs; 100-yd.
walk from first to second chairlift.

Top of 90-meter tower at Intervale Ski Jumps.* Usual access is
via short chairlift, 100-yd. walk, and elevator, but arrangements can
be made at the gate to drive to elevator level. Panoramic view of High
Peaks and Lake Placid from inside warming room at top of tower.

Trail Access

South Meadow (Marcy Dam) Truck Trail (trail 78). This 2.6-mi.
road is rarely driven and consequently the gravel is soft. Maximum
grade 16% at two locations. Numerous grades between 5% and 10%.

Newcomb Lake Road (trail 135). Easy grades, hard-packed gravel
surface. Farm buildings with view at 1.0 mi. make a good
intermediate destination. Total distance to Newcomb Lake is 4.5 mi.

Handicapped Access Nature Trail at Newcomb's Visitor
Interpretive Center. Rt. 28N, 1.4 mi. W of Newcomb Town Hall in
village of Newcomb.

Brewster Peninsula Nature Trails. Turn off Rt. 86 0.7 mi. W of
Main St. in Lake Placid. A small sign for the trails marks the road
that goes up between the restaurant and motor lodge of Howard
Johnson's. At 0.5 mi. from Rt. 86 there is a small parking area on the
L at a barrier gate. Past the gate is a gravel road with easy grades
leading 0.5 mi. to near the end of the peninsula. There are a few
interpretive displays along this road. The trail system also includes
approximately another 1.0 mi. of rougher trail (not wheelchair-

---

*Fee charged.

accessible) leading along a low ridge and down to the shore of Lake Placid. A map and nature guide to these trails is available at the Lake Placid Commerce and Visitors Bureau on Main St. in Lake Placid.

See also Appendix III for a table of short hikes.

Boat Access

There are several boat-launching sites close to roads where a boat may be put in for a trip away from a road into the High Peaks and surrounding areas.

Cascade Lakes. Rt. 73 between Keene and Lake Placid.

Chapel Pond. Rt. 73, 4.7 mi. S of Keene Valley and 4.2 mi. N of jct. of Rtes. 9 and 73. In addition to gravel turnout next to pond there is a primitive boat launching site at N end of pond with narrow road turning off Rt. 73 0.2 mi. N of gravel turnout, just N of road cut through rocks.

Chubb River. On Averyville Rd., 1.4 mi. S of Old Military Rd. A narrow, rough trail leads 200 yds. down to river starting from top of hill beyond bridge over river (opposite additional hiker's parking lot). After a 1-mi. paddle there is a 0.25-mi. portage to another 3 mi. of paddling. A challenging trip, as beaver dams may increase the number of times one must leave the boat, but the view of the Sawtooth Range and Street and Nye is about as wild as anything available to those with physical limitations.

Long Lake/Cold River/Raquette River.* Start at Long Lake village on Rt. 30. Part of the Adirondack Canoe Route, this section offers the chance for a multi-day trip with only a 1-mi. portage. Portage is road width, but too rough for easy wheelchair access. (See *Adirondack Canoe Waters: North Flow* for more information.)

Taylor Pond. * See trail 103 for driving directions and scenic attractions.

Adirondak Loj Area. ADK's Wiezel Trails Cabin is wheelchair accessible. See Introduction for general information about Adirondak Loj.

Newcomb Lake. See trail 135 and Newcomb Lake Road (above, Trail Access) for more information. Boat must also be transported.

The DEC produces a brochure titled "Opening the Outdoors to People with Disabilities" which includes a list of Essex County recreational facilities with special access features. It is available from DEC, 50 Wolf Rd., Albany, NY 12233.

The DEC (Region 5 for the High Peaks) also provides a free permit for physically disabled people who want to take a motor vehicle onto a normally restricted access road in wild-forest areas. Allow three to four weeks' lead time for obtaining the permit. There is no restriction on the use of motorized wheelchairs (as long as they are the kind used in the home) in wilderness areas.

---

*Power boats permitted.

Appendix V

Lean-Tos in the High Peaks Region

The following is a listing of all lean-tos within the area covered by this guidebook. They are listed according to the six different sections, with information on USGS map and location.

Shelter	USGS Map	Location
KEENE VALLEY SECTION		
Bear Brook	Mt. Marcy	1 mi. W of Garden on Phelps Trail
Deer Brook	Mt. Marcy	1.5 mi. W of Garden on Phelps Trail
Wm. G. Howard	Mt. Marcy	On Phelps Trail near DEC Interior Outpost
Wolf Jaws	Mt. Marcy	On ADK Range Trail on side of the Wolf Jaws
Orebed Brook	Mt. Marcy	On Range Trail 2 mi. from DEC Interior Outpost
Bushnell Falls No. 1	Mt. Marcy	On Phelps Trail at junction with Hopkins Trail
Bushnell Falls No. 2	Mt. Marcy	On R bank of Johns Brook above tributary (Chicken Coop Brook)
Slant Rock	Mt. Marcy	On Phelps Trail, 1.75 mi. beyond Bushnell Falls

Shelter	USGS Map	Location
ST. HUBERTS SECTION		
Boquet River	Mt. Marcy	On Dix Trail, 2.5 mi. below the summit of Dix
HEART LAKE SECTION		
Marcy Dam Nos. 1-6	Mt. Marcy	At Marcy Dam, 2.2 mi. from Adirondak Loj
Hudowalski	Mt. Marcy	S shore of pond at Marcy Dam
Kagel	Mt. Marcy	On Marcy Brook near trail to Avalanche Pass
Marcy Brook	Mt. Marcy	On trail to Avalanche Pass
Avalanche Nos. 1 & 2	Mt. Marcy	At junction of Lake Arnold Trail on trail to Avalanche Pass
Beaver Point	Mt. Marcy	On SW side of Lake Colden
Cedar Point	Mt. Marcy	On SW side of Lake Colden
Winacomac	Mt. Marcy	On R bank of Opalescent River above Lake Colden Outlet
Opalescent No. 1	Mt. Marcy	On L bank of Opalescent River 0.2 mi. below Lake Colden Outlet
Rocky Falls	Mt. Marcy	Off Indian Pass Trail 2.5 mi. from Heart Lake on L bank of Indian Pass Brook
Scott Clearing	Santanoni	On Indian Pass Trail, 4 mi. from Heart Lake

Shelter	USGS Map	Location
NORTHERN SECTION		
Whiteface Brook	Lake Placid	On Connery Pond Trail, 0.8 mi above Whiteface Landing
Cooper Kiln Pond	Lake Placid	At Cooper Kiln Pond, 2.8 mi. from Franklin Falls Rd.
Taylor Pond	Lake Placid	SE bay of Taylor Pond Nos. 1 & 2
Taylor Pond No. 3	Lake Placid	SW bay of Taylor Pond
Copperas Pond	Lake Placid	On N shore of Copperas Pond
South Notch	Lake Placid	At end of South Notch Trail
Placid	Saranac Lake	On trail to McKenzie Mt.
Wanika Falls	Santanoni	On N-P Trail, 6.5 mi. from Averyville Rd.
Moose Pond	Santanoni	On the N-P Trail, 8 mi. from Averyville Rd. and 4 mi. from Duck Hole
EASTERN SECTION		
Poke-o-Moonshine	Ausable Forks	At saddle just below summit
Biesemeyer Memorial	Ausable Forks	On Lost Pond
Gulf Brook	Ausable Forks	On N trail to Hurricane, 1 mi. from Crow Clearing
Hurricane Mt.	Elizabethtown	SE side of Hurricane near observer's cabin
Giant	Elizabethtown	On N side of Giant, 1.8 mi. below the summit

Shelter	USGS Map	Location
SOUTHERN SECTION		
Slide Brook	Mt. Marcy	On Dix Trail, 2.5 mi. from Elk Lake
Lillian Brook	Mt. Marcy	On Dix Trail, 3.8 mi. from Elk Lake
Panther Gorge	Mt. Marcy	On Elk Lake-Marcy Trail, 9 mi. from Elk Lake
Calamity Nos. 1 & 2	Mt. Marcy	On Calamity Brook Trail on W side of Flowed Lands
Griffin	Mt. Marcy	At Flowed Lands Dam
Livingston Point	Mt. Marcy	On a point on SE side of Flowed Lands
Flowed Lands	Mt. Marcy	On a point on SW side of Flowed Lands near Hanging Spear Falls Trail
Henderson	Santanoni	On Indian Pass Trail, 1.8 mi. from Upper Works
Wallface	Santanoni	On Indian Pass Trail, 2.8 mi. from Upper Works
Duck Hole Nos. 1 & 2	Santanoni	On NE shore of Duck Hole
Santanoni (Bradley Pond)	Santanoni	On Bradley Pond Trail, 4.5 mi. from Upper Works road
Cold River Nos. 1 & 2	Santanoni	On Ward Brook Truck Trail, 1.3 mi. W of Duck Hole
Number 4— Nos. 1 & 2	Santanoni	On Ward Brook Truck Trail, 6 mi. from Coreys
Ward Brook	Santanoni	On Ward Brook Truck Trail, 5.3 mi. from Coreys
Blueberry	Santanoni	On trail from Coreys, 1000 ft. W of Ward Brook Truck Trail

Shelter	USGS Map	Location
Calkins Brook	Long Lake	On Calkins Brook Truck Trail between Coreys and Shattuck Clearing
Raquette Falls	Long Lake	E bank of Raquette River at Raquette Falls Carry
Raquette Falls Nos. 1 & 2	Long Lake	E bank of Raquette River below Raquette Falls
Hemlock Knoll	Long Lake	E bank of Raquette River
Stony Creek	Long Lake	E bank of Raquette River at junction with Stony Creek
Calkins Creek	Long Lake	On Cold River at junction of Calkins Brook
Catlin Bay Nos. 1 & 2	Long Lake	Near N-P Trail on E shore of Long Lake
Kelley's Point	Long Lake	Near N-P Trail on E shore of Long Lake
Rodney Point Nos. 1 & 2	Long Lake	Near N-P Trail on E shore of Long Lake
Plumleys Nos. 1 & 2	Long Lake	Near N-P Trail on E shore of Long Lake, where N-P Trail leaves the shore of the lake
Cold River Nos. 3 & 4	Long Lake	On R bank of Cold River near Shattuck Clearing where N-P crosses Cold River
Seward	Santanoni	On N-P Trail at Millers Falls on Cold River
Ouluska	Santanoni	On N-P Trail below Rondeau's "Hermitage"
Moose Pond Stream Nos. 1 & 2	Santanoni	On Cold River Horse Trail, 1.5 mi. from Shattuck Clearing

Shelter	USGS Map	Location
Northern Nos. 1 & 2	Santanoni	On Cold River Horse Trail, 2 mi. S of Ward Brook Truck Trail
Ward Pond Brook	Santanoni	On N shore of Newcomb Lake
Newcomb Lake	Santanoni	On S shore of Newcomb Lake

Appendix VI

State Campgrounds near the High Peaks Region

Public campgrounds have been established by the DEC at many attractive spots throughout the state. Listed below are those campgrounds that might be useful as bases of operation for hiking in the High Peaks region. A complete listing of all campgrounds is contained in a brochure of New York State Forest Preserve Public Campgrounds titled "Come Back Next Summer." This brochure is available from the DEC, 50 Wolf Rd., Albany, NY 12233.

Below are the campgrounds near the High Peaks Region, listed generally from S to N:

Paradox Lake. Entered from Rt. 74, which meets Rt. 9 2 mi. N of Schroon Lake Village. Hiking trails, boating, fishing. A small campground.

Sharp Bridge. On Rt. 9, 7 mi. N of the village of North Hudson. A fine place to camp, with fishing and swimming in the Schroon River.

Lake Harris. 3 mi. N of Rt. 28N in Newcomb. A good base for hiking in the Santanoni Preserve and Sanford Lake areas.

Lake Eaton. On Rt. 30, 3 mi. W of Long lake.

Fish Creek and Rollins Pond Campgrounds. On Rt. 30, 12 mi. E of Tupper Lake. Two large campgrounds with good boating and swimming.

Meacham Lake. On Rt. 30, 19 mi. N of Lake Clear Jct.

Buck Pond. Between Rt. 30 and Rte. 3 near Onchiota on Rainbow Lake.

Meadowbrook. On Rt. 86, 4 mi. E of Saranac Lake in Ray Brook. A convenient stopping point in the area.

Wilmington Notch. On Rt. 86, in a picturesque setting 3.5 mi. W of Wilmington on the W Branch of the Ausable River.

Poke-O-Moonshine. On Rt. 9, 12 mi. N of Elizabethtown.

Index

Note: Lakes are listed under their names instead of under "Lake."

Other Publications
of
The Adirondack Mountain Club, Inc.
RR 3, Box 3055
Lake George, N. Y. 12845-9522
(518)668-4447

BOOKS

85 Acres: A Field Guide to the Adirondack Alpine Summits
Adirondack Canoe Waters: North Flow
Adirondack Canoe Waters: South and West Flow
The Adirondack Mt. Club Canoe Guide to
Western & Central New York State
Winterwise: A Backpacker's Guide
Climbing in the Adirondacks
Guide to Adirondack Trails: Northern Region
Guide to Adirondack Trails: Central Region
Guide to Adirondack Trails: Northville-Placid Trail
Guide to Adirondack Trails: West-Central Region
Guide to Adirondack Trails: Eastern Region
Guide to Adirondack Trails: Southern Region
Guide to Catskill Trails
An Adirondack Sampler, Day Hikes for All Seasons
An Adirondack Sampler II, Backpacking Trips
Geology of the Adirondack High Peaks Region
The Adirondack Reader
Adirondack Pilgrimage
Our Wilderness: How the People of New York Found, Changed, and
Preserved the Adirondacks
Adirondack Wildguide (distributed by ADK)

MAPS

Trails of the Adirondack High Peaks Region
Trails of the Northern Region
Trails of the Central Region
Northville-Placid Trail
Trails of the West-Central Region
Trails of the Eastern Region
Trails of the Southern Region

Price list available on request.

NOTES

NOTES

NOTES

NOTES

NOTES

NOTES

Backdoor to Backcountry

ADKers choose from friendly outings, for those just getting started with local chapters, to Adirondack backpacks and international treks. Learn gradually through chapter outings or attend one of our schools, workshops, or other programs. A sampling includes:

- Alpine Flora
- Ice Climbing
- Rock Climbing
- Basic Canoeing
- Bicycle Touring
- Cross-country Skiing

- Mountain Photography
- Winter Mountaineering
- Birds of the Adirondacks
- Geology of the High Peaks
  . . . and so much more!

For more information about the Adirondacks or about ADK . . .

ADK's information Center & Headquarters
RR3, Box 3055, Lake George, NY 12845-9522
(518) 668-4447
Exit 21 off I-87 ("the Northway"), 9N South

6/15–Columbus Day:
Mon–Sat., 8:30–5

Tues. after Columbus Day–6/14:
Mon.–Fri., 8:30–4:30

For more information about our lodges . . .

ADK Lodges
Box 867
Lake Placid, NY 12946
(518)523-3441   9 a.m.–7 p.m.

(For reservations or free info. re. lodging and programs)

Join a Chapter

Three-quarters of ADK members belong to the chapter in their area. Those not wishing to join a particular chapter join ADK as members at large.

Local chapter membership brings you an easy way to join in the fun of outings and social activities or the reward of working on trails, conservation, and education projects at the local level. And you can still participate in all regular Club activities and receive all the regular benefits.

Adirondak Loj ....North Elba
Albany
Algonquin ....Plattsburgh
Black River ....Watertown
Cold River ....Long Lake
Connecticut Valley ....Hartford
Finger Lakes ....Ithaca-Elmira
Genesee Valley ....Rochester
Glens Falls
Hurricane Mountain ....Keene
Iroquois ....Utica
Keene Valley
Knickerbocker ....New York City & vicinity
Lake Placid
Laurentian ....Canton-Potsdam
Long Island
Mid-Hudson ....Poughkeepsie
Mohican ....Westchester & Putnam co., NY/Fairfield co., CT
New York ....Metropolitan Area*
Niagara Frontier ....Buffalo
New Jersey
North Woods ....Saranac Lake-Tupper Lake
Onondaga ....Syracuse
Penn's Woods ....Harrisburg, PA
Ramapo ....Rockland & Orange counties
Schenectady
Shatagee Woods ....Malone
Susquehanna ....Oneonta

*Special requirements apply

Membership

To Join:

Call 1-800-395-8080 (VISA or Mastercard) or send this form with payment to **Adirondack Mountain Club, RR3, Box 3055, Lake George, NY 12845-9522.**

Check Membership Level:

☐ Life $1,000*
☐ Forest Preserve $250*
☐ Patron $125*
☐ Supporting $75*
☐ Contributing $50*
☐ Family $40*
☐ Adult $35
☐ Senior Family $30*
☐ Senior (65+) $25
☐ Junior (under 18) $20
☐ Student (18+, full time) $20

School _____

*Includes associate/family members

Name _____

Address _____

City _____ State _____ Zip _____

Home Telephone (____) _____

☐ I want to join as a member-at-large.

☐ I want to join as a _____ Chapter member.

List spouse & children under 18 with birthdates:

Spouse _____

Child _____ Birthdate _____

Child _____ Birthdate _____

Bill my: ☐ VISA   ☐ MASTERCARD   Exp. date _____

☐☐☐☐☐☐☐☐☐☐☐☐☐☐☐☐

I have read and accepted the ADK pledge.

_____
Signature (required for charge)

ADK is a non-profit, tax-exempt organization. Membership fees are tax deductible, as allowed by law. Please allow 6–8 weeks for receipt of first issue of **Adirondac** or the **ADK Newsletter.**

Adirondack ADK Mountain Club

Membership Rewards

- **Discovery:**
  ADK can broaden your horizons by introducing you to new places, recreational activities, and interests.

- **Enjoyment:**
  Being outdoors more and loving it more.

- **People:**
  Meeting others and sharing the fun.

- *Adirondac* Magazine & the *ADK Newsletter*
  Ten times a year.

- **Member Discounts:**
  20% off on publications, 10% on lodge stays, and reduced rates for educational programs.

- **Satisfaction**:
  Knowing you're doing your part and that future generations will enjoy the wilderness as you do.

Adirondack
ADK
Mountain Club

Conservation
Recreation
Education